Boston D.A.

Boston D.A.

The Battle to Transform the American Justice System

Sean Flynn

New York

For my father, Mike Flynn, an honest cop

Library of Congress Cataloging-in-Publication Data
available upon request.

The publisher has made every effort to secure permission to reproduce copyrighted material and would like to apologize should there have been any errors or omissions.

TV Books, L.L.C.
1619 Broadway
New York, NY 10019
www.tvbooks.com

Interior design by Rachel Reiss
Manufactured in the United States of America

Contents

Acknowledgments

BEN GALE, A SOFT-SPOKEN BRIT WHO WORKS FOR A COMPANY called Lion Television in the United Kingdom, recruited me for this project, for which I am grateful. He and his colleagues spent the better part of a year traipsing around after assistant district attorneys and defense lawyers, chronicling the workings of justice in Suffolk County. The videotape that he and his associates recorded was invaluable in reconstructing the courtroom scenes recounted on the following pages. In many instances, Ben supplied me with tapes of trials and interviews that provided much-needed background and context; in every instance, he gave me the rough-cut footage from which Lion's documentary would be produced. That provided the narrative spine for this book. For that, I am both grateful and indebted.

On the other hand, Ben first approached me because I had spent nearly a dozen years chronicling crime and punishment in greater Boston. Indeed, much of the information, insights, and scenes in these pages are adaptations of newspaper and magazine stories I wrote between 1988 and late 1999. For that, there are so many people to thank I fear inadvertently overlooking some of them.

Working chronologically, however, the list begins with Richard Gaines, who hired a skinny young man from Ohio to write for the *Boston Phoenix,* and Mark Jurkowitz, who molded that same skinny guy into a decent reporter and who is still the best editor I've ever had the pleasure of being browbeaten by. At the *Boston Herald,* where I learned to distill the worst spasms of gory violence into six-inch blurbs, Andy Gully, Andy Costello, Jim McLaughlin, and especially Mike Bello taught me things I'm still trying to forget. Finally, at *Boston Magazine,* where I was both a staff writer and, later, a senior editor, John Strahinich and Craig Unger gave me both the freedom and the guidance to explore the deeper and more subtle crevices of Suffolk County justice.

In the days of Nexis and in a two-newspaper town, however, no reporter can afford to work in a vacuum. I've been honored to work with some of the best in the business: Ric Kahn, Beverly Ford, Ann E. Donlan, Helen Kennedy, Mariellen Burns, David Boeri, Mick Macklin, and Carl Stevens, to name only a few. I've also had the privilege of competing against an immensely talented corps of reporters, whose clips in some instances I have relied on in reconstructing some minor parts of this saga (always, I hope, with proper attribution): John Ellement, who for my money is the best damned cops-and-courts reporter working east of the Mississippi; Toni Locy; Ellen O'Brien; Michelle McPhee; and, bane of my existence, Sean Murphy, with whom I was perpetually being confused by cops who were pissed off at the latest whack he'd taken at them.

Because this is a book about crime, there is also a rather sizeable cadre of police officers whom I've befriended over the years. Unfortunately, most of them spoke to me on the condition of strict anonymity, so I can't acknowledge them by name. But they know who they are. And I thank them. Generally speaking, though, I have deep gratitude for the members of the Youth Violence Strike Force, who not only provided me with an invaluable education but also restored my faith in policing. They are a model to be emulated everywhere.

My friend, Sergeant Detective Donald S. Gosselin, has supplemented that education. There should be more cops like him. On the street level, there are also the people who have left me in awe: Emmett Folgert of the Dorchester Youth Collaborative has been doing the Lord's work for three decades and the Revered Eugene F. Rivers has risked his life to save kids no one else cares about. They are both inspirations.

Of course, none of this would have been possible without the cooperation of Ralph Costas Martin II, whom I first profiled in 1993. I confess that I am a fan of his, and am grateful for his cooperation and for what he's done for my adopted home. Finally, everyone needs a muse, someone to keep you calm and sane when you fear the latter and have abandoned the former. Thank you, Mars.

Sean Flynn
Boston, July 2000

CHAPTER 1
An Idea

ON A COOL AND CLOUDY NIGHT IN THE EARLY AUTUMN OF 1991, six people wove through a tight corridor that separates the bar from the dining room of 224 Boston Street, a bistro that takes its name from its address two miles south of downtown Boston. J.W. Carney, Jr., a sturdy, balding criminal defender whose full beard and tortoiseshell glasses made him look like a professorial biker, led, followed by his wife, Joy. Robert Gittens, a young and bespectacled lawyer with tawny skin, followed with his wife, Donna, a doe-eyed broadcasting executive. Behind them were a rising dermatologist, Deborah Scott, and her husband, a slim federal prosecutor with a thick black mustache and skin the color of creamed coffee named Ralph Costas Martin II.

They were old friends, the three couples, their lives tangled together by years of court cases and professional associations. But they didn't get out much anymore, at least not all together. They were all in their mid-thirties, their days occupied by burgeoning careers, their nights and weekends by toddler children. Finding three babysitters on the same Friday night happened only every three months or so, usually less.

They followed the hostess to a large round table near the window, where the view opened up to a scrubby vacant lot across the road. 224 Boston Street had always been somewhat out of place on its namesake block, a narrow strip of blacktop that ran between rows of weathered triple-decker homes and low-rising storefronts and the occasional abandoned patch of weeds. A few hundred yards to the east, the pavement rose over the Fitzgerald Expressway, a clotted artery of traffic slogging to and from the southern suburbs, then dropped again into the crippled remnants of a retail and light industry district. The bistro would have fit more gracefully along Newbury Street, Boston's storied lane of high-end clothiers and trattorias, or downtown, under the glass and steel towers rising above the harbor.

But Ralph Martin liked it. In fact, it was his favorite restaurant in all of Boston, with high-end food at mid-level prices and an eclectic crowd willing to trek away from the city's glittery districts. For a rare night out with his closest friends, it was comfortable.

Martin hadn't been particularly comfortable as of late, either. He was thirty-seven years old and a restless, if veteran, prosecutor. He spent the first years of the eighties as an assistant district attorney in suburban Boston, convincing juries to lock up drunk drivers and drug dealers and wife beaters. In 1984, wanting to put a higher gloss on his professional repertoire, he joined the United States Attorney's office for the district of Massachusetts. In the state-level courts, the fight against crime is a sort of trench warfare, endless waves of miscreants and felons overrunning a token force of prosecutors and probation officers and judges. A man who stays too long in the trenches, especially a black man, risks a reputation as a guns-and-drugs specialist, able to handle only the simplest grist of crime and punishment.

In the marbled corridors of federal jurisprudence, on the other hand, the engagements are more precise, more strategic. Prosecutors pick and choose their cases, deciding which suspects are worth running through a gauntlet of malleable criminal statutes. By their nature, the cases tend to be more complex, invoking esoteric concepts of racketeering and interstate wire fraud and multilevel conspiracies. And, by extension, the Assistant U.S. Attorneys are generally seen as more legally nimble, able to decipher a morass of alleged offenses into a coherent and compelling package of evidence. It doesn't hurt that reputation that the feds rarely lose: in the Boston office, roughly 97 percent of all prosecutions ended in guilty verdicts.

By the fall of 1991, Martin had been a federal prosecutor for six and one-half years, the longest time he'd held a job. He'd worked mostly in economic crimes where he proved to himself, and anyone else who cared to notice, that he could, in fact, handle big complicated federal cases. Truth is, though, he missed the trenches. In the state courts, the prosecutor is usually the last, best hope for anyone who's been mugged or beaten and stabbed. State prosecutors can't pick their battles—they have to deal with every alleged criminal the police arrest—but they can at least set the rules of engagement, deciding who gets charged with how serious an offense. Justice in the lower courts can be rough, dispensed with a coarse expediency, but the emotions are more visceral, the victories more tangible, the entire process somehow more gritty and real. Martin wanted to feel that again.

The appetizers hadn't arrived yet when Carney asked his friend what he supposed the future might hold for him. "Well, you know," Martin answered, "I'm thinking of running for district attorney."

There was a second or two of silence. Then laughter. Loud, raucous laughter. "Oh, c'mon," Carney said, forcing the words out through his guffaws. "Really, what do you want to do?"

"No, no, no, I'm serious," Ralph said. "I've thought about this, and here's how I'd do it."

He began to outline an anemic strategy. Actually, strategy would be a kind assessment. All Ralph Martin had was an idea, a hopelessly naïve notion, protected and nurtured by an absolute absence of any political experience.

"No, seriously," Ralph was telling his friends. "I mean it. And this is how I would do it."

No one was laughing anymore, settling simply for bemused smiles. Ralph is a soft-spoken man, allergic to hyperbole and even-keeled to an eerie degree. His wife, Debbie, calls him a Vulcan because he's so emotionally steady. "First," he said, "I'd have to quit the U.S. Attorney's office." Not a problem, since he'd already decided to leave, having run his course in six years. "Then, I'd have to run as an Independent, 'cause there's no way I'd get through the Democratic primary. And then . . ."

He hemmed and hawed, fishing for a third step in his campaign plan. He didn't have one. Problem was, Ralph Martin wanted to be the district attorney because he thought he would be good at it. To him, prosecutors were an almost ethereal force, not as numerous or visible as police, not wrapped in the stoic black robes of judges. But every case that ended up in the criminal courts, and a good many that didn't, had to flow through the D.A.'s office. If justice is an ever-teetering scale of good and evil, the prosecutor is the person who calibrates the weights. The D.A. decides who gets charged and for what crimes, determines the point at which a Saturday night killing rises from manslaughter to first degree murder, deciphers whether a fourteen-year-old arsonist is a competent adult who deserves to stand trial or a confused child who needs probation and intensive therapy. The role of the prosecutor isn't merely to convict people, but to decide who goes to trial and for what crimes and, all the while, assuaging the gut-level terror and rage of crime victims. From that perspective, the job is more of a social referee than simply a bulldog advocate for the people of Suffolk County.

The smiles finally gave way to more serious deliberation. It had taken Martin most of the meal to convince his friends he was actually serious about wanting to be the D.A. Eventually, they began to strategize with him. No one had to lay out his negatives. They were too obvious. Black, for one, in a city that had never been electorally kind to anyone nonwhite. No political experience, for another. And, worst of all, his own curious history with the Boston Police Department. Only a few months earlier, in July 1991, Martin authored a report for the U.S. Attorney's office on alleged police misconduct in the investigation into the murder of Carol Stuart and her unborn baby, Christopher. It was scathing. If he'd had his druthers, which he made quite public, he would gladly haul a number of Boston cops in front of a federal grand jury. For a man aspiring to be the lead law enforcement official in Suffolk County, pissing off the police who'd be working for him was a strange way to begin a campaign.

It would be difficult, Martin's friends agreed, but not impossible. They began to lay out possible scenarios, wild and fantastical visions of political realignments, of pols and prosecutors plunging into disrepute. Years later, Martin wouldn't even remember the details, they were so dreamily unreal. The crucial detail of campaigning—raising money—was never even mentioned. All Martin knew was that he wanted to be the district attorney.

RALPH MARTIN DID EVENTUALLY BECOME THE DISTRICT ATTORNEY for Suffolk County—which is essentially interchangeable with Boston—in 1992 and he changed the city. In the worst areas, the blocks that in the late eighties and early nineties were plagued by crack gangs and gunboys with wobbly aim, serious crime has been neutralized, beaten nearly into absolute submission. In 1999, for example, the city suffered only thirty-one homicides, an 80 percent drop from the peak year of 1990 and the low mark of a tide that had been ebbing for four years. Other violent crimes have been reduced by similar numbers.

There are many reasons for that plunge, most of which have been lauded, or, as the case may be, debated, in newspapers across the county exploring the so-called Boston Miracle. Some criminologists, for instance, attribute the drop in crime to demographics, arguing that a smaller population of crime-prone teens and young adults gave Boston and other cities a temporary reprieve and that, as today's twelve-year-olds grow into seventeen-year-olds, a crime spike will be inevitable. Others have suggested, more pragmatically, that crime fell so precipitously in Boston because of

efforts in the mid-nineties to get the worst hoodlums off the streets
and into jail cells. When they get out, as some have already done,
the violence of a decade ago could easily reignite. (The Commonwealth of Massachusetts, like most of the rest of America, has all
but abandoned the notion of prisons as places to rehabilitate criminals into upstanding citizens.)

Both of those theories have some truth. Unquestioned, however, is that the City of Boston for the past half-decade has been
better policed—more smartly policed—than at any time in its history. Not simply in the traditional sense, of cruisers screaming
around the city and cops bashing in doors, but in a more organic
way, a systematic rearranging of priorities and tactics that have
made the city's streets safer. Nor, oddly yet essentially, have the
people involved been limited to the usual assortment of law enforcement personnel playing their assigned roles. Probation officers, youth workers, and ministers, most notably those involved
with the nationally acclaimed Ten Point Coalition, have all been
instrumental in calming the city. Boston has waged a successful
war on crime and Ralph Martin has been one of the generals.

He is not the only general, of course. In order for any sensible
and cohesive anti-crime policy to work, the D.A. needs the cooperation, at a minimum, of two counterparts. One is the mayor,
who, under Boston's form of government, wields enormous clout
over every aspect of the city and as such can wreak havoc on the
district attorney. Mayor Thomas M. Menino was an early ally of
Martin's. In 1993, shortly before Menino ascended from city council president to mayor and when Martin was freshly appointed, he
cast the rookie D.A.'s fate both as a prosecutor and an icon.
"Boston has always had the rap that it's a racist city, and if Ralph
Martin doesn't get reelected the media's going to play that up,"
Menino said. "I think Martin is a sharp, classy guy. A class act.
Sometimes you just have to do things that are good for your city,
and I think he's good for my city."

In 1994, after he became mayor, Menino installed another Martin ally into another key position, appointing a soft-spoken vet-

eran cop named Paul F. Evans to be commissioner of the Boston Police Department. More importantly, the mayor allowed Evans to actually manage the force, as opposed to using him as a political strawman to appease critics, punish enemies, and reward friends. Evans, despite having to wrestle with the internal politics that police are notoriously adept at practicing, has redeployed his resources and redefined the department's mission in ways that have sometimes been revolutionary for their common sense. And the relationship between the courthouse and the stationhouse has blossomed. Martin and Evans like and respect each other. They have their disagreements, of course, but, unlike regimes past, their differences are settled in private, often over monthly breakfasts at a greasy spoon in the city's South End neighborhood.

As generals, however, neither man is often in the trenches. Rather, their impact has been more systemic, establishing a tone and creating an environment in which crime can be more effectively controlled. The story of the Boston D.A., therefore, isn't about one man. Instead, it is a collection of anecdotes and urban tales of detectives who don't abandon old cases, about assistant prosecutors who, in a new and ugly age, risk their lives, about investigators and prosecutors who are willing to admit their mistakes yet reluctant to sensationalize their successes. Taken as a whole, it is a story of reinvention bordering on redemption, of a city transforming itself from a caricature of racial intolerance and law-enforcement incompetence into a model of actual justice.

Since he was appointed by Governor Weld in 1992, Martin has been steadily infusing his office with his own curious prosecutorial philosophy. In the spring of 2000, during the second year of Martin's second full term in office, I asked him when he understood the power of a prosecutor. Not intellectually, but emotionally, in his gut. I expected him to yammer on about a murder case or perhaps a child rapist, some undisputedly rotten criminal he'd locked away. Instead, he told me about a minor case involving a young man accused of drunken driving and assaulting several police officers, which took place in a suburban courtroom.

When he interviewed the police officers in preparation for the trial, Martin was bothered by the stories they each told. It wasn't that their stories differed radically. Quite the opposite: they all told the exact same story, as if they were reading from a script. Later, during the trial, the booking sergeant said something on the stand that he hadn't told Martin.

"How did the defendant look when you first saw him?" the defense lawyer asked. "He looked like he'd been through a war," the sergeant said.

Martin was taken aback. It is not uncommon for police to rough up a suspect and then charge them with assault to explain away the bruises as the result of necessary retaliatory force. (Suspects are forever falling on their face when they try to get out of a cruiser, for instance.) The jury, apparently, was taken aback, too: they voted not guilty on all counts.

Afterward, the judge asked Martin what he thought about the verdict. "I'm not sure what to think anymore, Judge," he told him.

"Hey," the judge said, and quite sympathetically, "we both grew up on the streets, and we can both tell when someone's feeding us a line of bullshit. And there was a lot of bullshit in this case."

Some fifteen years later, Martin told that story with almost clinical dispassion. "On the one hand, I was disappointed because I really thought he was guilty of the drunk driving," he said. "But on the other hand, I was relieved. I would have felt terrible if he'd gone away for a longer time for something he didn't do."

And that, neatly encapsulated, is how Martin runs his office, how he approaches the dispensation of justice. One of these days, he swears he will take all his years of prosecutorial experience and write The Great American Novel. He doesn't have a plot yet, or even a protagonist. But he knows what the moral will be. "It's not putting the bad guys in prison that's the problem. That's the easy part. The hard part," he says, "is figuring out who the really good guys are."

Chapter 2

Boston

IT IS IRONIC, AND SOMEWHAT PROPHETIC, THAT RALPH MARTIN'S favorite restaurant would be on Boston Street. In a city of starkly demarcated neighborhoods, separated by such psychically solid barriers of race and class that they may as well be outlined by walls of reinforced concrete, Boston Street lies in a kind of no-man's-land, as if the carefully drawn borders of adjoining territories had smeared into a fuzzy, unclaimed blotch.

To the east, beyond the expressway, lies South Boston, a peninsula separated from the city proper by aging shipping channels and the goopy waters of Boston Harbor. Yet while it is physically isolated, tethered to the mainland by only two bridges, "Southie" is the spiritual center of Boston's Irish, which is to say of Boston's power elite. By 1991, the enormously popular mayor, Raymond L. Flynn, his enormously obsequious police commissioner, Francis "Mickey" Roache, and the enormously powerful president of the Massachusetts State Senate, William Bulger, were all sons of Southie (as was the city's mythically vicious Irish gangster, James J. "Whitey" Bulger, the senate president's older brother).

Immigrants from the Emerald Isle have long defined Boston, to one degree or another. In the beginning, which would be about

the time a failing potato crop forced hundreds of thousands to flee
for America in the middle of the nineteenth century, the City on
the Hill was notorious for its open hostility to the Irish. Yankee
dominance, historian Thomas H. O'Connor has noted, made
Boston "the one city in the entire world where an Irish Catholic,
under any circumstances, should never, *ever,* set foot." Forced to
flee English hegemony at home, the new Irish found themselves as
heavily trod upon by WASP overlords on Boston's soggy soil. The
signs—"No Irish Need Apply"—were ubiquitous; the anti-Catholic
bigotry, weird fears of papist conspiracies, was virulent. It didn't
help matters that the ruling Brahmins favored almost every other
ethnic and minority group over the Irish, most notably blacks, for
whom they founded the abolition movement and later fought and
financed a civil war. The Irish got to be cannon fodder.

Still, Celtics swamped the city, packing into West End and
North End slums, then migrating to South Boston and the new
public housing projects where a workingman could afford to keep
a roof over his family. As their numbers rose, Irish politicians of
the day manipulated historic grievances to rally electoral mobs.
And, in short order, Irish Americans came to dominate the city's
political landscape, which, in turn, meant they controlled the
city's patronage system. Two or three generations hence, the Irish
thrived in Boston as they had in no other city in America.

Not that it mattered. The Boston Irish are a unique breed, a surly
and indignant bunch that enjoy a low and chronic misery, a firm
and unshakable belief that life will never be kind or fair to you or
your kin people. Ancient grievances are still massaged decades
after they ceased being relevant. Well into his third term, for instance, Mayor Flynn would still grumble drunkenly about how his
mother, God rest her, used to scrub floors for Yankee bankers. And
Jack Connors, an advertising executive and arguably the mightiest
business executive of the city's modern era, never tired of men-
tioning that his grandfather had been a footman for Governor
William F. Weld's grandfather. It wasn't true, but that was hardly
the point.

West of Boston Street, past a gray stretch of tow yards and freight depots and beyond the gentrifying brownstones of the South End, the Back Bay spreads out along landfill at the base of Beacon Hill. The Statehouse sits at the top of the hill, its golden dome gleaming in the New England sun, glinting in the eyes of tourists peering up from the Common. This is the Boston of textbooks and mythology, of grand Victorian townhouses lining the wide Parisian green of Commonwealth Avenue; the place where the Cabots spoke to the Lodges and the Lodges spoke to God; and where a proper gentleman never took a drink before three o'clock or east of Park Street, the marker between the rarified and the rabble.

In the psychological topography of Boston, the Back Bay and Beacon Hill are the last bastions of goo-goo liberals and old-money Republicans with stiff underbites. They aren't there anymore, most of them having died off or drifted into irrelevancy. Instead, their mantle has shifted south, to Dorchester, where the *Boston Globe* is published. Until the New York Times Company bought it in 1994, the *Globe* assumed the role of Yankee overlord, its unflinchingly liberal editorials echoing the same stilted *noblesse oblige* of the fading Brahmins. As late as January 1998, by which time Irish-Americans controlled everything worth controlling in Boston, the local Hibernians were still spoiling for a fight with an English oppressor, or at least a reasonable facsimile. So they skunk-sprayed the *Globe* (whose top editors, it should be noted, are almost uniformly of Irish descent) for a mildly unamusing cartoon that suggested professional terrorists in Northern Ireland would rather fight with each other than get a legitimate job. A hundred protestors stamped around the pavement in front of the *Globe,* burning copies of the paper and demanding a boycott. "A shameful ethnic slur," huffed Bernard Cardinal Law. John A. Hart, Jr., a state representative from South Boston, cut to the chase. "The *Globe,*" he groused, "wouldn't portray other people like that, so it shouldn't do it to us."

South of Boston Street, the last straggling blocks still populated by white people quickly give way to a sprawling black ghetto. The contours were first marked in the late sixties on a map in red ink—from which the term "redlining" is derived—by bankers who steered black mortgagers to the blocks around Blue Hill Avenue, which at the time was a predominantly Jewish neighborhood where, the thinking went, the homeowners and tenants would be more inclined to accept black neighbors. They were for a time, but the area by the mid-seventies was populated by an overwhelming percentage of African- and Caribbean-Americans, a burgeoning community that began to bulge at its southern end, bleeding into most of North Dorchester, all of Roxbury, and most of Mattapan, a teardrop swath dripping to the southern edge of the city.

Just as the Irish had their litany of complaints against the Brahmins who once ran the city, black Bostonians had their own list of legitimate grievances. A variety of programs and policies, some well-meaning but gone astray, others outright venal, contained the city's black population to deteriorating streets, withheld the spoils of patronage and, in a particularly craven and—in the end, volatile—scheme, deprived the schools where minority children studied their fair share of resources. In a city of neighborhoods, where pride often revolved around the local high school, black students were leafing through yellowed textbooks in crumbling classrooms.

A goofy quibble between well-to-do men about whose grandfather was a servant and whose the master is one thing. But on the streets, where the working class scratched out a living, those tensions were palpable, and at times violent. In 1974, they exploded when a federal judge, W. Arthur Garrity, ordered the city's schools be desegregated. The one physical thing white ethnics could claim as their own—isolated tracts of land in Southie and Charlestown—were being threatened, not so much taken away as invaded. More aggravating still, the invasion was ordered by a suburban judge (close enough to a Brahmin) and championed by the then Yankee-owned *Boston Globe*. The Boston Irish, long conditioned to believe the world conspired against them, now found themselves under assault by two enemies: blacks and Brahmins.

The next two years were among the ugliest in the city's history. Yellow buses filled with black children were stoned as they rolled into Charlestown and Southie. Snipers fired bullets through the plate glass windows fronting the *Globe*'s office on Morrissey Boulevard. Senator Edward M. Kennedy, for years the favorite of working-class whites, escaped a rock-throwing mob by scurrying into the federal building named for his dead brother, President John F. Kennedy. In an ugly and iconic image captured by a newspaper photographer, two white men, their faces twisted in rage, speared a black man with an American flag on the steps of City Hall. All this in Liberty's chosen home.

BY 1991, THE VIOLENCE OF BUSING HAD LONG SINCE SUBSIDED. The reputation of the city, however, had yet to fully recover. And the tensions that spawned the stoning and the spearing, instead of dissipating, had in some ways worsened. The white working class in Southie had begun to erode into a white underclass, crumbled by a caustic epidemic of heroin and endemic plague of alcohol abuse. In 1994, *U.S. News & World Report,* drawing from U.S. Census records, anointed the Old Colony projects as the poorest white district in the country. Southie Pride had mutated into Southie Survival.

In the black ghetto, meanwhile, survival had a more literal connotation. The waves of gang violence that washed across the country in the mid-eighties began splashing into Boston by 1987. Police officials were loathe to use that word—gang—but bodies of young black boys were piling up on the city's streets. From 1985, the beginning of the crack age, until 1992, the national homicide rate among black males between the ages of fourteen and seventeen rose 300 percent. In Boston, those numbers were reflected in a horrific mirror: In 1990, the city morgue was stuffed with a record 153 corpses, some 70 percent of which were those of young black or Hispanic males. Moreover, the neighborhoods of Roxbury and Dorchester suffered all the other woes of being poor and black in modern America: an unemployment rate three times that of whites; an infant mortality rate twice as high; two out of three children born to single mothers; AIDS following homicide as the leading cause of death for anyone under forty. And fifteen years after busing's violent introduction, the Boston public schools were in shambles, abandoned by anyone, black or white, who could get out, and hobbled by the exorbitant cost of shuttling kids from neighborhood to neighborhood.

Yet despite the similar deterioration among both blacks and whites, the races had yet to find much, if any, common ground. Boston was still run by white Irish Democrats, save for two members of the city's politically weak city council who were elected from predominantly minority districts as a matter of routine. For a black man such as Ralph Martin to even entertain the notion of running for a citywide office—as an independent and as blow-in from New York City, no less—was silly on its face. To aspire to district attorney raised the gambit to the level of farce.

In a perfect world, District Attorney would be an apolitical title, a role filled by a dispassionate dispenser of justice. But in the eighties and early nineties, the Suffolk County District Attorney's office was an intensely political position. The incumbent, Newman Flanagan, an affable, glad-handing pol with a mop of silver hair and a collection of loud neckties, was never so much a prosecutor as a perpetual campaigner. And the tension between black and white in Boston paled in comparison to the cold détente between City Hall and the courthouse.

Mayor Ray Flynn was a true populist, back before the term was tarnished by crackpots like Ross Perot and Pat Buchanan. When he was first elected in 1984, the city was rebounding both from its earlier racial discord and from a legacy of downtown development at the expense of the far-flung neighborhoods. Flynn downshifted, casting himself as "the mayor of the neighborhoods," jogging sidewalks that had never echoed with a mayoral footstep, let alone a sweaty sneaker. He staunched the hemorrhaging race relations, stopping to shoot hoops (he was a basketball star at Providence College) on some of the ghetto courts where the serious ball was played. He insisted on a program called linkage, in which down-town development projects were forced to funnel money into the residential areas. And he had a savant-like gift for remembering names. In one 1991 survey, a boggling 43 percent of Bostonians claimed to have personally met hizzoner.

But not for nothing was Flynn also known as a limelight junkie. Boston was his city, and he never missed an opportunity to remind everyone and anyone. He rode snowplows in blizzards, negotiated with holed-up gunmen, and, to the consternation of a number of critics, repeatedly stuck his nose into police investigations and, by extension, the district attorney's policies and practices. Partly that was because his police commissioner, Francis "Mickey" Roache, was a boyhood friend and a reliable sycophant. So, for instance, when the mayor announced on live television in the first frenzied moment after a white man, Charles Stuart, claimed to have been shot along with his pregnant wife by a black man that "every available detective" would be put on the case, no one questioned the propriety of an urban executive commandeering a police matter.

At times, however, such grandstanding devolved into political spats between Flanagan and Flynn. In 1990, for example, the mayor demanded that prosecutors use a process called direct indictment to go after the worst urban hoodlums, bypassing lengthy probable cause hearings that often gave defendants ample time to intimidate witnesses into silence. The problem is, mayors aren't supposed to be pushing around prosecutors. More tellingly, after Charles Stuart committed suicide—revealing his claim that a black man had murdered his wife and unborn child was a cruel hoax to cover his own sociopathic tracks, and exposing the months-long police snipe hunt for a phantom black killer as terribly misguided at best—City Hall, police headquarters, and the district attorney all stumbled over themselves to both justify their investigation and blame someone else for how badly it was handled. "The blame game was a very big thing," Ralph Martin says now, years after the fact. "And because of the way it played out, it allowed the press, and therefore the public, to view prosecutions in terms of politics."

And, in the end, politics won out. In 1990, running for his fourth term, Flanagan faced no serious opposition. He coasted easily to another four years in office.

CHAPTER 3

The Early Years

THE MOST IMPORTANT STORY ABOUT RALPH MARTIN BEGINS IN 1954 in Harlem, in an apartment at 541 West 124th Street between Lenox Street and the green of Marcus Garvey Memorial Park. It is a murder story. He was only seventeen months old, able to babble simple syllables and toddle around after his sister, Kye, who was six years old. The two of them lived there with their mother, Delois, who was twenty-eight years old and worked as a switchboard operator for a black magazine called *Our World*. Near the end of March that year, she had separated from her husband and her children's father, a New York City police officer who walked a beat in Harlem's 30th precinct.

Ralph Martin, Sr. was a high-school dropout who hitched up with the all-black 369th Regiment as a private and mustered out as first lieutenant, with a snake tattooed on his forearm slithering around the words "Don't Tread on Me," which wasn't so much a motto as a creed. Nobody tread on Ralph Martin, Sr. When he pinned on the silver shield of the New York City Police Department in 1947, a black man with a badge was often treated as half a man in the stationhouse. But when he walked the streets, his leather shoes slapping the pavement in bolt-straight stride, his jaw set firm beneath his mustache, his brown eyes serious and stern beneath the gleaming brim of his cap, nobody moved. Everybody knew who Officer Martin was. He stayed on the job for only a decade until he was forced into early retirement by an ailing heart and a failing back. But in that time he disarmed fourteen bandits, all without ever firing a shot, and the police brass commended him on four separate occasions.

He was thirty-one years old when he and Delois split up. Their separation was mostly cordial, though it flared into acrimony on at least one occasion. In the spring of 1954, Delois summoned her estranged husband to court for nonpayment of support, money she needed to raise two small children and pay the rent, which, as it happened, was in arrears. Her mother helped when she could, babysitting the kids while Delois worked or when she needed a night out with friends. In fact, she dropped them off at her mother's house on Tuesday, May 4, while she waited at the apartment on West 124th for Ralph Sr., who had agreed to drop by and help her straighten out an eviction notice she had been served by her landlord.

Delois was supposed to pick up Ralph and Kye that evening. She never came. She didn't telephone, either. Night passed into dawn, then into late morning, and still Delois didn't come for her children. That afternoon her sister Justine reported her missing.

Men working for the New Jersey Highway Department found her six days later, on May 11. They were in a town called Alpine, grading Route 9W, a highway bordered by a rock wall on one side and by a drainage ditch, seven feet deep, on the other. At 2:30 in the afternoon, one of the laborers spotted Delois's body in the ditch. She was wearing black slacks and a pink sweater and one sandal. Her left leg was bent awkwardly up under her chest; rocks covered her other leg and part of her corpse, either part of a makeshift burial that had washed away or a smattering of rubble that had tumbled down onto her body. She'd been beaten to death, her skull fractured in two places, according to the Bergen County medical examiner, who also estimated she'd been dead for approximately one week. And near her body, resting upright among the rocks, the detectives found a fountain pen embossed in gold lettering with the name Ralph C. Martin.

Officer Martin was taken to the Amsterdam Avenue precinct house that night and questioned for hours, all through the night and into the daylight hours. An assistant district attorney was called to the station to join the interrogation. The next day, however, Martin was released. He was never charged with any crime, and the murder of Delois Martin was never solved, the case moldering away in a filing cabinet until the leads dried up and the detectives forgot about it.

RALPH II BARELY REMEMBERED HIS MOTHER. EVEN KYE FILtered the trauma through the convenient screen of a six-year-old's mind. "One day my mother just didn't come back," she says. "So we got to stay at Grandma's house longer." For a year, to be precise, which wasn't so terrible for the children, except for the fact that they ran a very serious risk of being horribly spoiled by their mother's relatives. Their father came for them most weekends, but he had to fight for months to regain custody. Being the last known man to see his estranged wife alive didn't endear him to the family court judge, even though he was never formally considered a suspect, let alone charged. Worse was being a single man with a fulltime and dangerous job. In the spring of 1955, after Officer Martin bought himself a brownstone in the hardscrabble Bedford-Stuyvesant section of Brooklyn and hired a live-in housekeeper to watch after the children, he was finally allowed to take them home.

Young Ralph was a volatile child, prone to tantrums and fits of temper. When she was still bigger than her brother, Kye would cuff him around, which would ignite a rage in Ralph. He grabbed a broomstick once when he was seven or eight years old and started swinging at his sister, tearing down the hallway after her, through the kitchen, and back around through the den and the living room. He never caught her but later—perhaps in some other snit, perhaps in throes of the same one—Ralph snipped the ties from Kye's favorite Angora hat.

He was no more subdued in school, either, ranting and screaming over some perceived slight or another, occasionally exploding so violently that the principal would call Ralph's father to the school to cart his son away for the afternoon. After the third such outburst, perhaps the fourth—the details have faded and fuzzed over the years—Officer Martin wrapped his hand around his son's skinny bicep firmly enough for the boy to know he was in trouble. "Ralph," his father told him, his voice level and measured but brushed with a stern resonance, "if I have to come here one more time, I'm going to pull your pants down and whip your bottom in front of the whole class."

Ralph stared back, wide-eyed and silent. He could tell his father was serious, hear it in the deep, whispered voice, see it in the eyes glinting with more anger than he'd ever seen. "Yes, sir," he managed to whisper.

Officer Martin never had to administer that whipping. Ralph's temper dissolved away that afternoon, neutralized as if by the acid in his father's tone. Forty years later, Ralph's friends, and even his enemies, would marvel at his equanimity.

That was his father's way: a strict disciplinarian, but rarely physical with his kids. He wasn't trying so much to keep them in line as he was to temper them, smelt a certain pride into their young psyches. "Don't you let anyone take advantage of you," he would tell his kids, his tattooed snake coiling and rippling over the muscles in his forearm. As Ralph grew older, his tantrums long since held in check, his father saved his sternest voice for his son's teachers, the ones who told him he wasn't good enough or smart enough. When Ralph was a student at the predominantly white Walt Whitman Junior High School in Brooklyn, he dreamed of being an aeronautical engineer, of building planes and soaring into the sky. That, in turn, led him to consider Brooklyn Technical High School, a citywide magnet school in Flatbush with a heavy emphasis on science and math. One of Ralph's teachers, a Mrs. Gladstone, knew how grueling the entrance exam could be. She also knew that the kids who passed it went on, with stunning frequency, to become Nobel Laureates and CEOs and senators. She told Ralph not to waste his time, an unsubtle hint that a cop's kid from Bed-Stuy had no business aiming so high.

Officer Martin was enraged. "You don't let anyone tell you you can't take that test," he nearly growled at his boy. "How in the hell am I going to let my boy take that from anybody? Out the window. Impossible."

So Ralph took the exam for Brooklyn Technical High School and, much to Mrs. Gladstone's chagrin, passed it easily. But after one endless semester of math and science—topics that, in practice, are much less gratifying than dreams of flight—he asked his father if he could transfer to Boys High School in Bed-Stuy. It was a much less rigorous institution and, unlike the schools Ralph had attended for the previous nine years, nearly all black. His father considered the idea for a few days. He'd never tried to direct Ralph, never told him to become a cop like him or a scientist or a day laborer. Rather, he'd tried only to expose his kids to as many sides of life as he could afford to. "I just tried to put him in front of things that would make him his own man, not belong to anybody," Ralph's father explained years later. "I didn't want him to owe a living ass."

But at fourteen, the one niche Ralph hadn't experienced firsthand was life among other black kids. His father told him he could enroll in Boys High School.

RALPH USED TO ASK WHAT HAPPENED TO HIS MOTHER. WAIT until you're older, his aunts—his dead mother's sisters—would tell him. You're not old enough to understand.

He was nearly twelve years old when he finally was told the whole story. He'd already figured out that it would be pretty awful, that anything that had to be kept secret from a little boy couldn't be good. His sister, Kye, knew most of the details by then as well, gleaned from her aunts and grandmother in the decade since her mother's body was found in the ditch.

Neither Ralph nor Kye, however, considered their father might have been the killer. Kye had concrete reasons: one of her aunts, for instance, had told her that Delois Martin was last seen leaving her apartment in a car that none of the neighbors recognized. In 1954, of course, they initially suspected Delois's estranged husband—spouses and boyfriends are, as a matter of routine, the first suspects whenever a woman turns up dead—but over the years even they came to believe Officer Martin had nothing to do with his wife's death.

Ralph, on the other hand, never even considered the possibility. Sure, Dad could be strict and stern, but not violent and certainly not evil. The only guilt he ever saw cloak his father was over the separating itself, a self-loathing hunch that maybe if he'd stayed with his wife he could have protected her. Sometimes, but not often because his father spoke of grief only rarely, Officer Martin would tell his children how terrible the rest of 1954 and most of 1955 had been, enduring a terrible accusation he couldn't possibly prove wrong and, worse, being kept away from his children. "If I hadn't been a police officer," he would tell them, "I would have kicked the door in and gotten you kids back." He would pause and his voice would soften. "But I couldn't."

As time passed, Ralph developed his own theories about his mother's murder—or, more precisely, about how his father was forced to suffer both grief and the indignity of suspicion. The most damning evidence against Officer Martin (and, truth be told, it wasn't so much damning as conveniently circumstantial) was his embossed pen found near Delois's corpse. Years later, when Ralph would tell the story, and then only reluctantly and in the most abbreviated fashion, he would describe the pen as having been "stuck in a pile of rocks," upright and straight, like a cairn marking a trail. Perhaps such a positioning was meant as a message to his father, an unsubtle threat against a tough cop, he would suggest. Or, more darkly, maybe it was a crude attempt to frame his father, which, given the reaction of the New York City Police detectives, seems a more reasonable scenario.

But neither makes much sense. For one, the pen wasn't arranged in any deliberate way, at least not according to the press accounts of the day. It was merely lying in the rubble, as if it had been dropped by mistake rather than calculation. For two, Ralph's theories ignore more rational questions of motive and opportunity. Why, for instance, would someone want to either frame or intimidate his father, let alone travel out of state and hide the body in a ditch where it would only be found by chance? Moreover, there is a far more plausible explanation: perhaps Delois Martin simply borrowed her husband's pen, which could have easily tumbled out when she was tossed into a ravine.

On the other hand, it was not unusual that Ralph, both as a child and a man, would recast his mother's murder into the effect it had upon his father. The mind typically explores the parameters of the universe it knows: Delois Martin was never part of Ralph Martin's universe, except as a long-forgotten figure who had a devastating impact on his orbital center, his father. "He never knew her," is how Kye explains it. "There are some things you grow up with and they're just a fact of life. You don't think to question them."

THERE WAS A TIME WHEN RALPH MARTIN WANTED TO BE A PO-lice officer, mostly because he wanted to be like his father. He had graduated from Boys High School in the spring of 1970 with grades good enough to get him into Brandeis University, a small, Jewish-sponsored liberal arts college on 235 leafy acres in Waltham, a suburb nine miles west of Boston. Four years later, shortly before he graduated with a degree in political science, he told his father he was going to join the New York City Police Department.

Ralph had already taken the test and scored well into the nineties, and passed the physical as well, proving himself smart enough and healthy enough to chase felons around New York. He assumed that someday he would study the law, maybe even decide to practice. But for now, at the age of twenty-one, he would assume his father's legacy.

His father, as was his way, didn't discourage his son. But he wanted him to consider another option first—"to put things in front of him that would make him his own man." So he asked his son to travel to Manhattan to visit the son of another police officer, an assistant district attorney with a billowing Afro named Richard Lowe. Ralph, despite his interest in a legal future, had never considered prosecuting people for a living; in the early seventies, black men, let alone black lawyers, were generally disinterested in working for the government. Lowe knew he was an oddity of sorts, and he took it on the chin more than a few times. "Why aren't you out there defending the brothers instead of prosecuting them?" he would be asked, and in a tone more accusatory than inquisitive.

His answer, however, revealed a more principled vision of the prosecutor's role in the criminal-justice system. "I took a very strong position that it was more important to make sure they weren't charged when they shouldn't be," Lowe said years after that meeting, by which time he had been appointed to the bench in Manhattan. "I was a firm believer that in order to rectify institutional wrongs, you had to become part of the institution."

In the process from arrest to incarceration, assistant district attorneys—or, in the highest-profile cases, the district attorney himself—act as a filter, screening out the dumb and unlucky from the wicked and felonious. Prosecutors, with their rumpled suits and armloads of tattered manila folders, are certainly not as visible as uniformed police officers (or as numerous, for that matter). Nor do they enjoy the regal authority of a black-robed judge. But they are, in Lowe's philosophical architecture, the keystone of the bridge between crime and punishment.

Ralph Martin was enthralled, fascinated by the power a prosecutor could wield. He abandoned his notion of becoming a police officer and instead applied to law school. He was accepted at Northeastern University School of Law in Boston, and graduated in 1978, after which he joined the small firm of Budd & Reilly. The principals treated their associates as protégés to be mentored, a process that, in the long run, proved valuable to all concerned.

Wayne Budd and Tom Reilly had been friends since they were twelve years old and growing up in the same neighborhood in Springfield, Massachusetts. They couldn't have been more different: Budd, who grew up to become a Republican, was the son of Springfield's first black police officer; Reilly, who would become one of the brighter lights in the commonwealth's Democratic Party, was born to Irish immigrants. But their bond was tight, forged on the gridiron for Cathedral High School—Budd, an exceptional athlete, was an end while Reilly played halfback—and permanent. The firm they founded in 1972, small and multi-hued in a legal arena dominated by white-shoe behemoths, quickly became a breeding ground for some of New England's top tier attorneys. In 1979, the letterhead expanded to Budd, Reilly & Wiley with the addition of Fletcher "Flash" Wiley, who specialized in real estate development, enhancing the firm's repertoire of business litigation and corporate transactions.

Wiley eventually went on to head the Boston Chamber of Commerce. The roster of alumni eventually swelled to include Craig Brown, one of the city's premier entertainment lawyers; Melvin Miller, who publishes the *Bay State Banner,* New England's largest black newspaper; Oliver Mitchell, an in-house attorney for Ford Motor Company in Detroit; and Steven Wright, who served as deputy counsel to former New York City Mayor David Dinkins.

Budd arguably rose the highest. In addition to his positions among the state's legal fraternities—he founded the Massachusetts Black Lawyers Association and was both the youngest and the first black president of the Massachusetts Bar Association—his career has been a steady climb into the highest reaches of law. In 1989, he was appointed the United States Attorney for the District of Massachusetts; three years later, he was promoted to associate attorney general in Washington, the number three position in the United States Department of Justice. In 1996, he became the president of Bell Atlantic–New England, wrestling a telecommunications giant through the age after deregulation.

AS FOR REILLY, HE LEFT THE FIRM HE CO-FOUNDED IN 1983 TO become an assistant district attorney in Middlesex County, a monstrous swath of suburbia north and west of Boston, where the D.A., L. Scott Harshbarger was experimenting with all manners of prosecutorial innovation. Middlesex County, despite its girth, doesn't suffer an inordinate amount of violent crimes; most of the murders tend to be domestic killings, and outside of the Boston-border city of Cambridge—until recently a predominantly working-class town, despite the presence of the Massachusetts Institute of Technology, Harvard University, and the tonier districts near Harvard Square—and Framingham, on the western edge of the county, serious mayhem was a rarity.

When prosecutors aren't grappling with a heavy flow of felony cases, they are free to direct their staff and resources into pet projects, either certain troublesome criminal trends—child abuse, say, or domestic violence—or into prevention programs—funding youth centers and afterschool activities, for instance. The prosecutor as master social worker, in a sense. (Though in Middlesex, the tenor of the times overtook the office's best intentions. In 1984, when horror stories of ritual sexual abuse at day care centers swept the nation, Harshbarger's office prosecuted Violet Amirault, her daughter Cheryl LeFavre, and her unfortunately named son, Gerald "Tooky" Amirault for raping dozens of children at the Fells Acre Day Care Center in Malden. While nearly every other such prosecution has since been revealed as the unfortunate result of children's fantasies and investigators' zeal, the Fells Acres debacle is still dragging through the Massachusetts court system, albeit in sporadic spasms.)

Ralph Martin followed his mentor Reilly to Middlesex in 1983. As a rookie assistant district attorney, he was dispatched to the district courts, the lower-level system in Massachusetts where misdemeanors are adjudicated and felons are arraigned before progressing to superior court. For two years, he argued against drunk drivers and drug peddlers and car thieves, tackling the occasional thug who punched out his wife or knothead caught carrying an unlicensed .357 in his waistband. It was an education in the rote scripts of justice, the daily grind of victims and villains, the never-ebbing tide of small violations and maddening disorder. Yet it was visceral, the graffiti-tagged shop owner or bruised girlfriend no less tragic simply because of their anonymity. The prosecutor, or, more accurately, the assistant D.A., is the last, best hope any grieving or raging casualty has to squeeze any sense of revenge or justice from a faceless bureaucracy of cops and court clerks.

Yet the work could be limiting, as well. In Massachusetts, particularly eastern Massachusetts with its long and tortured history of racial discord, a black man is easily pigeonholed, forced into a narrow professional role. Martin knew that assistant district attorneys could easily be saddled with a reputation for being able to handle only the trifles of law. Worse still, a black A.D.A. risked being branded a gun-and-drug specialist, crimes that sound glamorous and gritty but in reality are the white noise of any quasi-urban (and, increasingly, suburban) courthouse.

So in 1985, Martin migrated to the U.S. Attorney's Office, where his other mentor, Budd, would be appointed in 1989. Federal law is a different beast, the neurosurgery to the public health clinic checkups. The feds select their cases as much by political whim as judicial necessity. Throughout the seventies and eighties—the decades following the pronouncement by J. Edgar Hoover, the weird director of the Federal Bureau of Investigation, that the Mafia posed "the greatest internal threat to the security of the United States"—federal prosecutors in Boston chased Italian mobsters with an unbridled glee, building cases that, as late as 1995, were celebrated as legal triumphs. After 1995, revelations that those investigations involved the FBI's use of so-called Top Echelon informants, or high-level rats (including James J. "Whitey" Bulger, the gangster brother of the former state senate president), reduced those cases to a national embarrassment.

Other U.S. Attorneys, political appointees all, indulged their curious notions of right and wrong. Dilettante William F. Weld, who later went on to be elected governor, spent most of his five years in

office trying to prove that former Boston Mayor Kevin White had
been corrupt (a failure) and that a handful of Boston cops took
free dinners from widowed restaurant owners (a success). His suc-
cessor, Frank L. McNamara, Jr., meanwhile, imploded soon after he
tried to prove Weld was an unreformed pot-smoker.

Personal peccadilloes aside, federal prosecutors still have the
luxury of selecting their targets, of choosing which tax evader or
drug dealer is worth going after. The cases tend to be more complicated, largely because they are built from the ground up as opposed to being an after-the-fact crime with a ready-made set of
facts from which to work. A state-level prosecutor, by way of example, begins an assault case with a victim, a suspect, and a police
report. His job, then, is to prove the suspect assaulted the victim.
Federal prosecutors, by way of contrast, often begin by suspecting
(deciding, critics maintain, and not unreasonably) that Mr. Smith
is laundering money for some criminal organization or another.
Then they investigate Mr. Smith, usually in conjunction with the
appropriate federal law enforcement office, such as the Drug Enforcement Administration or the FBI. When they have enough in-
criminating information, they proceed to a grand jury, which
almost always indicts, and then to the courts. Not suprisingly, Mr.
Smith is dead in the water: more than 95 percent of federal charges
end in a conviction, often by way of plea agreements.

Martin was assigned to the economic crimes unit, where his job
was to uncover people such as the fictional Mr. Smith.

ON OCTOBER 23, 1989, FOUR YEARS AND SIXTEEN DAYS AFTER
Ralph Martin joined the U.S. Attorney's Office, a pregnant white
woman named Carol DiMaiti Stuart was shot in the back of the
head while she sat in the passenger seat of her husband's Toyota
Cressida on a dark side street in a housing project two blocks from
Brigham & Women's Hospital. Stuart and her husband, Charles,
had left a birthing class minutes earlier when, according to what
Charles told police that night, a man jumped into the back seat.
Spooked by Charles's cellular phone—"Are you a cop?" the man

asked—he shot Carol in the back of the skull, fired another shot into the visor in front of Charles, and then put a third bullet into Charles's back. "I ducked," Charles told a police dispatcher.

Ralph Martin, like the rest of Boston, heard about the killing that night. The next morning, so did the rest of the country, a brutal and gruesome killing made more real by the *Boston Herald*'s front page photograph of Carol slumped forward in her seat, blood and brain tissue matting her brunette hair.

Martin's first thought that night was the reflexive fear of every black man in Boston: "I hope they're not saying a black guy did it." His second thought came the next morning, when he read the transcript of Charles's conversation with the 911 dispatcher. "He ducked? How in the hell do you duck in a Toyota?"

That thought was immediately dismissed by a third. "I guess the cops know what they're doing."

CHAPTER 4

The Stuart Infamy

CHUCK'S THICK FINGERS FUMBLED ACROSS THE KEYPAD OF HIS car phone, trying to find the three-digits—star-7-7—that would ring the Massachusetts State Police. He was half blind from the pain. Gut-shot is the worst kind of shot, a hurt so bad you wish the bullet had gone through your brain. Chuck took it in the back, in the fleshy pulp just above his hip on the right side, a .38 caliber bullet fired point-blank, the barrel of the gun so close it burned a small, black circle into his skin. The lead mushroomed when it hit the weak resistance of tissue, widening into a hard and rumpled ball that tore through the top of Chuck's colon, his liver and his lower intestine before ripping a hole in his stomach on the way out. Mother of God, it hurt.

"State Police, Boston."

"My wife's been shot, I've been shot."

Gary McLaughlin, the dispatcher who answered the call at 8:35 on the night of October 23, 1989, kept his voice steady. "Where is this, sir?"

"I have no idea," Chuck said. The words were pinched, forced out through a grimace. *Fuck, this hurts.* He was thirty years old, a fur salesman from the suburbs. Had a wife eight months pregnant.

Five minutes ago, they were learning how to breathe deep and
slow, how to push a baby out of her womb. Now she was slumped
forward, the seatbelt holding her off the dashboard, her shallow
breaths burbling through the blood draining down from the back
of her skull. "I'm off, I was just coming from Tremont." A pause,
Chuck trying not to black out, keep all his organs from exploding.
"Brigham and Women's Hospital."

"Try to give me an indication of where you might be,"
McLaughlin told him, still calm, "a cross street or anything else."

Another pause. Then Chuck's voice. "Hello?"

"Yes, go ahead," McLaughlin said.

"Hello. I got into the car at Huntington Avenue"—*oh, Christ, it
hurts*—"drove straight through Huntington Avenue."

"Where are you right now, sir? Can you indicate to me?"

"No, I don't know, I don't know," Chuck groaned. "He drove us,
made us go to an abandoned area."

"Okay, sir, can you see out the windows? Can you tell me where
you are please?"

"No, I don't know. I don't see any signs." White heat flashed
through Chuck's abdomen. "Oh, God."

McLaughlin ignored it, focused on finding Chuck and his shot
wife. "What kind of car do you have, sir? What kind of vehicle do
you have?"

"Toyota Cressida."

"Toyota Cressida?"

"Cressida. It's, it's a—" Another jab to his gut.

"You're in the city of Boston though?"

"Yes."

At least McLaughlin had gotten him to narrow it down. "Can
you give me any indication where you might be, any buildings?"

Chuck answered with a groan, rumbling out of his throat. "No."

"Okay," McLaughlin said next, still calm. "Has your wife been
shot as well?"

"Yes," Chuck said. "In the head."

"In the head?"

"Yes. I ducked down."

"How far..." No, wait, wrong question. "How long ago did you leave Brigham and Women's, sir, and what direction did you go?"

Chuck groaned again. "Two minutes," he said. "Three minutes."

"Okay, sir, bear with me now, stand by, stay on the phone with me."

"Should I try to drive or should I stay where I am?"

"No," McLaughlin told him. "The people that shot you, are they in the area right there?"

"No, they, they took off. They left."

"Okay, can you look out, can you get out of the vehicle and look around to see where you are, sir? I'm trying to get some assistance to you."

"Should I drive up to the corner of the street?"

Chuck didn't sound like he could breathe, let alone drive. "If you can drive, sir, without hurting yourself, yes, if you could," McLaughlin said. "Just try to give me a cross street. If you can drive, give me any street indication and stay there. I'll get someone right to you."

"I'll start the car. He took the keys, but I have a spare set." Chuck's muscles turned to fire as he leaned toward the ignition. "Oh, man. I'm starting the car."

"Okay, sir. What's your name, sir?"

"Stuart, Chuck Stuart." Another poker through his guts. "Ahh, man."

"Bear with me, Chuck. I'm going to get someone to you. Hang in with me now."

"All right—" He stopped talking, swallowed a bolt of pain. "I'm at a place, but I can't read it."

"Just try to read it, Chuck. Just calm down, just stay with me. I'm gonna get help to you, help is gonna be on the way."

"I'm coming up to a, an intersection, but there's no—"

"What color is your car, buddy?"

"Blue."

"Blue Toyota Cressida?"

"Yeah," Chuck said. Then a loud, searing groan.

"Okay, Chuck, try to give me a street."

"I'm coming to an intersection."

"Okay, Chuck, help's gonna be on the way. Bear with me. Is your wife breathing?"

"She's still gurgling," Chuck said. "There's a busy street up ahead. Oh, man." *Fuck me, it hurts.* "I can't see where I am."

"Bear, hang in with me, Chuck. Just try to give me any indication of where you might be, hospitals"—McLaughlin guessed Chuck had to be somewhere near a cluster of medical centers south of Fenway Park and west of a ghetto—"if you see a building."

"I'm turning onto a busy street," Chuck said. Wrestling the wheel was excruciating. "My lights are out."

"Chuck, just pull over. Pull over, Chuck." The cops had a better chance of finding a parked Cressida than one moving around a tangle of knotted streets.

"Are you there?" Chuck asked.

"I'm here, Chuck."

"Oh. I'm driving with my lights off. I can't reach forward, it's too painful."

"Is it Francis Street, Chuck?" If Chuck was retracing his route across Huntington Avenue, he should have ended up on the long block that leads back to Brigham and Women's. "Chuck," McLaughlin asked him again, "are you near Francis Street?"

Chuck mumbled something, guttural syllables that never made the transition into complete words.

"Okay, why don't you just pull over." Chuck was getting harder to find, limping around in his Cressida. "Is there someone there you can ask where you are?"

Another groan, shorter, sharper, an acute grimace. "I'm coming up on a busy street. Oh, man, ahh."

"Hang in there with me, Chuck."

"I'm turning onto a busy street. I recognize where I am now. Should I drive to the hospital?"

"Just tell me what the street is, Chuck."

"Ahh, man." *Sonofabitch, this is fucking agony.* "I'm pulling over. Tremont Street."

"You're at Tremont?"

"Oh, man, I'm gonna pass out."

"Hang in with me, Chuck. Tremont Street where? Help's gonna be on the way. Chuck." Silence. "Chuck. Chuck?"

"Yeah."

"Tremont Street where?"

"I don't know. I'm in front of—" His voice broke into gibberish. "Oh, man."

More silence. "I'm blanking out," Chuck said.

"You can't blank out on me. I need you, man. Chuck? Chuck?"

"Oh, man, it hurts, and my wife has stopped gurgling, she's stopped breathing."

"Chuck, I'm gonna get assistance to you, buddy. Open the door, talk to someone on the street."

"I'm gonna try to drive straight to the hospital."

"Can you drive?"

"I'm trying." Chuck was grimacing again, too, every short phrase interrupted by a sandpaper clinch in his throat.

"Are you driving now?"

"Yeah, I'm driving."

"Can you indicate to me exactly where you might be? I got Tremont Street, we got assistance on the way to you."

"I gotta pull over."

"Is there anyone on the street, Chuck? Stop a passerby on the street so they can tell me where you are."

Chuck moaned again.

"Chuck, pull over on the side of the street and talk to any passerby so I have an indication of where you are." McLaughlin was still calm, but his tone was firmer. If Chuck's wife wasn't gurgling, there was no time for the ambulance to be hunting a moving target.

"I can't move." Chuck said. "Oh, God."

"Chuck, can you see anyone on the street?"

"My car died. Oh man."

"Chuck, pull anyone over on the street, anyone you see on the street, pull over."

"I'm looking, I'm looking. There aren't many people."

"Okay, calm down, just hang in with me. I'm gonna have assistance right there to you."

Silence. "Chuck." More silence. "Chuck? Can you give me anything? Just look out the window. Can you see anything?"

A moan came back over the phone, then an eternity of dead air.

"Chuck, can you hear me? Chuck? Chuck, pick up the phone. I can hear you breathing there, Chuck. Come on, buddy."

No answer.

"Chuck? I don't know a definite location. We heard a siren, though."

Nothing.

"Chuck? Chuck Stuart, come on, Chuck, I can hear you breathing. Can you hear me, Chuck? Pick up the phone."

Still nothing.

"Chuck, can you hear me, buddy?" McLaughlin was edgier now, knowing time was running out. "I need a little better location to find you right away. Come on, Chuck. Damn! Chuck? Hello, Chuck, can you hear me?"

McLaughlin kept trying to rouse Chuck, shake him back into consciousness, keep him talking and alive for a few more moments. A half dozen cruisers were combing the area, blaring their sirens one after the other, McLaughlin tracking their positions and the relative volume of their wails through the phone, sonically triangulating a fix on the Cressida.

"Chuck Stuart, stay with me, buddy," McLaughlin said again. "I can still hear you moving. Can you pick up the phone, Chuck? Chuck Stuart, come on, Chuck. Can you pick up the phone? Chuck Stuart, are you there? Chuck? Hello, Chuck."

Chuck didn't answer. Seconds ticked off. Finally, he spoke into the phone, his voice weaker. "I hear the police."

"Chuck!"

"I hear the police."

"Chuck! Where are you, Chuck?

"Help, help," Chuck said. "Get in touch with the State Police. My wife and I've been shot."

"Chuck!"

"Right here," Chuck said, "There's Boston police."

In the background, over the dull rush of traffic, McLaughlin heard a cop holler, "We've located him."

Thirteen minutes had passed since Chuck had first dialed the phone. "Put the Boston police officer on the phone, Chuck," McLaughlin told him.

Chuck didn't answer. He was telling the cops, "Get my wife out."

NEWSPAPER PHOTOGRAPHERS WHO WORK THE NIGHT SHIFT drive battered Crown Victorias and bulky sport utility vehicles crammed with scanners that pick up the radio chatter of every cop and paramedic and firefighter within fifty miles, a cacophony of static and choppy, coded voices droning out of tinny speakers. With experience and instinct, those photographers filter out the routine of traffic stops and domestic beatings, waiting for the calls that might provide some news.

Evan Richman was cruising the city that night for the *Boston Herald*. He heard the first words—"I've been shot, my wife's been shot"—and keyed his ear to the state police frequency, deciphering which streets Chuck was most likely to be forcing himself to drive in his Cressida, circling the neighborhood between Brigham and Women's and, across Huntington Avenue, which is the main thoroughfare from Boston's Fenway neighborhood to the more southern reaches, the Mission Hill housing project. When the cops started firing their sirens, it was easy enough to follow them to Chuck and his gurgling wife.

The Cressida was parked on St. Alphonsus Way, a narrow street that forms the western border of the housing project before it empties onto Huntington directly across from Harvard Medical School. Richman got there at the same time the police and paramedics, scrambling to the front of the Cressida and pointing his Nikon through the windshield. He made a great and gory picture, the stuff of Pulitzers and utter revulsion, an image of a crumpled woman who was still pretty despite the blood matting her brunette hair.

Other reporters were stampeding to Mission Hill. A film crew from "Rescue 911," an early forerunner of the reality genre, happened to be riding with Boston paramedics that night, which meant the entire bloody extrication was recorded for a national audience. The city's two daily papers, the *Herald* and the *Boston Globe* scrambled to re-plate their pages for the late editions, the *Herald* splashing the shooting on the front cover, the *Globe* pushing 626 words onto the first page of the Metro/Region section.

No one—not the reporters and certainly not the police—had much information to work with. Carol DiMaiti Stuart, who was thirty-three years old, was rushed back to Brigham and Women's, where her son, Christopher, was sliced out of her womb. He entered the world two months ahead of schedule weighing three pounds, eight ounces. The doctors put Christopher into intensive care and listed his condition as critical, the same as his mother. Six hours later, Carol died. Seventeen days later, Christopher died. The paramedics raced Chuck to Boston City Hospital, where doctors were exceptionally well-practiced in treating gunshot wounds. Before he was put under anesthesia, though, Chuck regained enough of his senses to tell the detectives what had happened.

After leaving a Lamaze class with Carol, Chuck steered the Toyota toward Mission Hill, a route that took him across busy Brigham Circle and, eventually, would have led to Melnea Cass Boulevard and the expressway to their split-level home in suburban Reading, thirteen miles north. While he was stopped on Francis Street, waiting for the traffic light to change so he could cross Huntington, a black man jumped into the back seat, pointed a silver pistol at Chuck's back, and told him to drive and not look into the rearview mirror. Still, Chuck somehow managed to get a pretty good look at him: black running suit with red stripes down the side, leather racing gloves with open knuckles, a scraggly beard, about five feet, ten inches tall, maybe six feet, 150 pounds, give or take, thirty-ish, and a raspy, "singsong" voice.

The gunman directed Chuck to a desolate area—the best guess of the police that night was a dilapidated strip on the far side of the Mission Hill housing project—and told him to stop the car. He stripped Carol's jewelry, including her diamond engagement ring and the wedding band Chuck had slipped on her finger four years earlier. He also took their watches, a hundred dollars in cash, and Chuck's car keys. Finally, he demanded Chuck's wallet.

"I don't have one," Chuck told him.

The black man considered that. No wallet? Maybe the white man was a cop, had a badge in his wallet, didn't want to give himself away. The black man eyed the phone mounted between the front seats. That could be a cop thing. "I think you're five-o," he announced, at the time a voguish slang for police, strange homage to Jack Lord.

Then the black man shot Carol Stuart in the back of the head. The next shot went into the visor in front of Chuck. The third—"I ducked"—hit him in the abdomen.

After he told the police what had happened, the doctors wheeled Chuck into surgery to put his ravaged innards back together. Meanwhile, the mayor, Raymond L. Flynn, and the police commissioner, Francis "Mickey" Roache, hurried to both Brigham and Women's and Boston City Hospital to console the Stuarts' relatives. When he finished with that task, Flynn stood up in front of a small crowd of reporters at the police station in the Roxbury neighborhood, a half mile or so from Brigham Circle. The sweatsuit he happened to be wearing at that late hour couldn't conceal a swell of bewildered rage. "I demand that the Boston Police Department continue to be extremely aggressive in cracking down on people who are using guns and killing innocent people," he said. "It's intolerable. We will use every lawful tool to support our police officers in cracking down on gun-wielding criminals." Later, he told Roache he wanted "every available detective on the case."

IN THE YEAR BEFORE CAROL AND CHUCK STUART WERE SHOT,
Mission Hill had enjoyed an 18 percent drop in crime. On the
other hand, Mission Hill is actually two distinct neighborhoods.
One is the hill itself, a steep rise of pudding stone lined with Victorian homes and a few small apartment complexes, populated by
carpenters and plumbers who held out against the encroachment
of the ghetto below and a smattering of gentrifying yuppies drawn
by the architecture and the views and the location, close to the
medical centers and a short walk to a trolley line a block in one direction and a subway a block in the other.

The other neighborhood, the one across Tremont Street at the
bottom of the hill, was a miserable housing project, a collection of
squat and squalid brick buildings arranged around bare dirt and
weeds and potholed parking lots. In the late eighties, when heroin
first began its resurgence in Boston, the corner of Parker and Smith
streets, on the eastern edge of the project, was considered to be one
of the busiest drug bazaars in New England. The cops even had a
nickname for Annunciation Road—Assassination Road. Indeed, the
project was such a swamp of urban blight that rather than try to rehabilitate it, the local authorities bulldozed the entire thing in
1999. Most of the residents—most of whom were law-abiding folks
trying to survive in a horrible environment—were black or Latino.
In 1989, a lot of young men and boys with dark skin were shooting
each other: that year, 100 people were murdered in the city of
Boston, the overwhelming majority of which were minorities, a
ratio that would remain constant in 1990, when a record 153 were
slain. Two days earlier, a fourteen-year-old black boy was murdered,
which happened only a few days after a sixteen-year-old was killed.
In the fifty-three days before the Stuart shooting, according to fig-
ures compiled by the Boston branch of the National Association for
the Advancement of Colored People, 104 black Bostonians had
been shot. And in forty catastrophic days and nights beginning
September 1, 1989, officers in Area B, the police district that covers
the bulk of the city's black neighborhoods, responded to 170 shootings that left 5 people dead and 101 wounded.

Given that dreary drumbeat, Chuck Stuart's tale of urban murder and mayhem sounded terribly reasonable. In those first few days, no one seemed to doubt it, either. The very next day, the state's Republican leadership, who, despite a brief respite in the early nineties, have always been the lunatic fringe of Massachusetts politics, immediately called for the return of the death penalty. More compassionately, some three hundred people attended a Mass for Carol Stuart at Mission Church in Roxbury, the heart of the city's black community, on October 25. A week later, students and teachers at Mission Church High School held a candlelight vigil to mourn the escalating violence in their neighborhood. McLaughlin, the cool-headed dispatcher who can arguably be credited with saving Chuck Stuart's life, called Chuck "a hero." And City Councilor Bruce Bolling, the last vestige of a long political dynasty in Boston's black neighborhoods, proclaimed, "The Stuart family has become a symbol. People felt that as long as all this violence was in the greater Roxbury neighborhood, it's not going to affect us. Now we see it is not confined to a single race or ethnicity."

There were some mild and dutiful protestations about class and race, namely that the murder of a white suburban couple was somehow more important than the murder of a poor black man. In fact, James Moody, who was twenty-nine years old and black, was shotgunned in the back of the neck a few miles away and a few hours later on the same Monday night that Carol Stuart was killed. He made it onto page fifty-seven of the *Globe* on Thursday. Yet Mayor Flynn dismissed such concerns, and not unreasonably. "There will be the same aggressive and fair and consistent enforcement of all our laws, regardless of where it takes place," he said when a reporter asked him about the disparity at a press conference the day after the Stuart shootings. "Whatever area or color or ethnicity, it will be handled the same aggressive and fair way by the Boston Police Department." Which was true: by the time reporters got around to noticing James Moody was dead, the police and district attorney already had a warrant out for his alleged killer, who was arrested later that day, arraigned the next, and ordered held on $1 million bond.

Truth is, though, a pregnant white woman and her furrier husband falling prey to an urban stereotype is a better news story than yet another black kid dying. That is the very definition of "news"—something unusual. No one ever said it was fair or right or moral; it just is. And in late October 1989, there was no bigger news story than the Stuart shooting. The unfolding saga of funerals and frustrated police and mourning relatives played across the front pages for nine days, then haunted the inside pages of the papers for another three months.

The story became more tragic by the hour. A quick, and, in the end, shallow, portrait of the Stuarts cast them as almost iconic sweethearts. They had met in the early eighties in a restaurant in Revere, a working-class city on the shore just north of Boston, where Chuck tended bar and Carol waited tables. In the autumn of 1985, they married. By then, Chuck had been working for four years at Kakas Furs on Newbury Street, Boston's eight-block strip of high-end retail; Carol, who was three years older than Chuck, earned a law degree and took a job as a tax lawyer at a local publishing company. They kissed each other goodbye in the driveway every morning, kissed hello in the evening, and Carol always said, "I love you," before she hung up the phone when Chuck called her at work.

Carol's funeral Mass was held at St. James Church in Medford, the same place they were married. Nearly eight hundred people showed up, including Flynn, Roache, and Governor Michael S. Dukakis. They all wept, or at least fought back tears, when Brian Parsons, Chuck's best friend, read a letter the widower had written from his bed at Boston City Hospital.

> Good night sweet wife, my love. God has called you to His hands. Not to take you away from me or the happiness and gladness you brought me, but to bring you away from the cruelty and the violence that fills this

world. He said that for us to truly believe, we must know that His will was done and that there was some right in this meanest of acts. In our souls, we must forgive this sinner because He would too. My life will be more empty without you, as will the lives of your family and friends. You have brought joy and kindness to every life you've touched. Now you sleep away from me. I will never again know the feeling of your hand in mine, but I will always feel you. I miss you and I love you. Your husband, Chuck.

THE POLICE WERE STYMIED FROM THE BEGINNING. THERE WERE no witnesses, for one, though that seemed strange, considering Brigham Circle is a heavily traveled intersection where a black man forcing his way into a car could conceivably draw someone's attention. As for Chuck, he was either too sedated or in too much pain to add much to his original story. And while he had managed to give an exceptionally detailed description of the shooter, those same details were fuzzy enough to fit several hundred men in and around Mission Hill—several thousand if the bad guy was smart enough to shave off his scraggly beard.

So the police pursued three basic investigatory trails. The first was to race after every report of a black man with a gun, as two dozen officers did on the afternoon of October 24 when someone saw two men in Roxbury with a pistol. Wrong caliber. Wrong guys. The second was begging for help, pleading with the public to come forward with any scrap of information. And the third was more primitive: harass the bejeezus out of every known hoodlum, and some not known, until one of them finally gives up the shooter.

That tactic wasn't new. Police in Boston for nearly a year had been stopping young black males and patting them down for weapons, a practice that a judge in September, 1989 ruled was unconstitutional—which wasn't so surprising considering a police commander a few months prior told a reporter for the weekly

Boston Phoenix that "I don't care about their constitutional rights."
Still, the policy had broad support, especially in the neighborhoods then under siege by young men with guns. "Right now, the
police have to do what they have to do," Georgette Watson, who
ran a crime-prevention program called Drop-A-Dime in Roxbury,
told the *New York Times* shortly after Carol Stuart died. "Unfortunately, there are good kids who are stopped and searched. But I've
heard people say, 'In these times, I don't mind. My child being
searched and having nothing is better than me seeing him in a
coffin.' Instead of us yelling about the constitutional rights of the
kids, we have to explain to them that times are hard right now.
And we have to think about the constitution of safety. If you hand-
cuff the police, who do you have?"

In the days after the Stuart shooting, however, the police made
no secret of their third strategy. As one detective told a *Boston
Globe* reporter, "Somebody in Mission Hill is going to give this guy
up—if not to do the right thing, then just because it will get rid of
the heat."

That strategy, in turn, assumed that Chuck Stuart was telling
the truth. When a wife or girlfriend is murdered, the first suspect
is always the husband or boyfriend for the plain fact that the husband or boyfriend is most often guilty. Yet Boston homicide detectives did only a cursory check into Chuck Stuart. His health
made more thorough interrogations difficult, for one thing. More
importantly, Captain Edward McNelley, who commanded the
homicide unit, was firmly convinced that Chuck could not have
shot himself as a cover story for his wife's murder, that the angle of
the entry wound was such that only a contortionist could have
pulled the trigger. Plus, Chuck damn near killed himself: another
few minutes of puttering around lost in his Cressida and he could
have easily bled to death.

Officially, investigators never identified any suspects in the
murder of Carol Stuart and the wounding of Chuck. Unofficially,
cops started whispering names to reporters within forty-eight
hours. (Such reportage is standard on the Boston police beat—in-

ternal rules forbid all but a few key officers from speaking publicly—and it is not nearly so reckless a practice as critics sometimes charge. Because Boston still has competing dailies, reporters
are generally quite careful in building their stories on reputable
sources.) The first name dribbled out like so much chum to a
shark frenzy was Timothy Talbert, who was twenty-three years old
and fairly close to Chuck's generic description when he was arrested on a minor charge on October 26. At his arraignment the
next morning, Talbert was released on his own recognizance. He
left the courtroom to find a small swarm of reporters and TV cameramen who'd been told he was a suspect. He wasn't; in fact, the
story was knocked down so fast that his arraignment never even
made the papers.

The next fellow, a homeless junkie and ex-con named Alan
Swanson facing a trial for possession of a gun, wasn't so lucky. An
unusually large contingent of police found him squatting in a
friend's apartment in Mission Hill with his girlfriend, who also
happened to be the mother of his three children. He was charged
with breaking and entering, which gave them a reason both to
hold him and to make a cursory search of the apartment. In the
bathroom, soaking in a small plastic tub, the officers discovered a
black jogging suit with a white stripe.

Later that evening, Detective Paul J. Murphy wrote an application for a warrant to search the apartment where Swanson was living. Chuck had said the shooter wore a jogging suit with a red
stripe. Murphy's warrant application said the killer wore a suit with
"red or white stripes .... The white stripes appeared to have a pink-
ish color."

Swanson spent six hours being badgered by homicide detectives
that night. By Monday morning, the original charge of breaking
and entering in the nighttime had been upgraded to unarmed bur-
glary, which carries a twenty-year sentence, ten times that of the
lesser crime. Worse, a phalanx of reporters showed up for his arraignment. On Tuesday morning, October 31, Swanson was publicly anointed a suspect in the Stuart shootings.

He was never seriously under suspicion. The lead investigators knew the jogging suit was a weak link in an imaginary chain of evidence. And Swanson might have been a thug—he had spent time in state prison for armed robbery, a not-uncommon crime among addicts—but he wasn't cut out to be a killer. But that didn't stop the guards and the other inmates in the Charles Street jail from calling him a baby-killer, from spitting in his food, from threatening to shank him in a corridor.

Swanson was never officially cleared as a suspect, mainly because he was never officially named as one. But by early November, no one believed he'd pulled the trigger. By then, Willie Bennett was the new alleged bad guy.

THE BOSTON POLICE DEPARTMENT IN THE LATE 1980S WASN'T particularly good at solving crimes, and the Suffolk County District Attorney's Office was even worse at prosecuting them. The last years of the decade were a bloody serial of botched investigations, acquitted cop-killers, rogue police shootings, and man-handled hoodlums. Both agencies were so cloddish that a *Boston Globe* reporter named Toni Locy began a four-part, ten-thousand-word series on the era, under the heading "Bungling the Basics," with a devastatingly blunt assessment: "Boston Police lag behind many major city departments in bringing criminals to justice because of inept handling of some of the most basic facets of police work." And that was one of the kinder sentences.

Between 1985 and 1989, by way of damning example, the Boston police solved homicides (the crime, curiously, that is solved most often) at a rate lower than all but two of the nation's thirty largest metropolitan areas—which was actually an improvement from 1980, when Boston was dead last.

Partly the problem was procedural. As Locy noted, the B.P.D. was woefully lax in securing crime scenes, a fundamental first step in investigating a crime. (Which would explain, by the way, how a *Boston Herald* photographer was able to point his camera through the windshield of a Toyota that had just been the scene of a double shooting.) The most horrific instance came in February 1988, when a veteran drug detective was shot to death during a raid gone wrong, and the alleged killer and a number of police officers were dragged through the court system for nearly four years. Indeed, the murder of Sherman Griffiths—by all accounts an excellent and aggressive cop—revealed a department hobbled by layer upon layer of mismanagement.

It began with the raid itself. Technically, police were supposed to apply for search warrants only after a cumbersome investigation, including several days of watching a suspected crack house and, depending on the scenario, gathering evidence from informants or from so-called controlled buys, actually purchasing drugs from the bad guys. In the real world of Boston policing, that policy was designed to be ignored. Officers were promoted to the drug squad for a few months at a time, essentially as an audition. Make enough busts before your six months were out, and you had a better chance of staying with the unit. Yet if every aspiring drug cop had to spend three days sitting in front of a drug den, carefully noting the comings and goings of junkies—"heavy foot traffic," in the parlance of policing—his tally of arrests would be anemic. That is not to imply, however, that cops smashed into random houses in a snipe hunt for drugs; anyone who has worked the streets for a week can identify a crack house practically by glancing at it. So, as a matter of routine, they lied. "Testilying," to use civil libertarian and Harvard Law Professor Alan Dershowitz's phrase. Young officers and even some veterans fabricated informants, almost always identified by an untraceable first name of simply "IT," to whom they attributed information that appeared obvious. To bolster IT's credibility, they would list several other raids in which drugs were recovered, giving credit for the tip-off to the same fictional IT.

In mid-February, "John" told police that he had bought cocaine on the third floor of 102-104 Bellevue Street, a worn-out two-family triple-decker in the city's Dorchester neighborhood. A Hispanic man named Stevie, who was five feet, six inches tall, had sold him the drugs, "John" swore. With that information, which was cobbled together by a young detective named Carlos Luna, Griffiths and a squad of detectives were dispatched to Bellevue Street on the evening of February 17. Griffiths, a bearish man of thirty-six who been a cop for eight years, led, carrying a sledge-hammer in his massive hands. There was no need to announce themselves: the detectives had secured a no-knock warrant, which meant they were free to smash into the apartment.

Griffiths positioned himself in front of the door and drew the sledgehammer back, torquing his shoulders and back. Then he swung, the head of the hammer bashing the door with a tremendous thud. But it left only a dent. Damn. Stevie had reinforced the door. Griffiths swung again, then wound up for a third swing.

The bullets blew through the door like grenades. Forty-fives, big slugs designed for the battlefield, fast enough and heavy enough to drop a charging soldier in his tracks at fifty yards. One hit Griffiths in the left temple with more force than the sledge pounded on the door, throwing him down the stairs, already dead or only seconds away from being so.

All hell broke loose. Cops started screaming into radios, pleading for backup. More charged the door, crashing through and chasing down everyone inside. There were six people, including a white man, a white woman, and a six-foot, two-inch Jamaican with lampblack skin named Albert Lewin. There was no short Hispanic man, and no one named Stevie. Or, if there had been, he was long gone, having scampered down a back stairway that none of the detectives had bothered to guard. The two white people were allowed to leave after giving brief statements but before detectives swabbed their hands for gunpowder residue. No one claimed to have seen who pulled the trigger, but Lewin—the only black guy there—was arrested and charged with murder

The investigation went downhill from there. By March, Judge Charles Grabau was ordering the police and prosecutors to produce John, the informant who provided the information. They didn't, because they couldn't: John didn't exist. But suddenly other informants, "Y" and "Z," were conjured up as snitches who'd also contributed to the investigation. They didn't exist, either.

For the next two years, the murder of Griffiths produced one humiliating revelation after another. Luna, who was Griffiths's partner and who was eventually convicted of perjury for inventing an informant, testified that a month after the killing, a sergeant on the homicide squad told him to lie and claim "John" was dead. "A lot of people die in Boston," Sgt. Brendan Bradley said, according to Luna's testimony. "Some of them suddenly and some of them violently. And a lot of homicides go unsolved." The lead homicide prosecutor, Francis O'Meara "reinforced" that notion the following day, Luna swore. "My father was a police officer," Luna said O'Meara told him, "and I know sometimes police officers have to stretch the truth to get the job done." (Neither O'Meara, who is now in private practice, nor Bradley, who has since retired was ever charged with any wrongdoing and both denied Luna's account.)

Lewin was never convicted. For a while, it seemed he might never even go to trial. In March, Judge Charles Grabau dismissed the case in a ranting decision listing a litany of police perfidy. "A fair trial is not possible," he wrote. The misconduct from the day Griffiths died "has been pervasive, egregious, deliberate, and intentional." Max Stern, a bushy-haired lawyer with a thick mustache, went further. "It was not a lie," he said. "It was *hundreds* of lies."

Five months later, the Supreme Judicial Court, the commonwealth's highest judicial authority, reinstated the case, but only by a four-to-three majority and only while harshly criticizing the department's awful behavior. "In order to express its outrage at the reprehensible police conduct in this case," Chief Justice Herbert P. Wilkins ruled, "society need not punish itself by freeing a man who may be guilty of murder."

In the end, Lewin was acquitted. No one else has ever been charged, which means the killing of a police officer—the worst kind of killing, especially as far as the police are concerned—remains unsolved. But the Lewin case was only the highlight of the local constabulary's recent decades of shame. Police culture, a product of generations of professional inbreeding, is notoriously stagnant and resistant to change. Yet in the late eighties, fundamental and sweeping changes in the philosophy of policing were being slowly carved into most of the country's big-city departments. The notable exception: Boston. The obvious reason: politics, an almost creepy throwback to the patronage that controlled law enforcement in the nineteenth century.

Mayor Raymond Flynn had one paralyzing weakness: he ran his department as a political foil, parrying to deflect a criticism here, thrusting to give a friend a job there. Three mayoral chauffeurs, for instance, leapfrogged through the ranks from, respectively, sergeant detective, sergeant, and patrolman to become deputy superintendents, promotions that, not suprisingly, demoralized legions of honest cops who believed merit was a more reasonable route to the top. On the other hand, that notion should have been shot down in 1985, when, after the proverbial nationwide search for a new police commander, Flynn selected his boyhood friend and former altar boy Mickey Roache to run the department. Even Roache appeared flabbergasted by the move. "When I got sworn in," he said a few years later, "I was saying, 'Dear God, just get me through this.' That's all I wanted."

YET EVEN WHEN THE BOSTON POLICE DEPARTMENT PERFORMED gloriously—and, in fairness, the bulk of the rank-and-file have consistently been either competent or excellent, albeit frustrated—the district attorney's office was fully capable of bungling the prosecutorial phase. The trial of Albert Lewin would be a telling example: more than one legal scholar, not to mention anyone with the common sense of a houseplant, has wondered why the D.A. would insist on forging ahead with a case so clearly polluted.

But Newman Flanagan was never so much a professional prosecutor as he was an exceptional politician, a Boston native who grew up at a time when employment with the county was considered a life tenure. He made his reputation in 1975, when, as an assistant district attorney, he convinced a jury to convict Dr.

Kenneth C. Edelin for manslaughter after he removed a twenty-eight-week-old fetus from a seventeen-year-old unwed mother. Because Boston is a predominantly Irish Catholic city (at least when it comes to those who vote), it was a politically shrewd prosecution. Because both Edelin and the mother were black, and because the trial took place at the height of the busing riots, Flanagan was accused of racial bias. He denied any such thing, but even the suspicion wouldn't have hurt him among the working-class whites who believed their neighborhoods were being overrun by blacks.

Three years later, Flanagan ran against his boss, a legendary D.A. named Garrett Byrne who, at the doddering age of eighty and after twenty-six years in office, knew he was stumbling though his last campaign. His young assistant, glad-handing his way through the Democratic strongholds, a loud tie knotted around his neck, charming old ladies with gentle flirtation and riling up blue-collar workers with tough talk about crime and punishment, won handily.

Almost from the beginning, however, criticism rained down upon his office. There was a troubling theme threaded through his tenure, a series of cases tinted with politics and race, rising above the dreary landscape of criminal justice like bright red herrings. The first surfaced just months after Flanagan, then forty-eight years old, took over the office, when a serial rapist was preying on women in Brighton on the far western edges of the city. One night in the early winter of 1979, Flanagan and several Boston Police officials met with some five hundred frightened and angry residents in a local gymnasium, absorbing a torrent of criticism for allowing a serial predator to roam free. That same night, police arrested Willie Sanders and charged him with four rapes.

Juries acquitted him of the first two and a judge dismissed a third, ruling that the police investigation had been badly handled, even that the victim had been coaxed into identifying Sanders as the man who raped her. The fourth charge was dropped by Flanagan's office for lack of evidence—two years after Sanders was first charged.

A year later, in another rape case, the defendant was convicted despite having been locked up in the Deer Island House of Correction at the time of the rape, an inconvenient fact Flanagan's prosecutors tried to nullify by rewriting the indictment to fuzz the date of the alleged attack.

When confronted with questions about those and numerous other cases, Flanagan barely blinked. In a memorable interview with the *Boston Globe* in 1990, the district attorney defended himself by delineating a prosecutorial philosophy that was stunning in its idiocy. "We're in a position where we take all the evidence that we have, we present it to a grand jury, the grand jury makes a determination if there are sufficient facts to put this individual on trial, and that's the system," he said. "We take what they give us. That's our job. We're not investigators. We rely on the Boston Police Department, who do an outstanding job in difficult times. Are you going to have horror stories? Sure, you're going to have horror stories."

Perhaps horror stories are unavoidable. But a prosecutor's job is a far more nuanced task than to simply "take what they give us." Prosecutors are supposed to evaluate evidence to figure out what's credible and what isn't before throwing any scrap of tripe to the grand jurors, whose role is not-inaccurately compared to that of a rubber stamp. As civil libertarian and Flanagan critic Harvey Silverglate was fond of pointing out, "In America, you can indict a ham sandwich." And claiming to rely on the Boston Police Department is fundamentally untrue: In the Commonwealth of Massachusetts, district attorneys, not police departments, are formally in charge of murder investigations.

Beneath the spasms of ineptitude, meanwhile, was a more generalized chaos. Even in the administrative details, the office was trapped in a time warp. Computers were obsolete if they existed at all, the phones were one generation removed from Sam Spade's day, and the women employees were forbidden from wearing slacks. In a rapidly changing city, Flanagan surrounded himself with others of his kind, white Irish Catholics; of 104 prosecutors, a mere seven were black. Prosecutors in the district courts, those trenches of crime and punishment, were overworked, underpaid, and demoralized, flubbing cases for want of simple paperwork. Supervision was sporadic at best, nonexistent at worst. The superior courts, where the most serious felonies are tried, were infused with a low-level thuggery. Flanagan's lead homicide prosecutor, Francis O'Meara, for instance, famously boasted that he "likes to hurt people who hurt people." Murder cases, meanwhile, most often involve "one miserable maggot who says he saw another miserable maggot kill another miserable maggot"—which may, in fact, be true, but it's hardly an epitaph the dead maggot's mother wants to read in her morning newspaper.

WILLIE BENNETT ENTERED THE STUART DRAMA ON NOVEMBER 11, 1989. He never stood a chance. Not that he deserved one, necessarily. He was an ex-con with a criminal record that spanned twenty-five of his thirty-nine years, a litany of sixty arrests splashed with instances of egregious violence. He began as a petty thief, arrested in 1964 for looting coins from parking meters. By the seventies, he was armed and quite dangerous, as he demonstrated by shooting a Boston police officer in the leg in 1973. Bennett did five years in state prison for that crime. Three years after his release, in February 1981, Officer Francis X. O'Brien, who worked for the now-defunct Metropolitan Police Department, pulled Bennett over in Mattapan Square, a neighborhood on the southern tip of the city, for a minor motor vehicle violation. Bennett told the cop he'd left his wallet, with his driver's license in it, at home. The officer, noticing Bennett had two toddlers in the car with him, agreed to follow him to Dorchester, where Bennett lived.

Bennett pulled to the curb and stepped out of the car. In his right hand he held a sawed-off shotgun, which he leveled at O'Brien's chest. With O'Brien's hands in the air, Bennett reached to the officer's hip and pulled the pistol from the holster. Then he pointed the handgun at the left front tire of O'Brien's cruiser and pulled the trigger, blowing through the rubber, and putting the car out of service. He took the keys to the cruiser, climbed back into his own car, and drove away.

The police caught up to Bennett three months later, tracking him to his apartment in Boston's Roxbury neighborhood. Pointing a gun at O'Brien and wounding his cruiser wasn't the only the reason Bennett was a wanted man. Another warrant charged him with trying to kill another police officer, and a third accused him of robbing a legless cab driver. According to a *Boston Globe* account, the cabbie only had forty-two dollars to surrender. So Bennett shot him in the gut.

Eight cops stormed Bennett's apartment in May 1981. Bennett, startled by the crashing and bashing of a police entry team, crouched into a shooting stance, a .357 Magnum revolver clutched between his hands and loaded with hollow-point bullets—a type accurately known as "cop killers" because the dented front end forces the lead to expand, ripping a larger-than-usual hole through the target. "You'll never take me alive," Bennett told the cops in a raspy voice and with his best gangsta swagger.

It didn't work. Detective Tommy Montgomery shot Bennett in the left hand. End of standoff.

Willie Bennett got eight to twelve years for those assorted incidents, which meant he was paroled back to the streets on October 23, 1989, the night the Stuarts were shot. In addition to his criminal record, Bennett had several other strikes against him. He was living alternately with a girlfriend in Burlington, a suburb sixteen miles north of Boston, and with his mother in her apartment on Alton Court, which happens to be in the Mission Hill projects. He also had a scruffy beard and a "raspy, singsong" voice, at least according to the witnesses who later said they saw him stick up a video store with a silver pistol in neighboring Brookline on October 2.

On November 11, 1989, Boston police arrested him for defaulting on a traffic violation. They found Bennett at his girlfriend's house at about the same time they were raiding his mother's apartment on Alton Court, a search that turned up, among other things, a .38 caliber bullet. Neither the police department nor

Flanagan's office would comment about Bennett's connection to the Stuart case, but "sources familiar with the investigation" told reporters the ex-con was the prime suspect.

The news only got worse as the days wore on. After being arraigned on the traffic warrant, he was charged in Norfolk County with the video store robbery. Given the context—his name bubbling through the Stuart investigation, his habit of skipping court dates, and his propensity to shoot people and automobiles—he was held on an exorbitantly high bail. Three days later, Flanagan convened a grand jury to probe the Stuart case, the target of which (again, according to anonymous sources) was Bennett.

The police were building a strong case against a two-time loser, and had been for several weeks. They had no physical evidence, but enough convenient circumstances to make Bennett worth looking at. Through drips and drabs of unattributed newspaper ink and, later, formal investigations, the police by mid-November had found at least four people who could incriminate Bennett. One woman said she saw him with a silver handgun on October 23. Another said she saw Bennett in a Mission Hill hallway, pounding his fist against the cinderblock wall and moaning. Bennett purportedly told her Chuck wanted to buy a bundle of heroin, even though he was already in debt to Bennett. "The bullet wasn't meant for the lady," Bennett supposedly told that witness. "It was meant for the man." One seventeen-year-old said Bennett confessed to him. Another said he heard from Bennett's nephew, Joey "Toot" Bennett, that Bennett had admitted being the shooter. And a fourth witness was waiting in the wings.

Chuck, still convalescing at Boston City Hospital, was steering police toward Bennett as well, albeit awkwardly. Twice he was shown photographs of eight black men. The first time, he pointed out Bennett and another man as the two who most resembled his attacker. Then, on November 21, he was shown another array including Bennett and seven men he hadn't seen in the first set. Chuck picked up Bennett's photo and began to tremble, the photograph jiggling in his hand.

"What's wrong?" an assistant district attorney said.

"This is the best photograph I've seen so far," Chuck told him.

Eleven days later, Chuck was released from the hospital. He bought himself a new Nissan Maxima with the trade-in from his Cressida and a $10,000 certified check, part of the $83,000 Carol's life insurance paid on her $100,000 policy. He bought jewelry, too, including a diamond tennis bracelet for a lithe young blonde he knew in the suburbs. Finally, three days after Christmas, he was summoned to homicide headquarters on D Street in South Boston, led up a creaky stairway, down a long hall and around a corner to a room with one-way glass. On the other side of the window, eight black men filed in. Seven were police officers or civilian employees or friends of cops. The eighth, and the third one to file in, was Willie Bennett.

Chuck studied their faces, examined their builds. "Number three," he said after a moment, "looks the most like him."

Not a positive ID, but close enough for horseshoes and hand grenades and grand juries. Bennett's attorney waited for the indictment to come down.

CHAPTER 5

Hindsight

THE WINDS WERE CALM 135 FEET BELOW, BARELY RIPPLING THE sludgy waters of the Mystic River flowing into Boston Harbor. Up on the Maurice J. Tobin Memorial Bridge, though, the morning breeze felt like a cold sword, cutting through Chuck's sweatshirt and jeans, numbing his ears.

He looked over the edge. The upper deck of the bridge, the one that pumped traffic into Boston, would give him a longer fall. But the outbound side was high enough. A body falling from that height would hit terminal velocity before it hit the water, which, at that speed would be as hard and solid as concrete. Most of the Tobin jumpers—about a dozen leapt every year—are lucky enough to die from the fierce smack against the surface of the Mystic. The rest drop through the depths and get snarled in the muck or the rotting timbers or the abandoned cars that litter the bottom, sucking in brackish water until they drown.

Chuck's Maxima was parked on the berm behind him, the hazard lights flashing in the pale light rising from the east beyond the airport. He'd only been on the run a few hours, not even a full day, before he decided to surrender on the bridge. He knew the cops were looking for him, hunting him like a dog ever since Matthew,

his brother, went and told them what happened. He'd known all along that Chuck had killed his wife. Some of Chuck's other siblings knew, as well. But, damn, now the D.A. was getting ready to blame Willie Bennett for the whole thing. Matthew never thought Chuck would let a *real* guy take the fall. Chuck should have known Matthew didn't have the stomach for it. Mathew had spent New Year's Day drinking in a bar, mumbling over and over, I've got to do it, I've got to get it over with. His friends thought he was talking about killing himself. Two days later, on January 3, Matthew's conscience finally got the best of him.

At 8 p.m. that night, Matthew, accompanied by a lawyer named John Perenyi, met with Thomas J. Mundy Jr., who was in charge of the grand jury investigating the Stuart shootings. He told Mundy that he and a friend met Chuck in the Mission Hill projects the night of October 23, pulling his car next to Chuck's Cressida a few minutes before 8:30. He couldn't see Carol, most likely because she was slumped so far forward in her seat. Chuck leaned out the window and tossed a Gucci bag into Matthew's car. "Take this to Revere," Chuck told him. Matthew did. Matthew never questioned his big brother. A few hours later, when he heard his sister-in-law was dead, Matthew looked inside the bag. There was some jewelry and a silver-plated .38 caliber revolver. One more thing: Carol's engagement ring. Matthew put that in his pocket. Then he drove to a bridge over the Pines River on the border between Revere and Saugus, and dropped everything else in the water.

Flanagan's office told the Boston Police to go arrest Chuck once Matthew had told his story, which he backed up by handing over Carol's ring. But Chuck was already gone, driving south on the Fitzgerald Expressway to Braintree, where he checked into the Sheraton Tara Hotel. On a small pad of paper he found on the night stand, he scribbled a short note. It wasn't a confession. "I love my family," he wrote. "[But] all the allegations of the past four months have taken all my strength."

Chuck checked out of the hotel early the next morning, January 4, and drove north, following a long, swooping ramp off the

expressway and down before the pavement rose again between the sea-green railings of the Tobin Bridge. Halfway across, jersey barriers separate a strip of blacktop from the three main lanes, a spot for state troopers to monitor speeders and for overheated Chevys to pull over. Chuck parked in there, left his keys in the ignition and the note he'd written on the seat. Then he climbed over the railing and stared down at the water. Just after seven o'clock, he jumped.

BY THE TIME THE POLICE DIVERS FISHED CHUCK'S SOGGY CORPSE out of the Mystic River, which was less than six hours after he leapt, history was already being rewritten in broad, grotesque strokes. Some of the revisions were self-serving pabulum: in newsrooms and barrooms across the city—hell, across the country—reporters all pronounced themselves the true cynic who knew from the beginning that Chuck was the killer. True, some of them may have suspected as much, and a good many of them chased down rumors of Chuck's affairs, Chuck's cocaine habit, Chuck's general creepiness. Still, none of them got one word of it into print or onto the air, which is the way such scores are kept.

Others were self-serving, bordering on prevaricating. Willie Bennett, still awaiting a trial he would lose for sticking up the video store, was promptly cleared of any suspicion by D.A. Flanagan. No matter: "My life has been ruined," he told reporters. City Councilor Bruce Bolling, meanwhile, joined a number of other prominent blacks on June 4 to denounce the mayor, the police, and the media. The same councilor who a few months earlier had proclaimed the Stuarts "a symbol" of urban violence shifted hard into rhetorical reverse. "It's incidents like this that really make me angry and make all black people angry because it's incidents like this that characterize black people as vicious, as animals, as people who don't care about themselves or care about their neighborhoods or care about their families," he ranted, apparently forgetting his own contribution to that characterization. "The Mission Hill neighborhood was maligned, the greater Roxbury community was maligned and, through implication, black people were maligned because the alleged perpetrator was described as a black man."

Bolling aside (it is no coincidence that his family's long political dynasty ended with him), Mayor Flynn faced a serious racial dilemma, but one only partly of his administration's making. Chuck Stuart was able to fool so many people for the simple fact that Mission Hill *was* a dangerous place, that young black males in Greater Roxbury *did* have a wearily well-documented habit of shooting each other and the occasional bystander. To the average Bostonian, regardless of color, a black man carjacking and shooting a white couple was only slightly beyond the pale of conceivability. To reporters who'd been to the scenes of dozens of killings in the black community, including the slaying of a twelve-year-old girl who had the misfortune of sitting on a mailbox in the middle of the afternoon next to a hoodlum, Chuck's version of events was well within the realm of possibility.

Police commanders and homicide detectives, on the other hand, are not average Bostonians. In the hours, then days, then months after Chuck Stuart killed himself, nearly every facet of their investigation would come under serious scrutiny and, at times, outright attack. A policy of stopping and searching young black males—so reasonable, even among black anticrime activists, in October 1989—was now seen for what it was: fundamentally wrong-headed police work. Shrill commands made in the bright anguish after the initial shooting were, in the retrenched aftermath, respun in a more damning context. Ray Flynn's order that "every available detective" be put on the snipe hunt for Carol Stuart's phantom black killer, for instance, was dredged up ad nauseum as proof that he fanned the city's always-smoldering racial heat. Little emphasis, however, was put on the key word in that phrase, which was *available;* no detectives were pulled away from the murder of James Moody, who was shot the same night as Carol Stuart and whose killer was in jail within the week.

At first, police and prosecutors defended their investigation, albeit conceding they had taken only a cursory look at Charles Stuart as a potential suspect. (Of course, had Jay Kakas, who owned the Newbury Street fur store Charles managed, reported the nickel-plated, snub-nosed .38 caliber revolver missing from his safe in October, when it disappeared, instead of waiting until January 8, detectives surely would have stared more closely at Stuart.) "We worked as hard on this case as any other," said Francis O'Meara, the prosecutor who believes "miserable maggots" commit most murders. "We've come a long way down the truth road, yet some very good policemen are going to get maligned because they didn't solve it in three days." Well, no, actually: some very average men were going to be maligned for performing some very poor police work. The wake from Chuck's splash had barely settled, though, when disturbing tales began to bubble to the surface, distressing accounts of police coercion, of bullies in badges, of belligerent detectives threatening teenaged boys with beatings and prison. Some of the stories were either false or exaggerated. For example, despite all the tales of apartment doors being smashed apart in the Mission Hill project, the Boston Housing Authority received no requisitions for new ones. Others, however, all had the same chilling echo. One by one, Mission Hill residents came forward to say they had been pressured to implicate Willie Bennett.

By January 8, less than a hundred hours after Charles Stuart killed himself, the *Boston Globe* quoted defense attorneys complaining about detectives' heavy-handed treatment of the purported witnesses against Bennett. "The way they intimidated these kids into making statements," said Leslie Harris, a public defender who represented Alan Swanson, the man whose name surfaced as a suspect first, "some heads should roll." Over the next five days, reporters drew more details out of those same teenagers. On January 15, the commonwealth's attorney general, James Shannon, announced his office would investigate the allegations.

Ralph Martin had followed the twisting saga of the Stuarts as closely as anyone in the city. When Chuck killed himself, Martin didn't pretend to have known all along, didn't feign an all-knowing cynicism. But as the winter of 1990 wore on, he read the newspapers more closely, measuring the lengthening litany of complaints, weighing a new crush of suspicion. Boston police investigations were hardly his area of expertise: at the time, he was prosecuting economic fraud in the United States Attorney's office. Yet the first thought Martin had had when Carol Stuart was killed—*I hope they're not saying a black guy did it*—came screaming back to him. They did say a black guy did it, and the police tried damned hard, maybe too hard to prove it, too.

Sometime in the middle of the last week of January, Martin dialed the extension for Wayne Budd's office. "Hey, you got a minute?" he asked his boss. "I want to come up and talk to you about something."

"Come on up," Budd told him.

Martin rode one of the slow elevators in the federal courthouse on the edge of Boston's financial district up one floor and stepped into a wide, polished corridor. He turned left and, at the end of the hallway, swiped a magnetic card through the security lock that controlled the red double doors that led into the U.S. Attorney's suite of offices. He sat down in Budd's office. Both men were in shirt sleeves, relaxed and informal.

"I've been thinking about the Stuart case," Martin said.

"What about it?"

"Well, I've been thinking about all the articles that have been written. If they're true—if even half of it is true—it's an outrage," Martin said. "Somebody ought to take a look at it."

The two men went over the details for a few minutes, picking out the most egregious anecdotes, Martin building a case that the feds should investigate.

"Why not you?" Budd finally said.

"Huh?"

"You," he repeated. "How about you do it?"

BY THE BEGINNING OF FEBRUARY 1990, MARTIN HAD TWO agents from the FBI working under him to begin picking apart the Stuart case. In some ways, it was a difficult investigation. The fact that Martin and his boss were black men warmed the already-simmering racial climate. Plus, the feds' long history of snooping into Boston's police and politicians made cops who would be reluctant to cooperate downright recalcitrant.

On the other hand, murder investigations, especially aggressive ones, leave a trail of detritus in their wake, notes and recordings and human recollections that, when everything goes right, are pieced together to convict the killer. If things go terribly wrong, as they did in the Stuart case, those same scraps can be reassembled into a rough recreation of the actual events, much the way a million fragments from a shattered airliner can be pieced into a crinkled shell.

For fifteen months, agents interviewed police, prosecutors, and the key witnesses against Willie Bennett, read the transcripts of their interviews with police, and, when they could, listened to recordings of those same or similar conversations. Finally, on July 10, 1991, Budd's office released Martin's fifty-four-page report outlining its version of the Stuart investigation. It was ugly. And it went like this:

Bennett's name was initially mentioned by people calling a hotline Boston police had installed to receive tips in the aftermath of the Stuart shooting, the first call coming on October 27, the second three days later. There was no physical evidence—or even one reliable witness—to link him to the crime. But Bennett, one detective scribbled in his account of the investigation, "had a criminal record consisting of shooting police and civilians, indicating he is capable of the crime of shooting and robbing Carol Stuart."

On November 3, Erick Whitney got involved, and things went downhill from there. Erick was familiar with the police in a number of different ways. For one, they wanted to arrest him on two warrants, one for larceny and one for trying to break into a car. Moreover, a cop named Trent Holland, who patrolled the Mission Hill projects, had used Erick's mother and little sister to make undercover drug buys and had been a Big Brother to Frank Whitney, Erick's older brother. Erick's girlfriend, Angela, meanwhile, was the niece of a Boston police officer.

In the late autumn swirl of rumors and gossip and ghetto machismo, Erick started telling a few people—Angela and his mother being two of them—that he'd heard Willie Bennett had bragged about shooting the Stuarts. Which is how Angela ended up at the homicide division on November 3, driven there by her uncle and talking to a detective named Peter O'Malley. O'Malley could safely be called old school, broad-beamed and balding with a salt-and-pepper beard, a Bogart scowl and a Sipowicz mouth, only he never spoke so much as growled. According to what Angela later told the FBI, O'Malley said he heard Erick had some information and that he wanted to talk to him. In exchange, he would help Erick clear up his two warrants. If Erick preferred not to talk, O'Malley promised he'd see the boy do twenty years.

Not surprisingly, Erick went to South Boston later in the day with Angela. O'Malley asked him what he knew about the Stuart shooting. Erick said he only knew what another kid, Derek Jackson, had told him. O'Malley told him, "Don't fucking lie to me." The conversation continued along those lines for awhile—"I don't know anything," Erick would protest; "You're bullshitting me," O'Malley would answer—until Erick began to change his story. He constructed, poorly, a scenario in which he was in Joey "Toot" Bennett's bedroom the day after the killing when Toot bragged that his uncle Willie had shot the Stuarts. Unfortunately, Erick didn't know where Toot lived, let alone had ever been there, so he had to feed off cues from O'Malley and another officer, Billy Dunn.

Eventually, O'Malley had had enough of Erick. He told him to have Derek call homicide.

Shortly after three o'clock in the afternoon, Erick, Angela, and Derek all ended up back at homicide. O'Malley, Dunn, Holland, Detective Miller Thomas, and another officer Derek didn't recognize were all waiting for them. O'Malley, according to Martin's report, told Derek to tell the truth. So Derek explained how he and Black Mike and Junior were drinking beer and smoking weed in Toot's bedroom the day after the Stuart shooting when Toot passed around an old newspaper clipping about Uncle Willie. Derek read it and said, "This guy is ruthless." Then he asked Toot if Willie was involved in shooting those white people. "Yeah," Toot said, stoned and giggling. Wide-eyed, Derek pushed the point, asking again. "Yeah," Toot kept answering, his giggles swelling into laughter.

O'Malley listened intently. When Derek finished, he said, "Fuckin' liar."

That went on for ninety minutes or so, Derek talking about Toot being high, O'Malley swearing at him. The detective was chain-smoking, pacing the worn linoleum, sweating. Derek offered to take a lie-detector test.

"The only lie detector I've got," O'Malley told him, jerking his head toward Billy Dunn, "is him in a small, dark room."

"I'll get the room ready," Dunn allegedly chimed in.

O'Malley called Erick into the room and told Derek to listen. Erick started retelling his weak story. "Remember, D, how Bennett said how he shot them and came in the room and told you, and his eyes were bloodshot," Erick said, not so much asking his friend as telling him. It took some prodding, but eventually Derek came around. At 9:29 that evening, with O'Malley and Thomas in attendance, Derek started talking into a tape recorder.

His story got even better. Not only did Toot boast about his uncle, but the very next day Willie himself confessed, going so far as to act out the shooting. "The guy made a motion and Mr. Bennett said, 'You're five-o' and he shot them," Derek said. Willie even admitted he'd been wearing a black Adidas running suit with red stripes running down the sleeve.

At 10:39, Erick sat in front of the tape recorder. His tale was becoming more elaborate by the hour, like a fisherman whose blue gill grows into a great white shark after a few hours of drinking. Now Willie was in Toot's bedroom on October 24, telling all those young boys how he popped "the Stokes family." "He told them, 'Give me your wallet,'" Erick said. "So he sees the watches, he took that. So he got out, he saw the Stokes man reach for whatever. He thought he was five-o, and he shot both of them." Proof? Willie was passing around a silver pistol while he told the story.

Neither boy slept well. The next afternoon, Saturday, November 4, Derek called Erick and said they had to go back to homicide and tell O'Malley the truth. Trent Holland and another officer picked them up and, on the ride to South Boston, asked what they were going to say. "I want to talk with O'Malley," is all Derek would tell them.

When they arrived, Erick was summoned into O'Malley's office alone. Derek was left with Holland and the other cop, who reminded the boy that changing your story halfway through a murder investigation can get you sent to jail. Know what boys become in jail? "Faggots."

Erick apparently spent his time talking to O'Malley and another detective, again on tape. He retracted most of what he'd said the night before, admitting that he lied. O'Malley wanted to know why. "Well, my girl said you was going to . . . give me twenty years in Walpole [the state's maximum-security prison]. I mean, I flipped out. I was scared, you know, I came and said anything, you know, to try to get me out."

O'Malley wasn't going for it, countering every protestation of fear by insisting the police are only after the truth. "Does that mean you're nervous if your hands are sweating?" the detective asked Erick at one point.

"It means I'm scared," Erick answered.

"You're scared? Do I look like I'm going to beat you up?"

"No."

"What are you scared of?"

"Going to jail."

Erick was crying when he came out to talk to Derek. He was holding a booking sheet, too. O'Malley left him alone with Derek. "Just stick to the story," Erick begged his friend. "They're gonna send us to jail. Just stick to the story."

They did, even when they were called before the grand jury looking to indict Willie Bennett.

THAT WAS THE GENESIS OF WILLIE BENNETT, PRIME SUSPECT. Martin's report, however, went on to list a number of other alleged offenses committed by Boston police in their efforts to arrest Bennett. Toot Bennett, for one, was busted for possession of cocaine (later dismissed) after Holland allegedly planted a fine white powder in his room. In fact, the final report listed eight specific types of misconduct, including intimidating witnesses and then using their coerced statements to swear out affidavits for search warrants; and feeding information to witnesses to help them conform their stories to the Bennett-as-killer theory. Thrown in for good measure was the charge that detectives used "abusive, profane, and threatening language."

Wayne Budd, however, decided not to press federal charges against O'Malley, Holland, or any other Boston cop. Martin's investigation, while it covered a broad terrain, was legally quite narrow. There is no provision under federal law to prosecute simple police misconduct. Rather, Martin was working under the domain of civil rights statutes, which are quite specific. In order to win any convictions—and the feds don't indict if they can't convict—he would have to prove that two or more cops agreed to violate someone's civil rights. More crudely put, federal prosecutors would need Boston police officers to testify that, in the most notorious murder of the decade, their professional brothers conspired to screw a few black kids. And that wasn't going to happen.

The Boston Police Department's internal investigation, meanwhile, found no evidence of misconduct, save for O'Malley's abundant and varied use of profanity. But the repercussions from the Stuart fiasco set in motion of chain of events, perpetuated by a string of police steps that would have been comical had they not been so invariably violent and often deadly. In 1991, for example, a patrolman shot to death a teenager who was hiding under a parked car, claiming that his gun misfired when he stumbled, looking for the kid. Nineteen-ninety-two opened as badly as any other year, as well. The very first day, an off-duty officer shot an unarmed teenager. Then the attorney general requested an injunction against thirteen officers accused of beating a coked-up miscreant who led them on a high-speed, pre-dawn chase.

On January 14, 1992, a commission appointed by Mayor Flynn the previous year to study the Boston Police Department reported the obvious: the department was in chaos, devoid of leadership, floundering in a stew of managerial incompetence and political chicanery. After years of blundering, "the Department has adopted a purely reactive posture, and drifts from crisis to crisis," said the panel, headed by attorney James D. St. Clair, who worked for Richard Nixon during the Watergate hearings. The chief problem, the commission maintained, was the chief cop, Mickey Roache. And any hope of righting such a badly listing ship, it concluded, could only begin by tossing Flynn's boyhood friend overboard.

That wasn't going to happen. Instead, Flynn turned to the wundercop William J. Bratton to come in as the superintendent in chief, the department's number-two man. Bratton was already fairly famous in certain circles, mainly among fellow cops and New York City straphangers. A hawk-faced man who never lost his thick and native Boston accent, Bratton began his cop career, ironically, as Roache's patrol partner. Smart and ambitious, he rose rapidly through the ranks, climbing from academy recruit in the fall of 1970 to lieutenant before the decade was out. In September 1980, he was appointed superintendent in chief, and heir apparent to Commissioner Joseph Jordan. Eighteen months later, he told a magazine writer that, yes, he would like to be the boss. "My personal goal is to become commissioner," he told *Boston Magazine*. "Be it one year or four years, that's what I want."

What he got, however, was busted back down to lieutenant. So he left. In 1983, he took over the Massachusetts Bay Transportation Authority's demoralized police force. Three years after that, he took over the now-defunct and then-troglodytic Metropolitan District Commission Police, which was still recovering from an exam-stealing scandal. Then, in 1990, he decamped for New York City to command the perpetually downtrodden transit police. At all three departments, and by any measure, he was wildly successful. Morale went up, crime (or, at the very least, the statistical picture of crime) went down. By the time he was called back to Boston,

Bratton had a well-developed and well-deserved reputation as a managerial Rambo, parachuting into troubled departments, fixing what's broken, and spiffing up everything else.

He returned to Boston like a prodigal son. He was humble, no mean feat for a man with a very tight-fitting cap. The unspoken script had Bratton ascending to commissioner after a face-saving grace period for Roache. But in the interim, Bratton pretended to be happy as an underling, promising to work with Roache as "the management team." He was hired on January 16, two days after the St. Clair Commission issued its report, and assigned an office on the sixth floor of police headquarters next to Roache's, the two suites joined by a common bathroom.

Within the week, Roache had Bratton's side of the bathroom walled shut. It was not an isolated gesture. One of the first things Bratton did when he arrived, for instance, was assure all of the top officers that their positions were secure. One of the first things Roache did after that was reassign all the top commanders. Bratton lasted less than two years in Boston before quitting in frustration.

RALPH MARTIN WAS DEPARTING THE LAW ENFORCEMENT BUSIness right about the same time Bill Bratton was arriving in town. He'd been playing with the idea of running for district attorney for more than six months, and had even told his friends three months earlier. He was no closer to a campaign plan, of course. He was still a black man in very white Boston. It didn't help that he was also the same black man who accused all those Boston police officers of manhandling black boys while trying to frame Willie Bennett.

He reminded the city about that, too. In February, bored with the U.S. Attorney's office, he resigned for a private practice joining, of all places, Stern, Shapiro, Rosenfield & Weissberg, the first-named partner of which, Max Stern, had successfully defended Albert Lewin when he stood trial for shooting Detective Sherman Griffiths dead. On his way out of his federal office, Martin cracked to a reporter that the decision not to prosecute any of the Boston police involved in the Stuart case was "the biggest disappoint-

ment" of his career. It's not that he disagreed with Budd—Martin
knew he couldn't win a conviction—but more that he'd found
something wrong that he couldn't fix. "The wrongs we had discovered," he would say later, "the misconduct that we had uncov-
ered were going to go unaddressed by any institution."

Martin's first day at his new job was Monday, February 18,
which, as fate would have it, was the exact same day District Attorney Newman Flanagan told his staff he was resigning to take a
job with the National District Attorneys Association. Flanagan had
nearly two years left in his term, which meant Governor and former U.S. Attorney William F. Weld would have to appoint someone to take over until the next election.

Martin made two phone calls in rapid succession. First, he called
Weld to tell him he wanted the job. Then he called Wayne Budd to
ask for his support.

Five months later, on July 31, 1992, Weld announced that Ralph
Martin was the new Suffolk County District Attorney. Martin,
newly minted as a Republican to placate Weld's GOP genes, would
now be in charge of the same homicide cops he'd so harshly criticized. He would be prosecuting the criminals arrested by Mickey
Roache's police department.

He would last until Election Day 1994. That's what the smart
money said.

CHAPTER 6

Early Lessons

ON THE SATURDAY NIGHT BEFORE CHRISTMAS 1992, RALPH Martin slowed his Audi to a crawl along Centre Street in Jamaica Plain, then braked it to a full stop in front of a bank with an automatic teller machine in the lobby. He shifted into park, pressed the switch that turned on his blinking hazard lights, and stepped into the street. He stood there for a moment, zipping his black suede jacket and adjusting his creamy leather cap, pulling it down tight against the winter chill.

The short, screaming burp of a siren startled Suffolk County's chief law enforcement officer, who was, a millisecond later, briefly blinded by the strobing, high-beam headlights of an unmarked police cruiser that had edged up behind his Audi. The driver's side door snapped open and spit out a white man in a scally cap and civilian clothes.

"Move that fuckin' cah!" the cop snarled at Martin. "Jesus Christ, what the fuck ya pahkin' heah for? Move the fuckin' cah!"

Martin stared back, wide-eyed, the ferocity of the words stunning him into silence. For a half-minute, maybe longer, the cop kept hollering. Martin never made a sound in reply. Finally, almost sheepishly, the man who reigned supreme over every criminal prosecution in the county climbed back into his car. He shifted into drive and puttered up the street, the cruiser hard on his bumper, and steered into an open stretch of curb. The plainclothes cop pulled up flush with the Audi, slowing almost to a stop. And for a long, ageless instant, the lawman stared down the black man, then he drove away.

Ralph Martin sat there in his Audi softly chuckling. What could he say? Even he had to admit that a prosecutor shouldn't be breaking the law, no matter if the infraction is both minor and widely tolerated on Boston's narrow streets.

As anecdotes go, it was a throwaway line, an afterthought Martin tossed into an interview a few weeks after it happened. He brought it up in making a meandering point about the image of law enforcement, slipping it in as an example of why the public sometimes gets irritated with the police and, by extension, the whole criminal justice system. Yet it was telling for two reasons, the first being that it highlighted Martin's notoriously even temperament.

The other reason, and the more important reason against the backdrop of race and politics in Boston, is that it ran counter to the way such episodes historically unraveled. Consider, for instance, that less than twenty-four hours before Martin was chewed out on a Jamaica Plain street, City Councilor Bruce Bolling was being abused by a cab driver at Quincy Market, the city's touristy shopping plaza across from City Hall. He wanted a ride to Roxbury, the predominantly black neighborhood where he lived. The cabbie, a white woman, refused. Words were exchanged. A male taxi driver stepped in, physically dragging Bolling away while calling him, among other things, a nigger.

Bolling speed-dialed the *Boston Globe*, which, on the Saturday night Martin was looking for a place to park, inked the councilor's picture and his tale of transportational woe onto the front page of 800,000 Sunday newspapers. "This particular incident, with the way it happened, the tone, the disrespect, the racist attitude was so flagrant that I decided I could not let it go by," he told the *Globe*. For the next week, Bolling was the sympathetic recipient of a customarily brief and shallow exercise in racial soul searching. Then, in short order, he was sneered at, forced to endure the deep and ugly things the city always found in its soul. A black politician gets slurred and manhandled trying to hire a taxi and half the populace wonders why he was hassling a white woman for a ride to the ghetto at two o'clock in the morning. The backlash was so severe that, only ten days later, even Bolling was backpedaling. "In recent days," he wrote in a column for the *Boston Herald,* "there's been far too much media coverage of my unfortunate and discourteous treatment by a cabdriver who refused to take me to my home in Roxbury."

That was how the Boston's black-and-white featurettes almost always played out. And it was that same tired script of race and politics that Martin, black Republican and rookie district attorney, desperately needed to rewrite if he was going to survive beyond the token term he was appointed to fill. As it was, Martin had been cast in the conventional wisdom as the Great Non-White Hope, an avenging black man who would thrash about for two years, savaging the same cops he'd so harshly criticized in his incarnation as an assistant U.S. Attorney, bashing the police commissioner and the mayor. With one firm command, he could eliminate the homicide squad, assigning murder investigations to state troopers; if he couldn't put rogue cops in jail, he could at least take away their machismo. He was expected to rage about injustice, throwing the trump card of race in a noble high stakes poker game with the white police. He would be a hero, to be sure, at least to those who believed the police had never paid a price for mauling black Bostonians, circa Stuart and otherwise. There would be such a ruckus that all of Massachusetts, perhaps the whole of the nation, would hear tell of this brash, young prosecutor.

But then what? Nothing. There would be no second act. After the headlines faded, Martin would disappear into the private sector after he was predictably embarrassed at the polls by any white Democrat in a suit come November 1994. All he had to lose was time.

"People had an unrealistic expectation that Ralph would come in like a gunfighter, like Clint Eastwood, and clean up the town," says J.W. Carney, Jr., a defense attorney and one of the friends to whom Martin first confided his desire to be the district attorney. "And there were probably some people who were hoping he would do that—because it would doom him to failure."

The problem, though, was that Martin truly wanted to be the D.A. for more than two years. Sitting there, chuckling in his Audi, he understood he could have stopped the blatting simply by giving the white cop a little mau-mau. And when the story got out, no one would have been at all surprised. But then what? The black D.A. gets chewed out by a belligerent white cop? Half the populace would wonder where he got off double parking, which, all things considered, was a point even Martin had to concede.

FIVE MONTHS INTO HIS TENURE, MARTIN HAD MORE IMPORTANT things to worry about than one mouthy cop. If he was going to get himself elected to a full term, he first had to straighten out the district attorney's office, which by then was in shambles. After fourteen years, Flanagan had left an office devoid of passion or morale, a dull, gray machine that ushered some fifty-one thousand cases annually through nine district courts and one superior court in a rote process that passed for justice. "The hallmark of the office was compassion by incompetence," one prominent defense attorney cracked at the time. "Suffolk County was the best place to have a guilty client, and the worst one to have an innocent client."

It was an odd electoral strategy. The problem with campaigning for district attorney is that most people don't know what the job actually entails. Among the branches of the legal system, it is the most anonymous: no badges or sirens, no black robes, no jokes about how many lawyers it takes to shingle a roof (Answer: depends how thin you slice them.). But Martin's political qualifications—affable, sure, and able to work a roomful of Rotarians without appearing too terribly uncomfortable—were too thin and untested, his persona too unknown to make him a viable marquee. Plus, there was his party affiliation, newly switched from unenrolled independent (as most Massachusetts voters are) to Republican, in deference to the governor who appointed him. "Doing a story about a Republican in Boston," sniffed a GOP consultant named Ron Mills before Martin's first election, "is like doing a story about a deli in Cairo. Who cares? He thinks he's actually supposed to prosecute people and that's going to get him elected? What a buffoon."

Actually, it was more of a well-reasoned desperation. Under the best of circumstances, Martin would have to rise above race and party affiliation to have any chance of winning a full term on his own. In the summer of 1992, however, his situation was far from ideal. There were two other agencies with which Martin would have to work if crime, and the fear of it, were to be tamed in the city. One was the Suffolk County Sheriff's Department, which at the time was run by Robert Rufo, a young, smart, reform-minded manager who liked and respected Martin. The other was the Boston Police Department, which, as an institution still stinging from the Stuart debacle and the St. Clair Commission, despised the new district attorney. By extension, Raymond Flynn—who still saw the BPD as his personal force—wasn't making Martin's job any easier.

The taunting began immediately. The day after Governor Weld announced Martin would fill the remainder of Newman Flanagan's term, the police department released its report on the Stuart case, in which every officer was cleared of all but one minor offense. Officially, the timing was coincidental, but no one believed that. The department had reverted to its old ways, despite the presence of Bratton. After a brief PR flurry the previous winter, reality settled in. Though Bratton had a proven track record as a law-enforcement wunderkind, he had no real authority to revamp, or even substantially tinker with, the Boston police force. By midsummer, he was being bandied about as a candidate to take over several big city departments, including New York's.

As for Mayor Flynn, he simply snubbed Martin. Requests for meetings were routinely dismissed. In fact, the only real face time the two shared didn't come until October, after Martin had already settled into his new office. The two men, along with Martin's first assistant, Robert P. Gittens, Roach, Bratton—who had just been eliminated from the running for the NYC job—and a police superintendent named Joseph Carter met for pizza and beer at Doyle's, an Irish pub in Jamaica Plain with a long, dark bar and pressed tin ceilings that's long been haunted by local pols.

"So, Ralph," the mayor asked him, dripping with sarcasm, "what do you want to be when you grow up? We know what Billy here wants to be. What do you want to be?"

Bratton grimaced. Martin never even blanched. "NBA commissioner," he deadpanned.

Deadpan was the only tone Martin could afford. Throughout the fall, he ignored the slights from City Hall, dismissed the hostility from police headquarters. The rookie D.A. couldn't afford a fight with the police unions, either. "You'll get your head handed to you," Martin's confidants warned. "Look what they did to Michael Dukakis." During the 1988 presidential campaign, the Boston Police Patrolman's Association had wimpified Dukakis by endorsing George Bush for the Oval Office. Martin could only imagine the damage they could do to a black Republican in white Democratic Boston.

So he went about restructuring the office as quietly and diplomatically as possible. There were no bloody purges when he took over, although more than a dozen staff attorneys were either encouraged to leave or outright fired. And his public statements, which were few and far between, were conciliatory. "Give us a chance," he pleaded with people who expected him to go to war with the police. "If people had seen me playing the pol from the beginning instead of focusing on the office," he explained later, "they would have thought I was a hypocrite."

Still, he made a good faith effort to smooth things over with Roach. In the fall of 1992, he began negotiating to have six detectives transferred out of homicide, including Miller Thomas and Peter O'Malley, the two he criticized most severely in his Stuart report, and replaced with four youngbloods. After four months of listening to Martin's careful, gentle pleadings, Roache, on the afternoon of Wednesday, January 6, 1992, agreed. Word of the deal spread through the grapevine with lightning speed. By the weekend, there were whispers of a mutiny among the department's detectives if the transfers went through. The following Monday, January 11, Martin answered a telephone call from Roache: the deal, already public knowledge, was off. Only three men would be transferred out of homicide; Thomas, the union representative for the homicide unit, and Detective William Dwyer, the secretary of the detectives union, would stay, as would O'Malley, who would be retiring in the spring anyway. After twenty years in homicide, a full two-thirds of his entire police career, shipping him out in his twilight, Roache reasoned, would be an insult.

It was a sucker punch, a classic maneuver from the annals of bare-knuckled South Boston politics. Martin absorbed the blow, and even tried to dismiss it as a little more than a light slap. He'd gotten his four new officers, he argued, which meant he didn't completely lose. But among cops—who Martin needed to do his job and who keep thorough scorecards in their heads—he appeared weak, a novice who'd been dropped in the first round. The president of the Boston Police Detectives Benevolent Society, Thomas Montgomery, wasted no time piling on. "He is obviously looking for his pound of flesh," he told the *Globe.* "There is no doubt in my mind that that's just a pound of flesh for the Stuart case ... It would mean something politically to him if he could move Peter O'Malley right now. He is not going to become the D.A. in two years by trying to ride on the backs of the Boston Police Department, and particularly the members of the detectives union. It's not going to happen."

The worst part was, it appeared Martin had lost a fight that he had picked to begin with. "I think he made a fatal mistake," one ranking officer said at the time. "He's dealing with cops and cops look at who wins and who loses. And cops think Mickey Roache won."

NINETEEN-NINETY-THREE WASN'T SHAPING UP TO BE A VERY good year. Martin got a brief bump of good press on the first day of the year, which was one day after one of his underlings convinced a grand jury to indict three high school students who allegedly marched into a classroom at South Boston High School, clubbed a kid named Angelo Bonilla with a chair and then beat him badly enough that an ambulance had to haul him away. Martin got one quote into the papers: "I want to do all I can to maintain stability in the public schools."

But it was all downhill from there. The very next day, January 2, Martin had Boston police officers guarding him after he received a death threat from a man who believed Martin hadn't done enough to investigate a few doctors after the man's mother died. Two weeks later, Flynn took another poke at the district attorney after two gangs in Jamaica Plain resumed their blood feud. The Goyas and the Mozart Boys didn't like each other for a couple of reasons, the main one being that they had some silly notion that each owned a particular corner, and another one being that the Goyas were mostly Puerto Rican and the Mozart Boys were mostly Dominican. This particular feud, however, began as so many stupid and deadly squabbles do, which is over a girl. Alex Reyes, a Mozart Boy who was sixteen years old, apparently was dating a girl who used to go out with a Goya. That simple fact in September 1992 had ignited a knife-swinging brawl at The Corner Mall, a small shopping center a block away from bucolic Boston Common. Reyes was slashed in the hand and a Goya took a knife in the back, but everyone lived to fight another day.

That day was January 15, when the Goyas found Reyes on an Orange Line subway train at about two o'clock in the afternoon, shortly after classes let out at English High School, which is two blocks from the train. More knives were flashed. Three kids were stabbed. One gun was pulled, the trigger was snapped back, and a bullet ended Reyes's too-short life.

Considering Reyes was the second young man to die violently in that particular neighborhood in a month, the people trying to live normal lives there were outraged. More than seventy-five residents jammed a hastily-called community meeting, demanding to know why the police weren't being more aggressive and why City Hall wasn't being more generous, or effective, with youth programs.

Flynn feinted, defending his and Roache's efforts, but then turning on Martin. The district attorney, the mayor declared, had to bring back the direct-indictment process, whereby prosecutors skip lengthy probable cause hearings and speed the worst hoodlums directly through a grand jury. Newman Flanagan had used that trick, and Flynn had taken credit for it, in 1989, when the police first conceded the city was indeed infested with gangs. It was a cheap shot, mainly because Martin had made direct indictments one of the cornerstones of his strategy.

It was a minor spat, one that passed quickly. But the following month, on February 19, 1993, the ghosts of Newman Flanagan's prosecutorial fumbling came back to haunt Martin.

Nine years earlier, in May 1986, two men robbed a record store in Codman Square, a neighborhood in the southern reaches of the city. One of them was named, or, rather, was then known as, Angus T. McCullough; the other was Raymond L. Hurd. And one of them shot the clerk, put a bullet square into the forehead of Angela Skeete, who managed to describe the two thieves before she died.

Hurd was captured on June 5 after he was picked out of a lineup as the man who tried to sell a television set looted from Skeete's shop. That day, he told police that McCullough had murdered Skeete. McCullough, meanwhile, stayed on the run for another eleven days, until he was tracked to North Carolina, where he was living with his girlfriend. When he was arrested, he told police Skeete had been the shooter, that he hadn't even gone inside the store.

Under the joint-venture theory—which holds that if two people are engaged in a serious crime that leads to someone's death, both are guilty of the killing—McCullough and Hurd were both charged with murder in the first degree. The case would be difficult, but not impossible, to prosecute, since each man would offer the same defense: the other guy did it. In such situations, it is not unusual for prosecutors to negotiate a plea to a lesser offense, guaranteeing a felony conviction as opposed to rolling the dice in front of a jury. Indeed, in Suffolk County, it was almost routine: According to a 1991 *Boston Globe* study, Newman Flanagan's office accepted plea bargains in 62 percent of first degree murder cases. For murder one, which carries a sentence of life without the hope of parole, the logical reduction is to second degree, which gives the killer a shot at getting out in fifteen years.

Not in Suffolk County in the eighties, however. Flanagan's office, in the person of Assistant District Attorney Phyllis Broker, dropped the charge all the way to manslaughter. On January 20, 1988, both men pleaded guilty. Hurd was sentenced to twelve-to-twenty years in prison, McCullough, on the prosecutor's recommendation, was sentenced to six-to-ten years. With credit for time served in jail before he pleaded, McCullough was back on the street in June 1990. A parole violation put him back behind bars in September 1991, where he stayed until June 16, 1992.

ANGUS T. MCCULLOUGH'S NEW NAME IS TERRELL MUHAMMAD, which is the name the Boston Police Department booked him under after he tried to steal an eight-hundred-dollar stereo system from a downtown department store. He'd chosen the name after embracing Islam while in prison for the record store murder. But it was only the latest in a long string of aliases, morphing from Mathis to Dixon to Dickson. Changing his name so often, as well memorizing a bogus address, has the distinct advantage of allowing a career criminal to confuse the police and the courts. And Muhammad had a great deal of experience jostling with the legal system, beginning with arrests for thieving as a teenager, assaulting a police officer, destruction of property and, two years before Skeete was killed, leading the police in tiny suburban Easton on a thirty-mile chase in a stolen Cadillac.

The police had a difficult time collaring Muhammad on February 19. He ran through Downtown Crossing, a pedestrian mall of department stores and boutiques, sprinting over the bricks and climbing over cars, security guards and cops puffing after him. He was finally wrestled into custody and hauled to the local police station, which was just on the other side of Beacon Hill. He was booked, allowed to make one phone call, and then locked into a holding cell to be arraigned the next morning in Boston Municipal Court.

For the next three hours, Muhammad demanded to be allowed to make more phone calls. No, the cops told him. He would have to wait until two officers were available to escort him. That happened at four o'clock, when officers Thomas F. Rose and Patrick F. Russell came on duty. They unlocked Muhammad's cell and led him to the booking desk, where the prisoner dialed a number and spoke to someone on the other end of the line.

Then Muhammad dropped the receiver and ran, barreling out a door and into the station's garage. He made it across the garage to another door leading to the outside before Rose and Russell grabbed him, knocking him off balance, toppling Muhammad so awkwardly and heavily that he took both officers to the pavement with him. Russell, who was sixty-two years old at the time, was pinned under Muhammad, the prisoner crouching on top of the cop. A third officer, Joseph O'Malley, heard the ruckus and tried to wrestle Muhammad into submission. Muhammad tossed him aside and turned back to Rose, who he had pinned to the garage door, his knee planted firmly into Rose's chest.

O'Malley and Russell heard three sharp bangs, followed by the terrible stink of cordite. The barrel of Rose's gun was pressed into his gut when the first report sounded. A second bullet went into his arm. He was forty-two years old, married and the father of two children when he died.

Muhammad waved the gun at O'Malley and Russell, who were trying desperately to get him into handcuffs. A fourth cop, Kieran Fitzgerald, piled on. Overwhelmed by the officers, Muhammad surrendered and was locked back in his cell. He told the cops, "I didn't mean to shoot the police officer."

Phyllis Broker was still a prosecutor—and, to be fair, widely re-
garded as a good at her job—one of the hundreds of people Martin
kept on staff when he took over. The week after Rose was murdered, as reporters pieced together Muhammad's wretched life, her
decision in 1986 was examined in detail, picked apart by legal
scholars and even other prosecutors, the primary thrust being that
Muhammad wouldn't have been able to kill a cop if he'd pleaded
to second degree murder seven years earlier because he would have
still been in prison. At the very least, Broker could have demanded
more time for the manslaughter. "That's an awful light sentence
for this kind of manslaughter, where some innocent store clerk is
killed," a judge and former prosecutor named Carol Ball told the
Globe in one of a series of articles on the topic.

Broker was on vacation and didn't get to respond. Martin simply didn't. And by March, the matter seemed to have been put to
rest. Even Roache was conciliatory. "I think it would not be help-
ful for any one of us," he told reporters the day Muhammad was
arraigned on murder and other charges, "to point fingers."

Three months later, Mickey Roache resigned. Bill Bratton was
appointed to replace him. And Ralph Martin's life got a whole lot
easier.

CHAPTER 7

Innocence Lost

THE BRAKE LIGHTS ON THE BUICK ELECTRA FLASHED ON MINDEN Street, the driver slowing the sedan to a slow roll near Gayhead Street, purring past the hoodies and the kiddies haunting the corner just outside the Bromley Heath projects. It was 9:20 on a chilly Halloween night, 1994. The car moved like a stalking wraith, the boy in the passenger seat cradling a shotgun across his lap, held down low, out of sight, the stock resting on the floorboard. He scanned the sidewalk through the open window, searching for the right cluster of bodies.

Howard Duckett was out there. In his twenty-three years, he'd been arrested nearly a dozen times but almost always for petty crimes, grabbed off the streets of Jamaica Plain for theft and driving without a license. Not the worst hoodlum in the city, but close enough. Kamiya Santos was with him, a man-child five years younger than Duckett but with a reputation five times worse. Three years ago, when he was fifteen, he'd almost shot a man to death. Put him in a wheelchair for life. It wasn't the guy he was aiming at—Santos didn't even know who he was—but it proved that Kamiya Santos wasn't afraid to shoot.

The boy in the passenger seat eased the shotgun up, pulling it level and laying the barrel out the window. The Electra was barely moving now, the driver steering straight and steady, trying not to jostle his shotgunner's aim. The shooter's finger was sweating in the cool autumn air, slippery on the trigger. He squeezed the lever back, then jerked, too hard and too fast, the barrel flinching to one side.

The sound was tremendous, a deep bass boom bouncing off of Bromley's red bricks. Pellets scattered from the gun in a tight cloud, a swarm of lead crashing into the crowd. A few of them found Santos, tearing into his leg and butt. A few more hit Duckett, ripping flesh from his back. And a few sprayed into Alexis Smith, who was twelve years old and bleeding from small, hot holes in her legs.

The driver crushed the gas pedal to the floor, the Electra lurching forward, tearing down Gayhead, away from the screaming on the corner. He turned left two blocks down, weaving and bobbing through the narrow streets of Boston's ghetto, finally pulling down Brinton Street. He slammed to a stop and bailed out the driver's side door. The shooter jumped out his side, a spotter from the back seat close behind him. Then they ran into the night, sprinting into the Halloween darkness with the rest of the goblins.

No one on the corner had gotten a very good look at the hunters. All they could tell the police—or, perhaps more accurately, all they *would* tell the police—was that there were three of them, all black males between the ages of eighteen and twenty-five, though they could have been as young as fifteen. But no one from Bromley Heath needed to see a face, needed to look into anyone's eyes to know where the shooters were from: Academy Homes. For fifteen years, Academy boys had shot at Bromley boys, crossing from one side of Columbus Avenue, blasting a few rounds, then running like hell. And then the Bromley boys would cross the street and pop a few caps into Academy. Sometimes, they didn't bother to cross, just stake out cover on one side of Columbus and open fire, bullets flying across six lanes of pavement. No one even knew what the feud was about anymore—the boys who started it were either long dead, long locked away, or, if they were lucky, grown up and moved away.

Now once again, the ambulance packed everyone away to the hospital so the surgeons could dig out the pellets and bandage the wounds. And once again, the counterattack was being planned. It didn't take long. Teenagers, as a rule, don't invest any military precision into their assaults. Run up, shoot, run away.

At 10:40, a white sedan turned right off of Centre Street onto Columbus, then made a left a hundred yards up, steering up a narrow driveway to the low white Academy apartments set on a rise of pudding stone. The driver killed the lights at the top of the drive, next to the fence that surrounded the small yard outside Dorothy Haskins's apartment. Two boys got out of the car, pulled black hoods loosely over their heads and turned left, around the corner of the fence. They continued past Haskins's apartment, past the next one, and stopped at the third, where Kevin Murphy lived. Murphy was thirty years old and old school, the man who all the boys in Academy looked up to, an ex-con who could almost remember why Academy and Bromley kept trying to kill each other.

There were nearly a dozen people in his yard, some of them adults but most of them children counting their trick-or-treat booty and celebrating Jermaine Goffigan's ninth birthday, which happened to be that night. Jermaine, who everyone called Manny, was still smeared with white makeup from his skeleton costume, his belly full of chocolate cake and ice cream that his grandmother, Dorothy Haskins, had treated him to before sending him out to play two doors down. In his pockets were five Tootsie rolls, a lemon drop, three dollars, and two rings he'd been given as birthday gifts.

The two hoodies stopped at the fence. "Who's that?" someone behind the fence asked. "Who's *that*?" one of the hoodies replied, mocking and snide. Then two pistols rose above the fence. Fire spit from the barrels. The shooters were fast, tugging their triggers without bothering to aim. Between them, they sprayed sixteen bullets into Murphy's small yard. "Heath Street's in the news!" one of them yelled before the last booming echo faded. Then they bolted back to the sedan, tearing back out onto Columbus and into the project across the street.

Dorothy heard the staccato *pop-pop-pop* of the pistols, heard the screams from the women and the children. She ran from her apartment to Murphy's. Crystal Brown, who was twenty-eight years old, was on the ground screaming in pain, her calf torn open by one slug. Manny had crawled through a patio door and into the kitchen, cowering under a table, clutching his gut and crying. His eleven-year-old brother, Jerome, still stinging from bits of gravel kicked up by the bullets, rolled Manny over. Blood was leaking from his little brother, pooling in a crimson puddle on the linoleum. "My stomach hurts," he said. "My stomach hurts."

He was still complaining about his tummy when the paramedics arrived, hustling him into the ambulance for the short, furious ride to Boston City Hospital three miles away. But the bullet had done too much damage, ripping through his ribs and innards. Manny suffered for the next four hours. He died just before three o'clock in the morning, the youngest child ever slain in Boston's gang wars.

BOSTON'S WAVE OF GANG VIOLENCE HAD ACTUALLY CRESTED four years earlier in 1990, when a record 153 people—the overwhelming majority young, male, and black—where murdered on the city's streets. The tide had been rising since 1987, when the official word from the Boston Police Department brass was that the city didn't have actual gangs; rather, the City on the Hill suffered only "groups of youths," loosely organized street-corner congregations. It was silly semantic nitpicking, considering those same groups had a disturbing propensity to shoot at each other, either to protect their cottage crack industries or, more often, over some adolescent slight, either real or perceived.

They weren't very good at it, the shooting part, which is what made them so scary. Very few children (and they were mostly children, no matter how well armed) can aim particularly well, for one thing. Hitting the wrong person was terribly common. Mervin Reese, who ran one of the local gangs, dodged so many bullets in the late eighties and early nineties that he earned a new nickname: Swervin' Mervin. Unfortunately, people around him—including a high school basketball star and Swervin's stepfather—kept stepping in front of bullets meant for Reese.

Still, Boston never was infected with the sort of sprawling urban armies that patrolled the ghettos of Southern California. The Crips and Bloods evolved into giant criminal corporations, their bloody street fights only a sidelight to a lucrative drug business. With a business plan not dissimilar from the Mafia, both groups expanded their territory, organizing branch offices through the Pacific Northwest and the Midwest, recruiting young dealers and controlling them under a loose rubric of gang fealty. But they never penetrated New England.

Boston has always been a parochial city, divided into neighborhoods that verge on the xenophobic. Borders are drawn starkly in Boston, turf sharply defined by geography and architecture, neighborhoods defined by the contours of housing projects and narrows strips of triple-decker homes. The Franklin Field project and the Franklin Hill project, for example, squat on the same two blocks of Blue Hill Avenue, in the Dorchester neighborhood. But they are separate places, small islands apart and, for a time, at war.

Some of the savvier hoodlums tried to emulate their West Coast brethren, though their models were drawn mostly from MTV and movies like *New Jack City* and *Boyz N the Hood*. The Humboldt Raiders would ally themselves for a time with, say, the X-Men, named for comic book superheroes, in Jamaica Plain and the Corbett Street Crew in Mattapan. But those allegiances were always short and volatile, dissolving in the wake of some petty squabble.

Finally, after the bloody year of 1990, the police started using the dreaded "g" word—gangs—and started counterattacking. Through a combination of arrests, pulling the hardest hitters off the street, and deaths, carting the unluckiest hoodies to the morgue, the tide of violence began to ebb. Old beefs were squashed or forgotten. By 1994, the homicide rate had fallen to half of its 1990 peak.

The only feud that endured was the one between Bromley Heath
and Academy Homes, the former a public housing development of
red brick high-rises, the other a federally subsidized strip of dilapidated townhouses. They sit kitty-corner from each other, straddling
the border between the neighborhoods of Roxbury and Jamaica
Plain. It had been raging for so long that no one even remembered
how it began. The shooting would flare for a few months, perhaps
a year, until the particular soldiers were either killed off or sent to
prison, leaving a void for a new generation to grow into. In the
mid-nineties, Bromley kids shot at Academy kids because Academy
kids shot at Bromley kids, which was reason enough.

The last flurry had happened in the spring of 1994. Shandell
Smith, who was nineteen years old and lived in Dorchester, a
neighborhood south of Roxbury, but who was affiliated with Academy Homes, was shot to death on a basketball court in the development. Retaliation came within minutes: Rodney Smith, a
Bromley boy, was shot less than a block away. The causalities
mounted the next day, a hoodie shot in Academy, followed by a
rival stabbed in Bromley Heath less than an hour later.

On April 5, five boys from Bromley rode up Blue Hill Avenue at
midnight in a rented white limousine. As they passed the
Caribbean Cultural Club, Brandon Bass, who was eighteen years
old, stood up in the back seat, poking his head and shoulders
through the open moon roof. He had a .357 revolver in his hand
and Kareem Tyler in his sights. Bass opened fire.

The limo driver abandoned his car when he heard the shots.
Tyler, an Academy boy, never had time to duck: he was hit in both
arms, the stomach and the back, wounded badly but still alive.

Security guards from the Caribbean Club grabbed all five boys in
the car and held them until the police arrived. Bass and another
eighteen-year-old, Benjamin Pocha, were charged with attempted
murder and assault and battery with a dangerous weapon. The police also arrested three sixteen-year-old boys from Bromley, who
were charged with the same crimes. Among them was Donnell
Johnson, a skinny high school sophomore with a toothy smile and

light skin covered in freckles and pimples. He was, to use the jargon, known to police, mostly from when he was thirteen and allegedly tried to stab a boy, partly from just seeing him on the fringes of Bromley, running with a crowd of dealers and shooters.

Johnson was already struggling against the gravity of the streets, a case study of a boy trying to decide if earning his ghetto props is worth going to jail for or, worse, dying. A few weeks earlier, one of his friends, Jeffrey Toney, ignored the Lenox Street boys when they told him to stop dealing crack near their project. So they shot him dead, blowing him off his bicycle in front of a church on a Sunday afternoon, just as the ladies in their finest hats were leaving their worship service. Jeffrey's blood all over the pavement took some of the luster off the streets.

April 5 would be the last time Donnell would be arrested. In the end, a Suffolk County grand jury decided all three sixteen-year-olds had simply been in the wrong place, that they didn't know anyone had a gun, let alone that anyone would get shot. After that, Donnell seemed to be pulling away from the hoodlum life, tugged by a pastor named Bruce Wall into the Dorchester Temple Baptist Church.

Yet he was still a black boy with a record of arrests. And with his freckles, he looked an awful lot like one of the hoodies who pointed a gun over a fence and killed a nine-year-old boy.

At 7:15 on the night of Tuesday, November 1, less than twenty-one hours after Manny Goffigan died, two Boston Police homicide detectives arrested Johnson at his grandmother's apartment. Donnell put up his best street swagger. "You ain't got nothin' on me," he told the cops. "I wasn't even there."

Actually, the police had a lot on him. Three eyewitnesses swore they saw Johnson standing behind the fence, his hood pushed back and a gun in his hand, his finger jerking the trigger like a cold steel rubber band. Three people told the police they saw Donnell Johnson kill a nine-year-old boy.

DYING YOUNG MAKES A BOY FAMOUS. MANNY GOFFIGAN WAS ON the front pages of both the *Boston Globe* and the *Boston Herald* the

next day, under bold and splashy headlines, his short life resurrected by his wailing mother and sobbing grandmother.

The village mob was properly rallied. In a city grown numb to black boys dying—an eighteen-year-old shot to death in a gang feud would likely have been reduced to a news brief in the *Herald*, if he got any ink at all—Manny's tender age stirred a deep rage. "He's Just a Baby!" the tabloid screamed that morning, its entire front page devoted to Goffigan's short life. With the details tumbling across the newspaper pages, his birthday, his lemon drop and Tootsie rolls, Manny became Everyboy. In the projects, where a mixture of fear and resignation routinely silenced witnesses to most every crime, a score of residents passed every whispered rumor and every suspected shooter's name to the police. One family's tragedy became the entire city's shame.

And from personal tragedies such as these arise political problems, or, depending on which side one happens to be on, political opportunities. For Ralph C. Martin II, a dead nine-year-old was a problem. In one week, he would face his first real election, running against Gerry Malone, a former assistant district attorney and a white Irish Democrat of the kind who had historically led prosecutions in Suffolk County. For Malone, a dead nine-year-old was an opportunity to be exploited. His backers in the unions representing Boston police detectives and patrolmen went on the offensive, ostensibly blaming Martin for Manny's death. Johnson had been arrested in connection with a shooting only months earlier, then released by grand jurors who prosecutors failed to convince to indict the boy. "Donnell Johnson should not have been walking the streets Halloween night," growled the president of the detectives union, Tommy Montgomery. "He is known as a violent individual, and a threat to decent people. Yet on Ralph Martin's watch, he was allowed to walk." (Neither union mentioned, curiously, that Malone was the chief prosecutor for the district courts under Martin's predecessor when a 1992 assault and battery case against Johnson was dropped.)

Truth is, however, Martin wasn't so much concerned with the

politics as he was merely aware of them. For a year and a half, Martin had run a low-key campaign, trudging through the politicking of his job like a reluctant and fidgety child, more concerned with running his office as opposed to running for it. In his campaign commercials, he was uneasy revealing even the most basic elements of his life. Instead, he believed he could survive on the strength of his work, proving himself a competent prosecutor without relying on the political hackery of generations past. For Boston, it was a radical notion.

So Martin approached the murder of Manny Goffigan with a tempered passion. While reporters and critical union bosses elevated the boy to martyr, seizing his death as a watershed of urban horror, Martin at first kept his distance. Years later, he couldn't even remember when he first heard about the shooting, though it was surely after the microwave trucks had packed up after their live shots in the projects. It was Halloween night, which meant he would have been out with his children, first collecting trick-or-treat loot, then helping them count it all at the dining room table. If indiscriminate gunplay is an accepted routine in the ghetto—and, faux outrage aside, it is—then it was inevitable that a child eventually would be caught in the middle. There was no more point to the D.A. grandstanding his outrage that night than there would have been every time an eighteen-year-old ex-con got popped. There was no need for the boss to trample over the crime scene. He never liked squinting into the glare of the television lights anyway.

THE PHONE IN STEPHEN HRONES'S OFFICE RANG EARLY ON THE morning of Wednesday, November 3, his number culled from the list of lawyers who represent murder suspects for the public defender's office. A wild-eyed Czech with blond hair frizzing off his head and around his jawline, Hrones was a veteran to the Massachusetts court system and a specialist in defending young kids accused of murder. He didn't win very often—most murder defendants are, in fact, guilty—but his record was better than most.

Even keeping a kid in the juvenile system, as opposed to the more draconian adult courts, counted as a victory.

Donnell Johnson had been under arrest for more than twelve hours, waiting to be arraigned in Roxbury Juvenile Court, the courthouse closest to Academy Homes. He figured he'd be out soon enough, that the police were only trying to scare him when they knew he hadn't done anything. "I know you beat other cases," one of the detectives had told him the night before. "You're not gonna beat this one."

"I wasn't there," Donnell had insisted.

"You were there. You were there. We know you were there," the cop told him.

Donnell offered to take a polygraph test, offered to have his hands swabbed for gun powder residue. The police were unimpressed. "You're going to get life if you don't help us out," one of them told him. "Please help us out."

No way Donnell was going to do that. He was no snitch. In the light of day, with a lawyer by his side, the judge would realize he was innocent and Donnell would go home. He just had to keep telling everyone he didn't do it until someone believed him.

Hrones didn't. In thirty years, he'd heard those four famous words more times than he cared to count. Experience had taught him that almost everyone did it, or did something bad enough for the courts to get involved. "Most of the guys, let's face it, they're guilty," Hrones says. "They"—meaning prosecutors and police— "just don't have the evidence. I mean, how many *purely* guilty guys do you have?" Then again, how many guys does any lawyer have accused of killing a nine-year-old counting his Halloween candy? As of that morning, the count in Massachusetts was exactly one.

Hrones explained the next few dreary steps to his new client. First Donnell would be arraigned, where the prosecutors would formally charge him in juvenile court as being delinquent (a quaint concession to youth) of murder, attempted murder, and possession of a firearm. Then Hrones, as a matter of routine, would enter a plea of not guilty on Donnell's behalf. Next, the lawyers would briefly argue about the amount of bail to be set. Technically, bail is meant only to ensure a suspect will show up in court, sort of like a human pawnshop. Realistically, it's a leg-iron prosecutors use to keep people locked up until trial, especially in high-profile cases. All things considered, Donnell would be better off locked up anyway: people had already threatened to kill his family, given the nature of the crime, and some vigilante would surely take a crack at Donnell if he was on the street.

"But I didn't do it," Johnson said. He was still forcing his words to sound tough, nonchalant. It wasn't working. He was soft-spoken by nature, born to weakly drift in the prevailing winds of the streets rather than tack with or against them. His bravado was forced, a lame mimicry of a real hoodlum.

"So what happened?" Hroncs asked. His mouth twisted with the words, which was normal because his face always seemed askew, and more so when he talked out of the left side of his mouth, which he almost always did.

"I was home the whole time," Donnell told him. "The whole time." His alibi—and, at the point, that was all it was, with all the pejorative connotations—was that he spent the night on Shawmut Avenue, more than a mile from Academy Homes. His grandmother, Lorraine Johnson, cooked a dinner of steak and onions and Spanish rice, after which Donnell watched the Green Bay Packers embarrass the Chicago Bears in a 33–6 stomping. He played Nintendo for a while, then talked on the phone with Corey Washington[1], who happened to be the brother of Willie Horton, the iconic convict who, while on a furlough from a murder sentence, escaped to Baltimore, raped a woman, beat her husband, and assassinated Michael Dukakis's presidential campaign.

"Winston's[2] here," Corey told Donnell at one point during the conversation. "He's looking for the gun."

---

[1] Because of both legal and privacy reasons, some names have been changed.

[2] A pseudonym.

Donnell didn't know what he was talking about, but he pretended not to care. The two boys talked for a little while. After they hung up, Donnell got a glass of iced tea from the refrigerator and went to bed. That was all he knew about Jermaine Goffigan dying until the police arrested him.

Hrones scribbled notes on a yellow pad. As alibis go, it wasn't half bad. Donnell's grandmother would back him up, as if that would matter to a jury. Outside, in the courtroom wedged between beige cinder-block walls, TV cameras were lined up in the box where jurors normally sit, and another half-dozen reporter from the newspapers and radio stations were crammed into the gallery. The murder of Manny Goffigan, Hrones knew, would be page-one news the next morning, too, only with the coverage more focused on the beast who slew him. "A little kid, all that press," Hrones thought to himself. "We're dead."

JUDGE MILTON L. WRIGHT CLIMBED BEHIND THE BENCH AS A white-shirted court officer told everyone else to stand. "Be seated," the judge said as he settled into his own high-backed chair and motioned to his clerk to start calling the day's cases. "Commonwealth versus Donnell Johnson," she read.

Robert Tochka rose from behind the prosecution's table, said good morning to the judge and began to outline the case against Donnell. Clipped to a short courtroom synopsis, it appeared solid: three eyewitnesses had fingered Johnson as one of the shooters who opened fire outside Kevin Murphy's apartment at 86 Academy Terrace. And because the state would "absolutely" attempt to have Donnell tried in adult court—where the maximum sentence leapt from twenty years to life without parole—Tochka asked the judge to hold the boy without bail.

Given a hard look, however, the state's case was as crinkly and thin as stale rice paper. One of the witnesses, Dorothy Haskins, Manny's grandmother, insisted she recognized Donnell by looking through her kitchen window into a badly lit parking lot at a fast-moving and hooded figure. Two others, Kevin Murphy and

Manny's little brother, said they recognized Donnell when he threw back his hood in that same dark lot and started spitting booming orange flames and a cloud of cordite toward them. And all of them picked him from an array of photos, Hrones charged, that included only one light-skinned and freckled face.

But no one was looking very hard, at least not at that moment. Crime stories are cast in terms of good and bad, of innocent victims and savage villains. Though Donnell had no criminal record, a fact Hrones took pains to point out, both Tochka and the anonymous police sources who feed reporters made clear that Donnell surely flirted with the gangsta life. He had been arrested twice, and both times for violent crimes. The shooting outside the Caribbean Cultural Club, for one. Even through Donnell wasn't charged, such an assault—a black man with a gun popping up though the sunroof of a limo and opening fire on a crowded street—dredged up the worst sort of *New Jack City* visions. Just being in the same orbit with an urban caricature tugged Donnell into the same hoodlum shape.

Then there was the time in January 1992 when he was thirteen years old, that Donnell was arrested for assault and battery with a gun and a knife in what police sources described as a gang attack. In reality, it was a petty squabble between two knothead kids, albeit armed ones. In fact, those charges too were eventually dismissed. But in painting Donnell as a villain, no brushstroke was too thin. "Face value?" one anonymous cop told a reporter the day Donnell was arraigned. "Victim intimidation. Anytime a case like that ends up being dismissed it's because the victim wouldn't come forward." In one pithy phrase, Donnell was elevated from garden-variety hoodlum to sophisticated urban terrorist. Properly crafted, the portrait of Donnell was of a wannabe gangster graduating into full-fledged felon.

Hrones spoke next. He asked Judge Wright to release Johnson on his own recognizance. The boy had strong ties to the community, as evidenced by the presence in the courtroom of his mother, his grandmother, and his pastor, the Reverend Bruce Wall from Dorchester Temple Baptist Church, where Donnell over the summer had found refuge from the streets. He was still in school, studying at East Boston High School. Besides, with a case so weak, why would Donnell bother to run? Better yet, where would he run?

"My client's position is he wasn't involved," Hrones said. "So it certainly is a case of mistaken identity if he wasn't there. And what's an eyewitness? An eyewitness's testimony is generally the weakest of all evidence."

The judge considered both arguments, and then reached a hollow compromise. Donnell, he ruled, could be released on $250,000 bail. Donnell, in other words, would sit in a juvenile lockup until his next court date.

RALPH MARTIN WAS NEVER ONE FOR THE LIMELIGHT. HE LACKED the showbiz glamour, the loose tongue that could roll a few short, searing words into a dazzling soundbite. Tochka, a thin and understated man in his late thirties, was a seasoned prosecutor, and the investigating detectives—a rumpled Irishman named Billy Mahoney and a shortish man in well-tailored suits named Danny Keeler—were both veterans of their trade. There was no need for the boss to get in their way. Plus, Martin was uncomfortable climbing into his bully pulpit to preach about any one instance of mayhem, even with an election looming only days away. He never bothered with the marches for instance, Taking Back the Night or Stopping Domestic Violence, leery of freighting his office with the voguish disorder of the day. Outside the courtroom that morning, surrounded by reporters, he managed to torque his voice into its best semblance of outrage. "This is one of the most reprehensible acts we've seen," he said, but in words echoing more with disappointment and mild grief than rage. "It's a real setback for the city."

He didn't say much after that, though he did at one point, prompted by a reporter's question, acknowledge how residents in the project helped capture Johnson. "Due to the age of the defendant and the totally callous nature of the crime, the community coughed up the defendant pretty quickly," Martin said. The harshest words were left to Jim Borghesani, of the district attorney's press office. "He's sixteen years old, he knows guns are dangerous, and he fired a gun," Borghesani snapped outside the courtroom the morning Donnell was arraigned. "We'll put our best case forward to see that he's tried as an adult."

The drumbeat continued. With one shooter and a getaway driver still at large, reporters still had a hook on which to hang twelve inches of type every morning. Manny's family, meanwhile, was grieving in the most public fashion. The nuances of his short life spilled out like cast-off scenes from an after school movie. He was in the second grade, where his favorite subject was social studies and where his classmates threw a surprise party for his ninth birthday. His heroes were Michael Jordan and Larry Bird, and he knew he would grow up to be either a basketball player or a lawyer or a doctor. He liked to ride his bike in the back parking lot and hug his grandmother, who taught him the Hail Mary because she worshiped as both a Pentecostal and a Catholic.

Yet he lived in a neighborhood where dodging bullets was apparently a way of life, despite a plummeting crime rate and dutiful patrols by two officers assigned to the project. "This isn't the first time it's happened, them shooting," Manny's best friend said. "Manny would come over my house saying how the boys from Heath Street would come over here shooting whenever they felt like it. It was an open door."

Sadly, they'd had some experience with the media horde that follows a young death. Three months before Manny was shot, Dorothy Haskins's fourteen-year-old grandson, Willie Ellebee, was shot dead in Atlanta, where his mother had moved him away from Boston's meaner streets. "The boy that shot my Willie was jealous of him, and that's all I'm going to say about that," Dorothy Haskins said, which was substantially more than she said about Jermaine's father, George, who'd died in July at the age of forty-six. "But I know my two boys, Jermaine and Willie, are in heaven tonight."

The boy was buried in a blue suit and white gloves, two stuffed animals laid gently in his casket and a crowd of mourners and reporters shivering in a cold wind blowing across the cemetery. His mother, Deborah Haskins, wailed to God, wailed for her baby. "It's all right, Debbie, the Lord is with him," someone in the crowd said while the reporters scribbled down all the words. It was death as dramatic theater. The night before, at Manny's funeral, a reformed hoodlum from Academy Homes, who had since found God and a job as a youth worker for the city, raised his voice to the rafters of the New Covenant Christian Center in Mattapan. "I'm tired of shedding tears," he bellowed to gentle rejoinders of amen. "Politicians keep trying to ask what the answer is, to come up with program after program. I'm so sick and tired of programs." He paused, gathering his breath, building momentum. "What in the world caused me to put down the nine millimeter and pick up a Bible? What did it?" Another pause. "The glory and honor of Jesus Christ!"

More amens. Louder, from the gut and the soul.

Jesus Christ saves young boys from guns. Donnell Johnson must be running with the devil.

CHAPTER 8

Swift Justice

THERE IS NEVER A GOOD TIME TO BE ACCUSED OF KILLING AN-
other human being. But there are some times and some places that
are worse than others in which to be called a murderer. At one
point in history, and not all that long ago, a suspect's prospects
were much improved if he was charged with murder before he hit
the mythical and arbitrary age of manhood. In Massachusetts, that
happens to be seventeen, an age at which the state forbids its residents from drinking beer or voting but has no qualms about ware-
housing them in prisons. So Donnell Johnson had that going for
him. He was only sixteen years old when he was accused of murdering Jermaine Goffigan.

On the other hand, Johnson was arraigned in the year of our
Lord nineteen-hundred-and-ninety-four, which also happened to
be the third year of the commonwealth's grim and eager progression toward a more severe juvenile justice system. Massachusetts
legislators, unlike their counterparts in many other states, had
once restrained themselves from smelting new laws into sledge-
hammers, hoping to beat into submission the bloody spike of
youthful violence that began poking through the nation's crime
statistics in the mid eighties.

107

Between 1985—the beginning of the crack epidemic—and 1992, for instance, the murder rate among black boys between the ages of fourteen and seventeen skyrocketed a boggling 300 percent; among white males in the same age bracket, homicide rose a still-alarming 50 percent. Massachusetts was suffering a similar surge in youth crime. In 1993, juvenile courts across the state arraigned 20,109 kids for all manner of delinquencies, a 9.1 percent increase from 1988. More disturbing was the escalating level of violence. In 1989, only 20 percent of the juveniles on probation had committed a violent crime, such as robbery, assault, and the like. By 1992, nearly one out of every three young probationers fit that profile. And in the Department of Youth Services, the state agency assigned to supervise delinquent kids, the number of children committed for violent offenses swelled 160 percent between 1988 and 1994, rising from 25 percent of the D.Y.S. caseload to 45 percent.

Indeed, Massachusetts appeared to be grappling with the violence better than most areas of the country. D.Y.S., which used a system of small, community-based group homes, a few secure lockups, and a network of outreach workers and monitors, was then considered to be one of the most effective agencies of its kind, in terms of both cost and in rehabilitating kids. Granted, it was a more generous system—by law, kids, with a few exceptions, could be held only until their twenty-first birthday—and its budget was atrophying like an unwatered plant, but it was working well enough that the juvenile justice code was in no dire need of revision.

Legislators rarely fret over statistics anyway. In order to overhaul the laws, they typically require a cathartic event, an especially brutal killing or a particularly tragic victim. In 1990, Boston's ghetto provided the former: a gang rape and torture killing of a prostitute by eight people, including five under the age of seventeen. In April 1991, the city's ghetto provided the latter: Damien Bynoe, who was then fifteen years old and a fledgling member of the Orchard Park Trailblazers, fired a pistol up a dark street. Two of the bullets hit two children, a fifteen-year-old named Korey Grant and an eleven-year-old named Charles Copney. Both died, immortalizing Copney as the youngest child at the time to be killed by gang violence.

The Suffolk County District Attorney's Office, led by Flanagan, decided Bynoe, as well as two boys who were with him, should be tried as adults for the murders. So they embarked on a lengthy hearing before a juvenile court judge, arguing that the crime was so heinous and the accused so irredeemable that only an adult prison sentence would be appropriate. Bynoe was defended by J.W. Carney, Jr., the close friend of the future D.A., Ralph Martin. Carney shopped Bynoe's life story to reporters, who wrote lengthy and sympathetic pieces, first in the *Boston Phoenix,* then in the *Boston Sunday Globe* magazine. In court, Carney lined the walls with teachers, counselors, youth workers, and psychiatrists, all of whom were willing to swear that Bynoe could be salvaged by a mere five years in D.Y.S. custody. A judge agreed.

The rabble were roused. Demands for the juvenile code to be stiffened came immediately, loudly, and angrily. The legislature acceded. Before the year was out, the so-called transfer hearing that determines whether a child will be tried as an adult or a juvenile was mandatory for a number of violent offenses. And the burden was now on the defendant to explain why he shouldn't be tried in superior court. Not that it mattered much. A juvenile delinquent of murder would do at least a decade behind bars (and twenty years for first degree killings), first in D.Y.S., where he would grow up, then in adult prison.

Other states, most notably Florida and New York, had long experimented with treating kids as adults. Invariably, the results were the opposite of the intentions. In Florida, for example, most of the five thousand or so kids sent to adult court every year in the early nineties ended up on probation or serving shorter sentences than they would have in the juvenile system. In New York, meanwhile, only 4 percent of the children bumped automatically to adult courts in that era received longer sentences than they would have as juveniles. The cause is rooted in basic human psychology: in all but the most heinous instances, adult jurors and adult judges still see a child sitting in the courtroom, a youngster whom they are loath to send to prison with hardened cons.

In Massachusetts—where Governor William F. Weld once proudly proclaimed himself as being "to the right of Attila the Hun" on crime and punishment—the purportedly tough new rules had a similar effect. Because they were now mandatory, the number of transfer hearings, time-consuming and expensive affairs that clog the court docket and absorb precious beds in juvenile holding facilities, increased from 155 in 1991 to 229 the following year. Yet the number of kids actually transferred into superior court *declined* from seventeen, or 11 percent, to ten, or barely more than 4 percent. One reason, a number of judges maintained, was that the recent changes also gave them the authority to commit a kid to D.Y.S. until the age of twenty-one, which made the decision not to send them to prison more palatable.

(For all the sympathetic press Damien Bynoe received, he turned out to be one of D.Y.S.'s worst failures. Released at twenty-one, he has been repeatedly rearrested. As of this writing, he was being held for violating probation in a carjacking case after he was charged with selling crack. His two co-defendants, meanwhile, were transferred to adult court. One was acquitted of murder. Charges against the other were dropped.)

From the perspective of a sixteen-year-old boy such as Donnell Johnson, however, the difference between twenty years as a juvenile and life without parole as an adult was worth roughly forty years of freedom. Keeping Johnson in the juvenile system would be the first challenge for Stephen Hrones.

RALPH MARTIN'S MAIN CONCERN DURING THE FIRST WEEK OF November 1994—getting elected—was less dire than Johnson's, but seemingly as desperate. The polls throughout the fall insisted Martin was in danger of losing his job to Gerald Malone, a young lawyer who, on paper, had far more going for him than Bill Weld's token appointee. Being a white man and a Democrat were his obvious advantages. So was his home turf: South Boston, the district that had long carried a disproportionate share of political sway in the city. Curiously, he even appeared to neutralize what could have been Martin's strongest suits. Malone was an experienced prosecutor, having worked under Newman Flanagan, then departing when Martin took over. And he had a curious specialty for a city with a rotten reputation for racial tolerance: He was the liaison between the Suffolk County District Attorney's office and the Boston Police Department's Community Disorders Unit, which was once a national model for its aggressive investigation into so-called hate crimes—assaults and threats and vandalism based on the race, ethnicity, or sexual orientation of the victim.

Goffigan's killing and Johnson's history of being arrested but unindicted didn't help Martin's odds. Malone had already picked up the official support of the Boston police unions, which used the Halloween murder as a cudgel to briefly bash the incumbent district attorney, as well as the obligatory endorsement from iconic senior Senator Edward F. Kennedy, which never hurt anyone's chances in Boston. What's more, the commander of the C.D.U., a well-respected cop named Billy Johnston, was stumping for him, albeit behind the scenes.

Then again, Martin wasn't running as the Black Avenger. Quite the opposite. In June 2000, the *Boston Globe,* under the page-one label "special report," strongly suggested that Martin backed off on civil rights violations in exchange for support from white South Bostonians, who were so frequently charged with harrassing black and Hispanic tenants in the local projects that they dubbed the C.D.U. the Caucasian Detainee Unit. City Council President James Kelly and City Councillor at Large Stephen Lynch, both of whm hail from the district, claimed they lobbied Boston police commanders to transfer aggressive cops out of the unit. "I'm not convinced a weakened C.D.U. is a bad thing," Lynch told the paper. Martin, who denied making any such deal—"That would mean I'm corrupt," he said—and Evans maintained that their investigations had simply become more focused, and that only the strongest cases were being taken to court. Whatever the reasons, complaints to the C.D.U. increased 57 percent between 1993 and 1999, according to the paper, yet the rate at which charges were filed after those complaints were investigated dropped 56 percent.

At times it was difficult to tell if Martin was campaigning at all, at least in the traditional sense. He made the rounds of the Rotarians and Kiwanis groups, of course, and he'd hired a political consultant to manage his efforts, a vegetarian named Michael Shea who broke his Democrats Only rule to work for Martin. But even Shea was frustrated, albeit with no small measure of pleasant surprise, with the candidate's lack of political cravenness. "Look, he's a decent guy with a core who doesn't take the easy punch," Shea explained once. "I mean, it's clear where you should stand on the death penalty if you just want to get votes. But Ralph has taken a very principled stand," which was also a very public stand, against killing prisoners.

Even crafting a television campaign with the proper tone was a struggle. TV advertisements are vital to elections in that they target a small percentage of voters with short attention spans who know little about the candidate or the issues yet still insist on trying to govern themselves. The point, therefore, isn't to convey too much detailed information but instead to wrench one visceral response from those swing voters who make their final decisions between reruns of "The Simpsons." Martin had two powerful pieces of information Shea could use to his advantage. One was his father's career as a police officer, suggesting he is a law-and-order type by dint of his genes. The other was the murder of his mother, which hints that he understands more painfully than most people the horror of crime. Problem was, Martin was reluctant to allow his mother to be mentioned. Too personal, he said.

In the end, Shea swayed Martin on the value of such a tragic tale. "The son of a police officer," the ad began with a solemn voiceover. "His mother was murdered." Then the candidate appeared to talk about locking up gangbangers and cracking down on domestic violence and demanding mandatory sentences for kids caught with guns. And it ended with Martin's campaign slogan: "Tough Minded Justice."

It was a good spot, an award-winner even. But such a short spot reduced Martin to a caricature of a prosecutor—granted, by design—but one that while not entirely deceptive, was still conveniently misleading. "If you've got thirty seconds to talk to people—and that's what you've got—you talk about being tough, because that's what people want to hear, especially people who are influenced by TV," Shea said.

Behind the rhetoric, though, is a more subtle and complex reality. Martin did, in fact, want gun-toting kids locked up for a specified period of time (later decided to be six months when, in 1996, a bill he co-authored was signed into law), which sounds quite severe. But when he initially broached the idea in 1994, it was based on a more pragmatic, even compassionate notion. Martin knew that a kid with a gun in some neighborhoods wasn't necessarily an assassin in the making; instead, he could be simply terrified of the neighborhood's serious thugs or looking for a touch of adolescent status. The problem with that, as any cop or psychologist will attest, is that a fourteen-year-old with a pistol is infinitely more dangerous than a forty-year-old with the same gun, simply because children don't fully understand the damage bullets do to human flesh nor fully control the emotional impulses that send a jolt of muscle-spasming electrical current from their brains to their trigger fingers. "We need to increase not only the penalties kids pay," Martin said when he first broached the idea in the spring of 1994, "but also the accountability of the system.... You have to have time to fight against the indoctrination they get on the streets."

The bulk of Martin's campaign, however, was constructed in his office, retooling the machinery of the district attorney to more effectively soothe troubled neighborhoods—the strategy one of his own GOP wags called buffoonery. Early in his tenure, for instance, Martin and his aides gathered with residents in various neighborhoods to suss out their concerns. Being prosecutors, they came equipped with the most current statistics on major crimes, the killings and beatings and burglaries that take priority in the county's courts and newsrooms. The lumpen prole, on the other hand, didn't much care about those numbers; even in the bloodiest of times, only a tiny percentage of people are directly victimized by crime. Instead, the citizenry fretted about the more subtle symptoms of decay, the fresh graffiti and swirling trash, the abandoned cars and loitering prostitutes, all the fearsome symbols that a neighborhood is losing control of itself.

The proper response, then, isn't demanding longer sentences for random categories of miscreants and felons. Jail cells, while costing taxpayers a fortune, only directly affect the handful of criminals who are dumb enough or unlucky enough to get caught and convicted. Instead, Martin's office, in conjunction with new Police Commissioner Paul Evans, Mayor Menino, and state and federal officials, developed broader approaches to deal not only with crime but with the fear of crime, which is arguably more crippling for any community.

So Martin rejiggered his office. In March 1993, he shuffled the staff of his organized-crime unit, which, he announced, would prosecute crimes "that disrupt neighborhood stability [including] more traditional organized crime activities as well as the recent resurgence of gang-related violence." In other words, teenagers who shot at each other would, in certain instances, be treated no less seriously than *La Cosa Nostra*. At the same time, however, Martin was actually softening his approach to younger delinquents, albeit carefully couched in the scripted tough-talk of a man who has to get elected. "None of us are shrinking violets when it comes to putting people in jail," he would say before uttering something that might be considered squishily liberal. Like, for instance, the sentence that followed that one: "We recognize that for people who are on the fringe, you're only going to reach them by showing them alternatives. It's not like you're revealing a weakness by demonstrating an understanding of the problem."

Six months later, he expanded the effort against youthful terrorism with what he called the Community-Based Juvenile Justice program, which involved the revolutionary technique (for Boston, anyway) of having different agencies that deal with troubled kids—police, prosecutors, teachers and school headmasters, probation officers, D.Y.S. officers—actually talk to each other. "The idea behind the program is simple," said Jack Zanini, the former head of the juvenile unit in Martin's office. "Through better communication, we're identifying the troublemakers and getting an early jump on kids who need help."

The office also began, in conjunction with all sorts of other agencies, to target especially troubled neighborhoods. Some began with dramatic shows of force. Before dawn one morning in October 1994, for instance, a small legion of local police and federal agents swarmed into the Franklin Hill projects, a bleak collection of red-brick apartments set across Blue Hill Avenue from the Franklin Field project, with which the local hoodlums, the Giants, carried on a sporadic shooting war. The police that morning carried with them a stack of arrest warrants and extra handcuffs, which they wrapped around the wrists of sixteen suspected criminals. After the cops cleared out, the carpenters and landscapers and painters and locksmiths swept in, replacing broken doors, hauling away abandoned cars, replacing burnt-out or broken street lights. Later, a permanent gang-prevention coordinator was assigned out of Martin's office to keep the Giants from regrouping or at least dragging in a new generation of recruits.

Similar sweeps were performed in other projects—Mission Hill, Beech Street in Roslindale. What's more, entire neighborhoods were saturated with anticrime efforts. Those initiatives began in early 1993 had actually come out of the office of Attorney General Scott Harshbarger, Martin's old boss when he ran the Middlesex County District Attorney's Office. Called the Safe Neighborhood Initiatives, it began with a squad of assistant attorney generals, Suffolk County prosecutors and victim-witness advocates, and a variety of police agencies descending first on the Four Corners neighborhood of Dorchester, a few square blocks long plagued by gangs and guns. Because the idea was to involve residents in fighting crime on their home turf, Neighborhood Advisory Councils were established to guide the cops and prosecutors. Those three pay phones the drug dealers use? Gone. The billboards for movies where actors are waving big pistols? Vanished. Eventually, the program spread to five concentrated tracts in Dorchester. Long term, the results would be impressive. Between August 1995 and August 1996, for instance, violent crime in those areas dropped 22 percent, including an astonishing 60 percent decline in aggravated assault; and property crime fell 40 percent.

In the summer of 1994, the S.N.I. idea was moved across Boston Harbor to Maverick and Central squares in East Boston, an area in the throes of a demographic overhaul as working-class Italian-Americans were replaced by impoverished immigrants from South and Central America and the Far East. Sergeant Detective Donald S. Gosselin, who worked in the district, went to his first S.N.I. meeting at the East Boston District Courthouse, a hundred feet or so from where he routinely made undercover drug buys, in the middle of the summer of 1994. The people already in the room included a judge in his robes, three people from Martin's office, officers from the Massachusetts Bay Transportation Authority and the Boston Housing Authority, and two other Boston cops, including the captain of the district.

It was not, to everyone's pleasant surprise, a rancorous meeting. "It was the first time in my career I'd ever seen so many people from that many different law-enforcement agencies in the same room in that community—in any community—and not be trying to punch the shit out of each other," Gosselin said. "Instead of talking about how we're not doing our job, how they're not doing their job, it was, 'How can we help you do your job better?' I can't imagine that meeting taking place under Newman Flanagan. It wasn't about politics, it wasn't about getting votes. It was about coming up with strategies."

What the police classify as Part One Crime—murder, rape, assault, and the like—was already dropping, in no small part because Martin's office had been steering the hardest-core hoods onto a fast conveyor to superior court. "The rest of it was a mop-up campaign," Gosselin said. Educating a new population of immigrants was part of it, instructing Colombian men, for instance, that it is not acceptable in America to drink a beer on the street, as it is in their home country. And a lot of it was, as Gosselin puts is, "reglazing the broken windows," a play on a famous 1984 book, *Broken Windows,* that argued minor deteriorations led to first the fear of crime, then the actual crime. "It was an exciting time to be a cop," Gosselin said.

Those efforts didn't generate an enormous amount of press coverage, the free publicity most incumbents milk like a personal teat. (Indeed, an overriding concern among Martin's supporters has been his reluctance to claim credit for anything.)

A quick digression: On October 3, 1995, the day Orenthal James Simpson was acquitted of nearly decapitating his ex-wife and a hapless waiter who happened to get in the way, black prosecutors were a prime draw for the pontification circuit. A local radio show desperately wanted Martin on the air, and started hounding Carmen Fields, his press attaché. Could he come on at seven o'clock? How about eight? Hell, we'll take him anytime he can get to a phone. But Fields couldn't give the producer an answer for the simple reason that she couldn't find her boss. She finally tracked him down at home. Martin demurred. His wife was out, he was watching his three young kids, getting them ready for bed. "Tell them thanks," Martin told her, "but I think I'll pass." Fields was incredulous. "What?" she said. "Ralph, what kind of media whore are you? How can I peddle you if I can't even get you out on the street?" Martin burst out laughing. "Media whore? I guess I'm not a very good one."

In any case, the polls all turned out to be wrong. On Election Day, Martin crushed Malone by a margin of 52 percent to 37 percent. In South Boston, Gerry Malone's bastion of conservative, white Irish Democrats, Martin took an amazing 48 percent of the votes cast. The victory was so impressively solid that, four years later, none of the city's bright and eager lawyers would bother mustering a campaign against him. Almost immediately, whispers began that Martin was the odds-on favorite to become Boston's first black mayor, if and when his friend Menino stepped aside.

LATE ONE SATURDAY NIGHT IN AUGUST 1998, A SIXTEEN-YEAR-old boy went to his cousin's house in Boston's Roxbury neighborhood to hang out for the night. Among the people there that night was a man who was twenty-six years old, armed, and, at half past three in the morning, quite cantankerous. For some reason—the reasons are rarely important in such matters—the older man pulled out a nine millimeter pistol and poked it into the younger boy's throat.

"Yo, man," the boy's cousin told him in grand understatement, "you better get out of here."

The teenager wisely began to run, sprinting right out the door, across the porch and down the stairs. The twenty-six-year-old squeezed off a few rounds, the bullets tearing into the night, but missing any flesh. No one died, or even bled, but only for want of better aim.

Six hours later, the boy told his family what had happened. They, in turn, called the police. By ten o'clock on Sunday morning, Boston police, including officers from the Youth Violence Strike Force, were at the boy's house. The cops, in turn, summoned a young assistant district attorney named Matthew Machera, who for the past fifteen months had been summoned by police to the scenes of most major crimes committed in Roxbury. Machera listened to the boy's story and, after being convinced there was probable cause to search the cousin's house, helped prepare a warrant. That afternoon, police poked through the crime scene and found the nine millimeter, sixty rounds of ammunition, and 260 grams of crack cocaine. Before the night was out—a Sunday night, mind you—Machera had distributed subpoenas to the young victim and several witnesses, who all dutifully reported to a Suffolk County grand jury to give testimony the next morning.

Two weeks later, the twenty-six-year-old was indicted for assault with a deadly weapon, a felony charge that was delayed only because the ballistics lab had needed time to test-fire the gun.

Machera loves telling that story, which isn't so much about one anonymous shooting as it is about the revolutionary evolution of law enforcement in Suffolk County. "It's just something when you can go out and get the bad guys and look at the victim and say, 'Hey, yeah, we do care,'" he says, almost beaming. "Think about this: you're the bad guy, and you've got the Boston police *and* the D.A.'s office coming after you, and coming after you fast."

A veteran cop such as Donald Gosselin, who had been amazed at all those cops from different agencies sitting in the same room and not choking one another, can understand what an enormous change such a scenario represents. In the not-at-all-distant past, when the cops and prosecutors worked as separate, if not competing, entities, a Saturday-night, non-fatal shooting in the ghetto would have first slogged through the lower district court, beginning with an arraignment, a bail hearing, and then, most likely, a probable cause hearing—a process that would plod along for weeks, if not months. During that time, a sixteen-year-old who'd already been shot at once would have time to realize that he might get shot at again, and maybe even hit, if he testified. Witnesses would be able to ponder the same scenario. In that sense, justice delayed truly is justice denied, which means there are a great many technically unsolved shootings lingering on the books from the bad old days.

Machera, on the other hand, hadn't been a practicing prosecutor long enough to become so cynical that he would be surprised by a common-sense approach to crime suppression. Since assuming control of the district attorney's office, Martin had shifted not only its practice, but also its philosophy. And people such as Machera were hired not only for their legal ability but also for their willingness to buy into that philosophy.

Every potential rookie assistant district attorney must pass through the office of Elizabeth Keeley, a slim woman in her mid-

forties whom Martin hired as his chief deputy in 1992. Her career
nearly mirrored that of her boss: she'd spent seven years as an assistant D.A. in Middlesex County, and then prosecuted federal
crimes in the U.S. Attorney's Office, eventually specializing in the
distasteful task of locking up child pornographers. Keeley, like Martin, never enjoyed federal work as much as state-level prosecutions, where the victims are more real, the effect of crime more
visceral. Feds work in an ethereal vacuum; district attorneys work
in a tangible community. "We have an awesome power over people's lives," she says. Thus, she believes prosecutors need to be held
to a strikingly high level of ethical and moral conduct.

By the time job candidates get to her office, they've already been
through several rounds of interviews, leaving her as the fine filter
to remove the flotsam. In most instances, she asks eager young
lawyers how they would handle a simple scenario:

It's nine o'clock in the morning in a crowded district court, and
there is a stack of perhaps three dozen cases piled on your desk,
none of which you've had time to thoroughly review. Just as the
judge is taking the bench, a defense attorney grabs you in the hallway. "My client will plead out," he says, "if you recommend probation." You skim the case file, which consists mostly of a police
report. The alleged bad guy was stopped in his car after an officer
saw him make a "furtive gesture." After pulling the guy over, the
cop searches the car and finds a small quantity of cocaine.

"What," Keeley will ask the wannabe A.D.A., "do you do?"

Nearly one third of the candidates give her the obvious, and
easy, answer. Take the plea. District courts are the assembly lines of
justice; disposing of one case, and with a conviction to boot,
means lightening the load ever so slightly. Those candidates, on
the other hand, are the ones who fail the test.

The correct answer is to ask the judge for a second call, which
means to take a pass on the case until later. During that reprieve,
the savvy assistant district attorney will go talk to the cop, who is
most likely sitting in the back of the courtroom. "What's a 'furtive
gesture,'" he'll ask the officer, knowing full well the phrase is

generic catchall for bogus stops. If the policeman doesn't offer a plausible explanation, there is no shame in a young prosecutor dismissing the case.

Counterintuitive? Not really. At first glance, such a collection of facts suggests an illegal search, one made without probable cause. A smart defense attorney will realize that immediately and file a motion to suppress any evidence—namely, the cocaine—that was found. A duller one will figure it out later, sitting in his office mulling over the day's work. So, too, will an alert judge smell a case that isn't daisy-fresh clean. And both of those people, the judge and the lawyer, will cross paths with the prosecutor again. The cop, meanwhile, will have no reason to cease making illegal stops.

"Your position in front of the bench has been diminished" if you take the plea, Keeley says. "The next time you're up there arguing this guy or that guy should be held on bail, how much credibility is that judge going to give you? So it's not a question of being qualified. It's a question of whether you buy into the philosophy of this office, into what we're trying to do as part of our community."

DONNELL JOHNSON'S FIRST FEW MONTHS OF INCARCERATION weren't going too smoothly. He was depressed, withdrawn, the enormity of his circumstances beginning to crush down upon his thin shoulders. At first, he'd believed the police were merely trying to frighten him, give a kid on the fringe a good shake, but that they'd let him go once they realized he hadn't shot any kid, hadn't even been there when it happened.

November moved into December, then January. He was being held in the Plymouth County House of Correction, an adult jail that had set aside one wing for juvenile killers and suspected killers. Johnson didn't get along with his fellow inmates, with whom he got into a few minor fights, or his counselors with whom he was uncooperative, even defiant. By February, though, he'd begun to open up, slowly at first and never very widely, as he is reserved by nature. But the first step in his progression through the legal system was the transfer hearing. If he couldn't convince a judge that he belonged in the juvenile system, Johnson would be facing the chance of spending the rest of his life in prison.

So Johnson cooperated with the psychologists. He immediately exposed the flaw in deciding whether a child is redeemable before he's been proven to have committed a crime that requires his redemption. The killing of Goffigan, in the psychological parlance, was "a planned and predatory crime," which "raised serious concerns" of his amenability to rehabilitation if he'd pulled the trigger. "He does not," a shrink concluded, "presently exhibit signs of emotional distress, victim empathy, or remorse." The reason, of course, is that he insisted he was innocent. Still, those weren't favorable words to take before a judge.

But the boy had gotten a break in that he'd drawn Judge Leslie Harris, who in his previous incarnations had defended poor kids in Roxbury District Court and then had briefly headed the juvenile unit in Martin's office. "Why would Ralph Martin hire me—a public defender—to head the juvenile unit?" Harris once rhetorically asked. "Because he realizes we can't keep treating juvenile crime the same way. It's not the same. But you can't lose sight of the fact that these are still kids."

In April 1995, Harris heard reports from psychologists who'd interviewed Johnson. The one working for the state, Frank DiCataldo, called the boy "a danger to society," assuming he'd committed the crime. But he put the odds of Johnson being successfully rehabilitated somewhere where between "very guarded" and "very favorable"—a conveniently wide range. Meanwhile, a psychologist hired by Hrones testified that Johnson was "very amenable to treatment within the juvenile system." On the other hand, she agreed he was a menace to society if he was, in fact, guilty.

Harris decided to keep Johnson in the juvenile system, a decision he handed down during a court session at two o'clock on the afternoon of June 15, 1995. The ruling also fit the pattern of transfer hearings in the era of new and supposedly tougher juvenile laws in Massachusetts. Hrones called the decision "courageous." The prosecutor, a lanky, beak-nosed man named Robert Tochka, was naturally frustrated. "If a person is saying he didn't commit the crime and has never been in D.Y.S. custody in the past," he told a reporter, "how can you overcome the burden that he can't be rehabilitated?"

And Manny Goffigan's relatives were drenched in grief and rage. "It's not fair, it's not fair!" Manny's aunt, Donna Haskins, screamed at Harris. "They killed my nephew and you won't protect him." She ran into the hallway, where she pounded on a wall and wept.

IF JUSTICE DELAYED TRULY IS JUSTICE DENIED, THEN THE JUDICIAL system is shortchanging everybody. Moving a case from arrest to trial is a lengthy ordeal, delayed by hearings and investigations and pretrial motions and continuances and conflicting schedules of attorneys and judges and open courtrooms. Plus, the entire system is clogged like a slop sink, plugged up with felonious goop.

Donnell Johnson finally stood trial in March 1996, nearly a year after Judge Harris first ruled he would remain in the juvenile system. Under a state law at the time—which has since been eliminated in yet another round of get-tough crackdowns—juveniles accused of felonies were granted two trials, first before a judge and then, if they lost, before a jury. Johnson would need both.

Kevin Murphy, the by-then thirty-two-year-old O.G., or Original Gangster, who police believe was the actual target when Goffigan died, got on the witness stand and told Judge R. Marc Kantrowitz that he recognized Donnell Johnson as one of the shooters. Eight times, in response to one question or another involving Johnson, a gun, and a dead kid, Murphy pointed across the courtroom and said, "That's him."

More devastating, though, was Jerome "Romey" Goffigan, Manny's brother. "I saw flames coming from the gun when he pointed it at me," he testified after identifying Johnson as the gunman. "I felt the sparks and I crawled along the gravel to get away."

Kantrowitz found Johnson guilty. The boy took it stoically—
"showed no emotion," as reporters always put it. "Don't worry
about it," Hrones told his client, wrapping his arm around his
shoulder. "The jury trial's the big game."

CHAPTER 9

Naming Names

THE NEEDLES TWITCHED AND JERKED, SQUIGGLING LINES ACROSS a scrolling sheet of paper, each one recording the physiological responses from Donnell Johnson's sweat glands and heart and lungs every time he answered a question. Some were mundane. "Is your name Donnell Johnson?"

"Yes." Since he was responding truthfully to an innocuous inquiry, the man watching the polygraph machine, a retired lieutenant detective from the New York City Police homicide squad, had a base against which to measure the more serious questions, all of which pertained to the night of October 31, 1994. The most important was, "Did you kill Jermaine Goffigan?"

"No."

The needles skittered back and forth in the same pattern. Donnell Johnson was telling the truth. Probably, anyway. Later, David C. Raskin, a specialist in psychophysiology and arguably the leading authority on polygraph tests, reviewed the charts and came to the same conclusion. Not that it would do Donnell any good.

Judges are generally reluctant to allow polygraph, or lie detector tests, to be used as evidence in court, mainly because even the most skilled technicians admit their machines are substantially less than 100 percent accurate. Using them can be a valuable investigative tool, helping to exclude weak suspects, digging the guilty farther into the hole, even spooking away people who fear failing, which in itself can help detectives in weighing how much effort to put into a particular target. But foolproof? No. Even though the machines measure supposedly uncontrollable changes in blood pressure and respiration and the like when someone is lying, sociopaths, the delusional, and exceptionally skilled liars can beat them. Even the most ardent fans of polygraphing put their reliability at 90 percent or so.

Massachusetts courts used to allow such evidence in a handful of cases, but eventually judges began accepting that the tests weren't sound enough for the courtroom. In 1989, the Supreme Judicial Court agreed, banning polygraphs—as well as testimony referring to a defendant having passed or failed a test before trial—from criminal proceedings. With nothing to lose but a second trial, Hrones tried to convince Judge Robert W. Banks to allow Johnson's test to be admitted. As a matter of course, the request was denied.

Donnell Johnson's trial before a jury began on Tuesday, November 19, 1996, and it followed much the same course as the first. Dorothy Haskins, Manny's grandmother, identified Johnson as the shooter. Jerome Goffigan told the story about seeing the flames spitting from the barrel of the gun and seeing Donnell's light skin and dark freckles. Kevin Murphy, who was now thirty-three years old, also identified Johnson again. Hrones attacked both of their memories, trying to shake them from identifications they made in the dark, from a distance, and, in Murphy's case, while he was diving for cover. Hrones also managed to bring out Murphy's life of thuggery, including his own participation in the long-running feud with Bromley Heath hoods and his 1983 conviction for attempted murder.

Defense attorneys generally prefer to keep their clients off the witness stand. For one thing, testifying allows the prosecutor to ask questions, which typically are not presented politely. A rattled defendant or an angry defendant is a losing defendant. Moreover, putting the suspect on the stand takes the focus off of the witnesses presented by the state, which bears the burden of proving guilt beyond a reasonable doubt. If a defense lawyer can poke enough holes in the state's case, raise enough questions and plant large enough seeds of doubt, there is no sense risking a not guilty verdict by giving the client an opportunity to stumble on the witness stand.

Prosecutor Robert Tochka wrapped up his case by the weekend. Hrones, preparing his defense, still had no intention of putting Donnell on the stand. On Saturday morning, November 23, the lawyer drove to Plymouth to talk with Donnell, considering and reconsidering his options along the way. Donnell, despite having been arrested before, had never been convicted, so there was nothing that Tochka could use to prove he was a bad guy. And Hrones knew that Johnson could name names, that he could tell the jury who everyone on the street already suspected, one of whom had even told Donnell that he'd pulled the trigger.

But Donnell didn't want to do that. He was holding fast to the code of the street. Why should he snitch? His pastor, the Reverend Bruce Wall, had been begging him for two years to give up the names, telling him he'd help Johnson and his family move out of state so none of them would get shot for speaking up. Donnell steadfastly refused. The jury would see the truth, he would walk free, and he wouldn't be a rat.

"Hey, it's your life on the line," Hrones told Donnell that morning in Plymouth. "Are you going to not implicate the real shooter just because the law of the jungle says that you don't rat?"

Donnell considered that. He was still reluctant.

"It's Judgement Day," Hrones finally said. "You've got to think about yourself."

NEICO SANTOS WAS USHERED INTO THE COURTROOM MONDAY morning, looking angry and nervous all at once. He'd been brought from a jail cell, where he was being held for an unrelated crime. Now his name was about to be dragged into Johnson's trial. Judge Banks told him he could assert his rights under the Fifth

Amendment not to incriminate himself. He also told Santos, who was then twenty-three years old, that he didn't have to testify if he didn't want to. He didn't. So, as a formal gesture, Banks noted for the record that Santos had denied that he was involved in shooting a nine-year-old boy on Halloween Night 1994.

None of that was surprising. Neico Santos was a well-seasoned hoodlum, practiced in the art of shooting, albeit not with any terrific accuracy, and accustomed to the slow grind of the criminal justice system. He knew what it meant to take the Fifth, and he knew it was the smart thing to do.

A few hours later, Donnell took the stand. Hrones asked him the right question. The boy gave the right answer: Neico Santos did it. He'd kept the secret all these years, he went on, because he was scared. "I would be a snitch," he said, "and people don't like that. I had nothing to worry about because I didn't do anything."

In the annals of Boston gang-banger trials, it was a monumental moment. Even Tochka was stunned, according to three of his colleagues (Tochka declined to be interviewed for this book). Prosecutors, after years of weary experience, are used to hearing defendants blame someone else for their crimes. But, usually, they say something along the lines of, "Junebug did it."

Then the prosecutor says, "Do you know Junebug's real name?"
"No."
"Do you know where we could find this Junebug person?"
"No."
"Do you know what he looks like?"
"No."

All of which is because Junebug in most instances is not a real person, merely a phantom to take the fall. But Johnson was fingering a real person, with a real last name. If Johnson beat the murder case, he would be back on the same streets with Neico and Neico's associates. Even if he didn't, his mother and his sister were still out there. The manchild accused of killing was now a boy risking his life, and the lives of his family members. Would a guilty thug risk so much?

Not that Tochka lightened up on Donnell Johnson. The next morning, in his closing argument, Tochka pushed all the emotional buttons, reminding the jury how, when a bullet tore through his chest, Manny said only the words of a young child: "Oh, shoot." When the paramedics came to try to keep him from bleeding to death before he got to the hospital, all the little boy wanted to know was, "Are you going to help me?" Packed into the ambulance, he told an emergency medical technician, "It's my birthday. My candy's all over the floor." And then, "I have a pain in my chest."

Tochka moved closer to Donnell, his arm out, pointing at his freckles. "Would you forget this face?" he asked the jurors, but in a way that was more of a statement than a question. "Would you forget this face?"

"Back off," Hrones snapped.

Hrones was no less aggressive in his argument to the jurors. The case against Donnell Johnson, he maintained, was built on shaky eyewitnesses, and crafted by bungling cops, and polished by disingenuous district attorneys. "This case stinks," he nearly snarled. He told the jurors, "Send out the message that there isn't enough evidence in this case to convict even your worst enemy . . . Send a message to the Boston Police and the district attorney's office that you are not going to tolerate this type of sloppy, incompetent, Keystone Kops investigation that more than borders on the unethical."

Perhaps the five men and seven women considered that message during the two days they deliberated. But they dismissed it. No, it seemed, they wouldn't forget that face, all those ebony freckles across the café-au-lait skin. On Thursday, November 28, 1996, the jury convicted Johnson of first degree murder.

Judge Banks sentenced him immediately. Donnell Johnson would spend at least eighteen years behind bars, first in the custody of D.Y.S., then in the state's adult correctional system.

TRUE FACT: VIRTUALLY EVERY SINGLE PERSON IN PRISON TODAY is guilty. Perhaps not of the exact crime for which he or she was convicted—some of the details always get blurred between the event and the conviction—and perhaps not of a crime that deserves a long stretch behind steel bars and razorwire fences. But very few inmates are innocent.

As far as Hrones was concerned, Donnell Johnson was one of those very few. "In twenty-five years of practicing criminal law I have never felt that way about a client who was convicted," he wrote in a letter to Ralph Martin a week after the conviction. Given that, he wasn't about to stop pleading Johnson's case. He would file all the requisite appeals, all of which were shot down over the next two years. (For appellate judges to smile favorably on a convict, he generally needs to demonstrate an error of law was committed during the trial, not simply that the verdict is wrong.) On December 6, 1996, one week after Johnson's conviction, he sent a letter to Ralph Martin, the first volley in what would be a long and at times cantankerous squabble with the district attorney's office.

"I write to you," he began, "because of deep concerns I have over the highly improper and unethical conduct of members of your office in the prosecution of Donnell Johnson."

He went through the litany of evidence he and his investigators had dredged up concerning Neico Santos, including a statement taken from a witness to an earlier shooting in Bromley Heath that wounded Santos's cousin, Kamiya. Neico, according to that witness, said, "We got to go get those niggers." Hrones also brought up Arthur Brice, who goes by the name Cano, and Al Wilson, who would later be indicted for selling cocaine in Bromley Heath and whom Donnell also fingered on the stand. "I would hope at the very least you would have a new set of investigators and staff look very closely at the roles played by the individuals named by Donnell in his testimony as being the real murderers," Hrones wrote.

On the second page, he got into the meat of his complaints, which was "the disgraceful performance of members of your staff in the prosecution of this case." Some of it revolved around a victim-witness advocate who, to Hrones's thinking, veered too deeply into the advocate part of her title, telling one witness, for example, that Donnell was "a bad actor." Most of his ire—pages three, four, and five, to be precise—was aimed at Tochka and, by extension, Sergeant Detective William Mahoney, a veteran homicide cop and one of the lead investigators in the Goffigan killing.

Before the trials, Hrones wanted any statements Donnell had made to police the night he was arrested. Tochka, according to Hrones, said there were none. Then, during the bench trial, Mahoney testified that Donnell refused to talk to police that night.

"So you took absolutely no statements from the defendant relating to that incident?" Hrones had asked Mahoney.

"No."

"So absolutely no questioning was done?"

"No."

Actually, there had been, not formally and not by Mahoney. Instead, there was a three-page summation of what Donnell had told Sergeant Detective Danny Keeler, which Tochka faxed to Hrones's office on November 21, 1996, in the middle of the jury trial. Keeler said he gave all his records to Mahoney, who in turn said he turned his entire file over to Tochka. "All this evidence makes it inconceivable that Mr. Tochka did not know of these statements and reveals he committed a fraud on the Court, as well as denying this youngster a fair trial both before the judge, initially, and then before a jury," Hrones complained on the fifth page of his letter.

It was, in many ways, a worthless point of contention. Though Hrones made a valid point, the sudden appearance of Donnell's statements made Mahoney look like a liar and Tochka like a bumbler, both of which should have worked to Donnell's advantage during the jury trial.

"I look forward to hearing from you in the very near future," Hrones closed his letter. "If I do not, I will take it upon myself to refer the matter to the U.S. Attorney."

IN SOME CIRCLES, STEPHEN HRONES IS REFERRED TO AS THE MAD Czech. This reputation is largely derived from letters such as the one he typed to Ralph Martin. Plus, he looks like he might go berserk at any moment, wild-eyed with wiry brown hair woven with gray and a beard and mustache that don't so much adorn his face as attack it.

These are not negative qualities in a defense attorney, a profession Hrones is quite good at. In fact, he received the Edward J. Duggan Private Counsel award, which is given to particularly aggressive lawyers from the Committee for Public Counsel Services, the state's public defenders. For prosecutors who have to deal with those attorneys, however, the nickname Mad Czech is not an endearing one.

Thus, it was not terribly surprising that Hrones did not get a response in the near future. Rather, Martin's office waited until March 12, 1997—more than three months—to respond, and then the letter came from Elizabeth Keeley, Martin's chief trial counsel, rather than from the boss. Keeley wrote a much shorter letter, only three paragraphs.

"Please be advised," she wrote in the one sentence of any importance, "that we have reviewed your allegations and find them to be conclusory and unsubstantiated."

She did not, however, mention that investigators were still digging into Neico Santos and the rest of the Bromley Heath gang. Though the district attorney's office believed they had one shooter behind bars, there were still two accomplices—one shooter, one getaway driver—on the street. Flushing them out would not be easy, considering the fear a few toughs with guns can put into an entire housing project.

But Bromley Heath, which once had been a model of tenant-managed public housing, had bigger problems than two killers hiding in its midst. The project was flush with crack cocaine, controlled by a few savvy and savage businessboys who were ripe for investigation. By March 1997, the Suffolk County District Attorney's Office, Boston Police, and federal agents were already months into a joint investigation.

CHAPTER 10

Bly and McLaughlin

LEE SIMMONS WAS AN ACCOMPLISHED MARTIAL ARTIST WHO ALSO happened to have a taste for crack cocaine, which is how he came to be in debt to the Theodore Street Posse. Because the first rule of a black market business is to extend no credit, a particularly aggressive member of T.S.P. named Jeffrey Bly repossessed Simmons's bicycle as collateral.

Bly could normally get away with such antics because he had an innate ability to frighten people. Even his street name could scare some people: Black, which was for the color he always wore when he was lurking on the corner of Theodore Street in Mattapan, the hood of his sweatshirt drooping around his face so he looked like the Grim Reaper, only shorter. Mostly, though, he frightened people because of his demonstrated ability to be exceptionally violent. Sometimes it came in hot flashes of rage that made his voice tick up to a falsetto stutter, and sometimes it exploded after bone-cold contemplation, his eyes dulling to stone while he considered his most lethal response.

Bly was not the boss of Theodore Street so much as its lead muscle. (Not that the lines didn't get blurred. The gang's titular leader, Richard "June" Frank, was once accused of shooting a man nine-

teen times with a Mac-11 submachine gun. The victim, astonish-
ingly, survived, and Frank was later acquitted of attempted murder
after his hairdresser testified he was braiding Frank's hair at the
time of the shooting). The second of four children, he lived with
his mother until he was thirteen, when he moved in with his father, Jerry, and stepmother, Rosie, on Walk Hill Road, which is also
in Mattapan. His mother tried to put salvation into the boy. "Jeffrey," she told him once, "you need to find Jesus." Jeffrey answered, "Fuck Jesus. What did Jesus ever do for me?" Still, his
grandmother Gennie Lue always believed the Lord would someday
bring Jeffrey home from the streets.

The Lord apparently never got around to it. Bly came of age on
the wrong side of Theodore Street, his role models a rogues' gallery
of shooters and dealers and snitches. He was an accomplished
criminal long before the police started catching him. One of Bly's
associates—"I don't have no friends," Bly once said. "I have associates"—insists T.S.P. was "the original H.B.C.," which stands for
Hot Box Crew, a legendary ring of car thieves of which nearly
every hoodlum in certain areas of Mattapan and Dorchester claims
to have been a founding member. They were barely big enough to
reach the pedals, only ten or eleven years old, when they learned
how to pop an ignition and squeal away into the night, stealing
mostly for fun, sometimes for stereos.

Bly started getting caught when he was still awfully young. He
first stood before a judge in the district court in Quincy, a southern
suburb, in the spring of 1989, when he was fifteen years old, accused of robbery and assault and battery. Both charges were later
dismissed. But eighteen months later, he was committed to the
Department of Youth Services for attacking someone with a knife.
In 1991, the drug arrests started piling up. When he turned seventeen at the end of 1991, he graduated to adult court; by September
1993, when he was holding Lee Simmons's bike in hock, Bly had
already been charged as an adult with eighteen criminal offenses,
including drug trafficking, conspiracy, and assault and battery.

Simmons, who was twenty-five years old, didn't much care about any of that. Nor did he think Bly was any tougher than he was, both because Simmons had a black belt and, more to the point, on September 13 he had a pistol stuffed into his waistband. At about eight o'clock that night, he confronted Bly and two cronies on the street.

"What's up with my bike?" he asked Bly.

"I'll get your bike," Bly told him.

Simmons pulled his gun, pointed it straight into Bly's face. "I want," he said through clenched teeth, "my fucking bike."

"All right, all right," Bly said. "I'll go get your bike."

Bly dashed into a building on Morton Street and sprinted up the stairs to one of the upper floors, grabbed a .380 semiautomatic pistol and opened a window. Simmons saw him, saw the gun, tried to run. One shot hit him in the ankle. A second hit him in the head, killing him.

The police were there within moments. They found Bly in the Morton Street building along with an associate, a 9 mm. pistol, and the .380, which the lab technicians would later determine had Bly's fingerprints on it. But Bly was never charged with murder. For one thing, detectives couldn't find any witnesses willing to testify, owing to the fear that T.S.P. had spread through the neighborhood. A man who'd kill over a bike would surely kill a witness, after all. For another thing, by the time the ballistics work was finished, the police were on to more pressing matters.

On September 25, a dozen days after Lee Simmons died over a crack debt and a bicycle, a Boston Police detective named John Mulligan was shot five times in the face as he dozed in a Ford Explorer outside a drugstore where he was working a security detail. No police commander will ever say so publicly, but a cop killing is instinctively treated with more urgency than the slaying of a ghetto crackhead. Lee Simmons simply slipped to a permanent backburner, followed up neither by the homicide squad nor a grand jury.

IN THE LATE 1980S AND EARLY 1990S, SMALL GANGS FLOURISHED throughout certain Boston neighborhoods, sprouting on street corners like so many dandelions. The line between a group that claimed a corner as their personal sanctuary and a gang that occupied a patch of pavement like guerrillas claiming their spoils of war was thin and blurry. Most youth workers and cops simplified the distinction: if they carried weapons and sold drugs, they were more likely a gang than a group.

The Theodore Street Posse was clearly a gang. Among the pantheon of local crews, T.S.P. was never the most notorious. Darryl Whiting and his New York Boys, who took over the Orchard Park project by force in the late eighties and didn't decamp for federal prison until the early nineties, sold more cocaine. The Intervale Street Posse and the Humboldt Raiders probably accounted for more corpses. Yet T.S.P. was known among police officers and terrified locals as aberrantly violent, often careening into the realm of sociopathic. There were the pit bulls, for instance, that they used to raise to fight behind the garage at Gus "Flip" Swafford's house. One day, one source says, the boys from T.S.P. hung a small dog and a cat by their tails from a tree and turned the pit bulls loose, just to see how mean they could be.

More often, however, the violence was colder, more calculated, igniting in rage but then tempering into revenge or, from the perspective of the Theodore Street Posse, necessity. One Friday night in the late winter of 1994, for example, the T.S.P. boys spent the evening at a nightclub in Mattapan where they happened to get into an argument with a local Haitian gang. Angry words inside the club spilled into a heated brawl outside. A gun came out, shots were fired, and Ricardo Gittens, a high-ranking Theodore Street hoodrat, got shot in the shoulder before everyone, Haitian and T.S.P., scurried into the night.

Since street gangs operate on the most basic tit-for-tat level, T.S.P. was required to shed the blood of a Haitian gangster. A few nights later, at a house party, Theodore Street had their first opportunity. The same Haitians were at the party. More words ensued, followed by more shooting, much of which was directed at the tail end of a red sport utility vehicle in which the Haitians fled. A few bullets hit the truck, but no human was injured.

Finally, on Tuesday, March 22, a handful of Theodore Street boys were walking down Hosmer Street when they spotted a red Chevrolet Suburban and a black man bent over, working on something inside. His name was Hans Pierre. He was twenty-five years old and lived in Sharon, a quiet suburb south of Boston, but at the time was visiting his girlfriend. "It might have been the wrong person in the van," Errol Moses, one of Bly's associates, said a couple years later. "But it was definitely the right van." No, it wasn't. It wasn't even the right make. Plus, there were no bullet holes in the rear. No matter. One of the T.S.P. hoodies pulled out a pistol, put it next to Pierre's left ear and pulled the trigger, the blast scattering powder burns across his head. Two more bullets were fired into Pierre's back. He died on the front seat.

Anthony Regis died on his front porch, another young man who'd had the misfortune of pissing off Ricardo Gittens. Regis was twenty-three years old and a former honor student at West Roxbury High School who, on April 7, 1995, got into a fender-bender on the Cummins Highway, a long, winding road that swerves across the southern part of Boston. It was a minor accident, except that the other car involved happened to be carrying Flip Swafford, Gittens, and another T.S.P. associate. The dents led to an argument, which, in short order, led to Regis bleeding all over the street from a stab wound allegedly inflicted by Gittens.

Regis survived and planned to testify at Gittens's trial for assault and battery. But on February 27, 1996, just a few days before the opening arguments, Regis was reading a book on his porch on Westmore Road, which is also in Mattapan. Two men walked up to the house. One of them opened fire, just blew poor Regis away. A number of detectives suspect Gittens was involved, but he has never been charged. Nor did he ever stand trial for the original assault and battery. With no victim, the case was dropped.

All told, police suspect T.S.P. to have been involved in an even

dozen homicides. Errol Moses, when he was asked about that figure, didn't dispute it. "You know," he said, "Theodore Street don't
be playin' around. You best believe, everyone T.S.P. was s'posed to
have killed, they died for a reason." All except Lee Simmons. "Lee
was like family," Moses said. "He grew up with us."

Moses didn't seem to mind talking about those things, all the
bloodletting, even the three times people tried to shoot him, and
never for any reason at all. If anything, he seemed more distracted
by the room next door, which was the gas chamber at Central
Prison in Raleigh, North Carolina. Unless the appeals courts smile
broadly upon him, Moses will one day sit there and suck poison
until he is pronounced dead. He had left Boston in September
1994 "to sell drugs" in North Carolina, mostly in the Winston-
Salem area. He brought with him a peculiar business style, one
gleaned from the teachings of Jeffrey Bly and his other associates.

About a year after Moses first traveled south, he went to the
home of a man named Ricky Nelson Griffin to work out the details
of a drug deal. Instead, Moses shot him three times, twice in the
head and, for good measure, once in the mouth. Two months after
that, Moses went to visit Jacinto Dunkley to settle a seven-hundred-
dollar cocaine debt, which he accomplished by shooting Dunkley
to death and ransacking his apartment. Moses and his partner
grabbed a few hundred bucks and Dunkley's car, but missed eleven
thousand dollars stashed in a drawer. Then, a short time after that,
while making a beer run, Moses caught the attention of the local
police, who allegedly had to chase him until Moses crashed Dunkley's car, killing his female passenger.

Moses was sentenced to death for killing Griffin, and then sentenced to a second death for killing Dunkley. If he manages to beat
either one of those on appeal, the state has promised to try him for
the vehicular homicide. In a mean quirk of law, he will be eligible
for the death penalty in that case, too.

Moses does not believe he will ever be strapped into the gas
chamber (though he does make a point of standing on his tiptoes
to look into the small room on his way back to his cell). In his cur-

rent fantasy, he will beat both of those cases on appeal and be released, whereupon he will return to Boston and be promptly shot to death. He does not know by whom, or why. "How many people want to kill Jeff? How many people want to kill Richard Frank? How many people want to kill Slash?" he said, ticking off the names of his associates from Theodore Street. Then he shrugged, his bony shoulders barely rising under his too-loose prison jumpsuit. "T.S.P., that's all."

SELLING DRUGS WASN'T THE ONLY REASON MOSES MOVED TO North Carolina. Had he remained in Boston after September 1994, police and other sources believe, Moses would have been killed. Someone already tried once, chasing him through the streets of Boston one Sunday afternoon until he crashed his car in front of the Mount Olive Temple of Christ Church. Two shooters, one twenty-eight years old, the other sixteen, chased him on foot, blasting away but never hitting Moses's skinny frame.

Moses had to worry about dying because a young man named Dana Alston did not die. Dana Alston, unlike Lee Simmons, was afraid of Jeffrey Bly, even though the two of them used to be quasi-friends. It was hard to be real friends with Bly, since most people who knew him didn't trust him. ("I don't trust nobody," Moses said once. "Okay, my wife. To an extent. Only Jeff don't have an extent." Then he laughed because he thought that was a very funny joke, especially for a man sitting next to a gas chamber.) In any case, Alston was at least comfortable enough with Bly to trade cars, his 1987 Volkswagen Jetta for Bly's 1982 blue Rabbit convertible and a thousand dollars in cash.

They made the trade in the late winter of 1994, when they were both nineteen years old, almost six months after Simmons was murdered and about the same time T.S.P. was shooting it out with the Haitians. By April, though, Bly's new car, the Jetta, had disappeared, and he got it into his head that Alston had stolen it. So he went out looking for him, prowling the streets with Moses in a rented white sedan. On April 12, just before 6:30 in the evening,

Bly spotted both the Rabbit—the car he'd traded to Alston—and Alston on Dunreath Street, the car at the curb, the man in an alley.

"Yo, there he is," Bly told Moses. "Pull over."

Moses steered to the curb. Bly called from the passenger side window. "Yo, Dana! C'mere."

Alston, who was visiting his cousin Orlando, looked back. He was wary. "No," he hollered. "You come here."

"C'mon, come over here," Bly persisted. "I got something to tell you."

Alston started walking down the alley. By the time he got to the end, Bly was out of the rented sedan, standing and waiting.

"What's up?" Alston asked him.

"I know who stole my car," Bly said.

"Yeah? Who?"

Bly swung his hand up from his waistband, his fingers wrapped around a .380 semiautomatic, the same type of gun that had killed Lee Simmons. "You did, nigga." He poked the muzzle into Alston's right temple. "Gimme the keys."

Alston, suddenly aware that Bly was planning to steal the Rabbit, the same way he'd repossessed Lee Simmons's bicycle, refused. Bly jabbed his head with the gun again. "C'mon, c'mon, gimme the keys, gimme the keys," he said. "I don't want to shoot you— gimme the keys."

Alston considered his options, perhaps considered Lee Simmons. He figured the odds were pretty good Bly would cap him for a car. He handed over the keys.

Cousin Orlando had been watching from the end of the alley. When Alston let go of the keys, Orlando let go of his pit bull. The dog raced down the pavement, a rippling mass of canine muscle snarling at Bly through oversized mandibles. Bly waved his pistol at the pit bull. "Get the dog, get the dog!" he screamed, backing toward the Rabbit, dragging Alston with him. "Get the dog!"

Orlando called off his pit bull long enough for Bly to slide behind the wheel of the Rabbit and release his grip on Alston. Then the dog charged back, leaping through the car's window and biting at Bly's head. Alston didn't wait to watch—he sprinted back up the alley. He heard one shot as he ran, then the sound of the Rabbit's engine and the squeal of tires as Bly sped away.

The police needed only an hour to find Bly and Moses. The two of them were pushing the Rabbit behind the house on Hannon Street where Moses lived with his grandparents. On the floor of the car, under the mat with a fresh hole in it, the police found a fragment of a bullet and a spent copper jacket. Apparently, the shot Alston had heard had been fired by mistake. And after Moses told them where to look, the cops found a .380 semiautomatic pistol inside the house.

MOSES MADE BAIL THE SAME NIGHT THAT DANA ALSTON WAS carjacked. Bly, because his bond was set higher, at three thousand dollars, had to wait until morning, when Moses could collect some cash from their Theodore Street associates. Still, Bly didn't remain out on the streets for very long. Four weeks later, he went back to court for an old attempted murder charge and was held for want of twenty-thousand-dollars bail.

Sometime later that spring, while Bly was locked up, Moses went to see Alston. He told him that the beef over the cars wasn't worth getting the law involved, wasn't worth dragging him and Bly into court. That's his version, anyway. Whatever he said, Alston absolved Moses of any responsibility. Of course, he also got his car back, so he didn't see much point in a legal drama, either. "I don't know how they met up afterward," Alston told a grand jury. "But Errol didn't have nothing to do with it."

The charges against Moses were dropped. But that didn't do Bly any good. From jail, where Moses kept depositing money into Bly's account at the canteen, Bly kept fretting about Alston. He worked on Moses, too, telling him how Alston could change his story and pull Moses back into the case. Among the Theodore Street Posse, a decree went out: "If he wants to snitch, he might as well die."

"It was just talking," Moses said years later, as if the topic had been last night's Celtics game. "Like all of us, sitting around. 'If he's gonna snitch, and someone else want to snitch, he should be killed.' That was it."

Someone tried to carry out the death warrant at about half-past midnight on September 10, 1994, five months after the carjacking. The way Moses tells the story, he saw Alston just minutes before the shooting at an autobody shop on Norfolk Street, Moses standing near the door, Alston sitting on a crate inside. They talked about nothing in particular for twenty minutes or so until a friend of Moses's picked him up. Then he rode to the Orchard Park projects to meet a girl. Moments later, riding back past the autobody shop, he saw the streets splashed with blue lights skipping off the paramedics who were trying to keep Alston's brains from leaking out of his head.

Several police officers tell the story in exactly the same way, right up until the point where someone supposedly picked up Moses. Oh, and their version of the conversation is different, too. They believe Moses told Alston to keep his head up, that someone might try to whack him. Then, they suspect, Moses stepped outside and around the corner, changed his sweatshirt and put a mask over face. He crept around the side of the building, slipped through a door, and put one bullet behind Dana Alston's right ear. Then he allegedly ran, firing another shot just to scare off a delivery man who happened to get in the way.

But Dana Alston didn't die. Two days later, Moses was ducking bullets outside the Mount Olive Temple of Christ Church, then running all the way to North Carolina. And sometime after that, the Boston Police Department issued a warrant charging him with the attempted murder of Alston. Considering Moses's legal circumstances, however, they have not yet formally served the warrant.

PAUL R. MCLAUGHLIN'S ROLE IN THIS WORLD WAS TO PUT PEOPLE such as Jeffrey Bly in jail. He worked for the commonwealth as an assistant attorney general, but since 1991 had been assigned to Suffolk County Superior Court, and, by practical extension, the Suffolk District Attorney's Office, where he prosecuted the most serious gang-related crimes.

Ralph Martin was pleased to see McLaughlin in the office when he took over in September 1993. The two of them practically began their careers together, sharing a small office with two other assistant district attorneys in Middlesex County. McLaughlin was a thin and unassuming man whose brown eyes looked through wide-framed glasses and matched the mustache that spread over his upper lip. He was a native son, one of six children born into a well-connected family in West Roxbury, a leafy enclave of middle-class Irish Catholics that rivals South Boston as the most politically muscular neighborhood in the city. McLaughlin's paternal grandfather, Edward, had been commissioner of the Boston Fire Department, and his father, Edward Jr., was a classic Boston pol who traveled in the better circles of the Democratic establishment: in addition to his public-payroll legal jobs—counsel to the Massachusetts Bay Transportation Authority, assistant United States Attorney—Edward Jr. had also served as president of the Boston City Council and as lieutenant governor under Governor John A. Volpe in the early 1960s.

Paul, as a young man, seemed destined to emulate his father, or at least approximate his career. After graduating from Boston Latin School, the city's premiere public school that uses a rigorous exam to select only the best and brightest students, he went on to Dartmouth College, in Durham, New Hampshire, the same Ivy League school from which his father had graduated. With his undergraduate degree in hand, McLaughlin took a job in politics, toiling at the State House as a senior research assistant for the Joint Committee on Education before moving on to become a budget analyst for the powerful Senate Ways and Means Committee.

But McLaughlin's heart was in the law. He studied nights at Suffolk Law School while working at the State House and, in 1981, he graduated with honors. On February 7, 1983, he started his new life as a prosecutor, joining the Middlesex County District Attorney's Office the same day as Ralph Martin.

He was never a flamboyant lawyer, never one to be mistaken as the inspiration for one of David E. Kelley's television attorneys. In-

stead, among the four men who shared the office, he was the plod-
der, the methodical, meticulous litigator who arrived early and left
late, organizing his thoughts and his cases and his legal arguments.
That is not to suggest, however, that McLaughlin was off-puttingly
serious. His lineage had blessed him with a politician's gift for connecting with people, looking them in the eye when he spoke, in-
quiring about how the kids were doing, if the wife was feeling
better. Yet he never played on his connections; McLaughlin rarely
mentioned that his father had once been a prominent and powerful public official and, if he did, it was never in a boastful way. He
certainly never used his father's connections to graft onto a cushy
job in the private sector, either. By 1995, a dozen years after his
first legal job, he was content to make $52,500 a year prosecuting
young toughs.

For McLaughlin, his chosen profession was almost a calling. He
lived alone in a small white colonial on Dwinell Street in West
Roxbury, a short block where neighbors still knew each other's
names and watched over each other's kids. The wave of youth violence that had swept other parts of the city had blessedly by-
passed Dwinell Street. To McLaughlin's way of thinking, there were
more such streets in the city, notorious gang-banger blocks like
Castlegate Road and Humboldt Avenue and Theodore Street, just
waiting to be reclaimed from the hoodlums who controlled them.

He tried once to pull himself away from the courtroom. In 1986,
he ran for state representative from West Roxbury and lost, after
which he melted into the private sector. But by 1991, he was back
prosecuting bad guys. Not that he saw his courtroom adversaries as
innately bad. In the late summer of 1995, he was talking with another prosecutor in the gang unit in Martin's office, mostly vent-
ing, frustrated by a tide of violence that never seemed to ebb. But
McLaughlin also understood, better than he had before he'd
picked through so many shattered lives, how different his own
could have been if he'd grown up in a ghetto, surrounded by crack-
heads and gunslingers and the pathology of chronic poverty. "It's
not hopeless," he said. "And I'm not without hope."

Which is stunning, considering the number of people he put in prison. By the time he had that conversation, McLaughlin had prosecuted 134 defendants in the four years he'd been assigned to Suffolk County. Of those, he won ninety-eight convictions.

Jeffrey Bly was not among the people McLaughlin convicted. He tried. Twice. In a span of only eight months. First McLaughlin tried to put him away for a drive-by shooting on Hosmer Street, the same block where Hans Pierre was shot to death. Bly was acquitted. McLaughlin went back after him for allegedly distributing cocaine within a school zone, a crime that carries a mandatory two years in prison. Bly beat that one, too.

Yet McLaughlin had one more felony waiting for Jeff Bly: the carjacking of Dana Alston. Alston, still in a wheelchair from the bullet someone put behind his right ear, was in hiding during the summer of 1995, mainly because police and prosecutors feared someone with more precise aim might shoot him again. With a live victim, the case would go forward. Trial was scheduled for late September.

Bly was fuming, irate that McLaughlin was going after him again and for a crime that, in Bly's mind, wasn't even gang-related, which was the type of crime McLaughlin usually prosecuted. "He saw Paul as on a vendetta against him," one source familiar with Bly said. "He started taking the professional interest personally." So Bly took it personally, too.

First he tried to spook McLaughlin. On Wednesday, September 20, after a hearing on a few minor motions in the upcoming carjacking trial, Bly caught McLaughlin's eye in a corridor outside the courtroom. He stared at him, his eyes turning that dull, stony color they always did when Bly was contemplating how ruthless to be. It didn't last long, only a few seconds, before McLaughlin turned away. He was uneasy about it, but not terribly frightened. Back at the office—to which one source said Bly may have made a couple of anonymous and menacing phone calls—he never told his bosses he was scared. He spent the rest of the week preparing for trial, which would begin on Tuesday, September 26.

THE WEST ROXBURY COMMUTER RAIL, ONE OF THE THIRTEEN
heavy-rail lines that ferry suburbanites to and from the city, begins
its outbound run at Back Bay Station, following the Orange Line
subway tracks south to Forest Hills, where it bends slightly to the
west. From there, it skirts the eastern edge of the Arnold Arbore-
tum, a mighty green hill of lilacs and exotic trees, then makes four
stops in rapid succession at stations named Roslindale Village,
Bellevue, Highlands, and West Roxbury before continuing on to
the western suburb of Needham.

Paul McLaughlin tramped down the three metal steps of the silver train at the Highlands station shortly before seven o'clock on
the evening of Monday, September 25. His rusting and aging Toyota Tercel, a dependable if noisy car he called Chitty-Chitty-Bang-
Bang, was across the station parking lot. He walked across the
blacktop, his keys already in his hand, and unlocked the door at
precisely three minutes before seven. As he twisted his body
around to slide behind the wheel, he heard a voice.

Jeff Bly came out from behind a tree. He knew where McLaughlin would be, knew what kind of car he drove, knew when and
where he could find him. A young underling, more afraid of Bly
than in awe of him, had followed his orders to tail McLaughlin
and report his routes and habits to Bly. Earlier that night, Bly had
another associate drive him to a side street near the Highlands station in a stolen burgundy Buick. A gold Dodge Colt was parked
next to it, the getaway car. Then he wrapped a green and white
bandana around his face and pulled his black hood down low over
his eyes. In his hand, which was gloved and now pointing at
McLaughlin's head, was a .38 caliber revolver. Bly shouted something, angry and loud, and yanked the trigger. The first bullet
crashed through McLaughlin's left temple, shattering his left eye
and shredding his brain until it blew out the right side of his skull.
The second bullet flew off into the distance.

Bly didn't stay around to see if McLaughlin was dead. He ran,
his short legs pumping along the railroad tracks, slowing only
enough to strip off the bandana and the sweatshirt, splattered and

nearly soaked with McLaughlin's blood, and the gloves. Bly and a getaway driver sped away in the Colt.

The paramedics found McLaughlin, who was forty-two years old, sprawled across the front seat of his car, his legs hanging out of the driver's side door, his keys still in his hand. They rushed him to Brigham & Women's Hospital, but the bullet had done too much damage. He was dead before the ambulance made it to the emergency room.

AN HOUR LATER, RALPH MARTIN WAS DRIVING EAST ALONG SOL-diers Field Road, a curving highway that parallels the Charles River until, closer to the city, it becomes Storrow Drive. He had just left the studio of WBZ radio, where he'd been a guest on "The David Brudnoy Show," discussing the intricacies of criminal sentencing and jousting with Brudnoy's generally more erudite call-in audience. Martin had just come out of a long, sweeping bend near the Harvard University stadium when his cell phone rang.

"Hello."

"Ralph, it's Carmen," said Carmen Fields, the woman who handled the press for Martin. "I'm getting some calls"—Martin knew that meant calls from reporters—"and they're saying one of our prosecutors got shot."

"What?" Martin wasn't so much stunned as confused. Prosecutors don't get shot. "Who?"

"They're saying it's Paul McLaughlin."

Martin's pulse quickened, his hand tightened on the wheel, slippery now from the sweat starting seep from his palms.

"Paul?"

"Paul. They're saying he's at Brigham & Women's."

Martin goosed the accelerator toward the city, and took the Kenmore Square exit, two short blocks from the hospital. By the time he got there, Paul was already dead. But Martin stayed for hours, grieving with his colleagues, trying to figure out what had happened.

Paul McLaughlin was not simply murdered. He was assassinated, a class of killing that is especially vicious because it is so

cold. At first glance, Bly's execution suggested a savage pragma-
tism: if he couldn't kill Alston, maybe popping McLaughlin would
make the case go away, or at least delay it long enough for him to
hunt down Dana Alston. The second glance, though, reveals how
thoroughly sociopathic Bly could be. He must have known Alston
was under police protection—indeed, he had spent months in a
rehabilitation hospital under an assumed name—and that prosecutors would line up to take over McLaughlin's cases. "You would
have needed one of those machines like they have in a deli, where
you have to take a number," Martin remembers. Which, in turn,
suggests the murder was more personal, a cold-blooded killing
rooted in nothing more than animosity.

As it was, McLaughlin's boss, a veteran prosecutor named
Michael Pomarole took the carjacking case against Bly. It was delayed by only two months, during which time Bly suffered an
enormous amount of scrutiny from detectives investigating
McLaughlin's assassination. A line had been crossed in Boston's
perpetual tension between the courthouse and the street corners.
Mafiosi, with only extremely rare exceptions, do not shoot at the
federal agents assigned to chase them. Likewise, young hoodlums
generally do not shoot at police officers, not counting those hot
and irrational moments when a gang-banger is trying to get away
from the cop huffing after him. And they certainly don't kill prosecutors, unarmed civil servants who are simply reciting facts and
making legal arguments before a jury. The risk of trial is, or was,
considered an inevitable part of the thuglife. By breaking that détente, however, Bly picked a fight he could never hope to win.
Some local officers used to wear T-shirts screened with a slogan
that was meant only partly in jest: "Boston Police: The Biggest
Gang in Town." McLaughlin wasn't a cop, but close enough; the
biggest gang in town was pissed.

Dana Alston took the witness stand on November 28, 1995, two
months and three days after McLaughlin died. One of the first
things he testified to, albeit unwittingly, was the frustration
McLaughlin was forced to deal with every day, the futility that still

somehow never drained him of hope. Shortly after he'd been car-jacked, Alston declined to name the people—Bly and Moses—who'd stolen his car.

Pomarole asked him, "Why didn't you identify someone who just put a gun to your head?"

"You just don't do that," Alston answered. "You've got to worry about other people that are around."

People, for instance, such as Errol Moses, who Alston also conceded he shielded when he was forced to testify before the grand jury. He changed his mind, Alston said, when Moses shot him in the head anyway.

The next day, the jury spent just two hours deliberating. When the court clerk asked them how they found the defendant, the foreman answered in a firm voice, "Guilty." For swiping Alston's car, Bly was convicted of carjacking, armed robbery, and illegal possession of a gun. The court officers put him in handcuffs and led him to jail, where he was held until December 7. On that day, Judge Patrick King sentenced Bly to spend at least a decade, and as long as fifteen years, in prison.

MCLAUGHLIN'S MURDER HADN'T BEEN SOLVED BY THE TIME BLY went to prison. Nor had the shooting death of Lee Simmons. A team of detectives were busting their humps trying to track down leads, but with only a few witnesses who only saw a shortish, hooded teenager in a black sweatshirt running away, there weren't many leads. Bly, of course, was on the early short-list of suspects, along with a dozen or so other particularly ruthless gang-bangers.

Meanwhile, the execution of a soft-spoken prosecutor naturally made national news. Given the backdrop of Boston, many of the stories delved deeply into the scars of the city, wounds just beginning to scab over. "Boston Killing Renews Fear of Police Roundup of Blacks," read the headline in the *Bergen Record* in New Jersey. The *New York Times* went with, "Boston Tries to Minimize Racial Anger," and the *Houston Chronicle*, reprinting the *Times* story, weighed in with, "Boston Tries to Calm Fears of Blacks in Wake of

Prosecutor's Killing." The reference, of course, was to the last time a black guy was said to have shot white people, which would be Willie Bennett and Carol Stuart. When there wasn't any rioting, no broad and brutish sweeps of young black men, the rest of the country seemed astonished. "Boston Averting Racial Strife After Slaying of Prosecutor," proclaimed the *Washington Post*. And the *Chronicle* followed up its first story (reprinting the *Post* piece this time) under the headline, "Racial Tensions Didn't Boil Over with Death of Boston Prosecutor."

Of course not. If anyone learned the bitter lessons of the Stuart fiasco, two people at the head of the class would be Police Commissioner Paul F. Evans and District Attorney Ralph Martin. Evans went so far as to appear on WILD-AM, a radio station with a largely black audience, where he conceded the description of the shooter was vague at best. And he asked for help from people on the street. Later, he joined the ministers from the Ten Point Coalition, most of whom are black and who had gathered to publicly thank the cops for not going berserk.

As for Martin, he relied on an economy of words. "We remember the mistakes," he said. "We do not intend to duplicate them."

CHAPTER 11
Cold Cases

MARK LEE PACED IN FRONT OF AN OAK RAIL, WORKING HIS GAZE across a dozen jurors and four alternates, every one of whom was a doppelganger of his wife. Jurors always looked like his wife or a close friend, at least when he had to stand up in front of them and convince them that a man should go to prison for the rest of his life. Mark Lee could always make a point with his wife, keep his thoughts organized and logical, his delivery appropriately theatrical, raising his voice just a tick in volume to make a particular point, then drop it low and somber to allow a certain image to linger. So he imagined every juror was his wife.

"Just listen to the story from the investigation to the arrest," Lee told the jury. "Just the sequence of events"—his voice started climbing—"will paint a stunning picture of the defendant's guilt."

Lee Perkins blinked, his eyelids falling slow and heavy, then rising again. There was no expression on his face, which seemed fatter than the rest of his body, fleshier, as if two globs of muddy dough had been mushed over his cheekbones. Perkins was the defendant, the man Mark Lee wanted to send to prison for life. Back to prison, actually, since Perkins was already locked up for raping a woman in 1991. Now Lee was trying to convince those people in the jury box that Perkins was a killer, too, that he threw that Sandra woman down all those years ago, raped her right in that tiny apartment, yanked her panties around her knees and climbed on top of her. And then, after he'd ejaculated, that he'd shoved a steak knife through her chest.

If Perkins was scared, he didn't show it. Sitting there in his dark trousers and white shirt and light gray sweater, a blue and silver tie knotted around his neck, he looked more curious than anything else, like he was wondering who Mark Lee could possibly be talking about. Another prosecutor had already tried to say he'd killed that woman, put him on trial for seven days in February and March 1999. Couldn't do it, though. One of those jurors—maybe more than one, how did he know?—wouldn't say he was guilty. "Hopelessly deadlocked," is what the forewoman said. Of course they were. It happened so damned long ago, almost nine years to the day the judge declared the mistrial. Just because he'd had sex with her—Lee Perkins admitted that much—didn't mean he'd killed her. He didn't remember at first, not when the detectives first asked him about it. At least he said he didn't remember, which made sense because the cops were asking him six years after the fact. A man can forget a lot of women in six years.

That's what Mark Lee was talking about now, how he forgot. "The evidence in this case is going to show that on the evening of March 22, 1990, the defendant in this case raped, stabbed, and killed Sandra Francis in her apartment." He hitched a quarter beat after each of the verbs—*raped,* pause, *stabbed,* pause, *and killed,* pause—letting each one echo for a dramatic instant. His left fist, gently curled around a yellow pencil, poked forward in cadence with his words, punctuating the last three violations of Sandra Francis's nineteen years on this earth. Lee is a sturdy man, not heavy or round but solid and squat, and when he turned his head to look at the jurors, his neck rolled over the collar of his suit, a proper prosecutorial shade of bluish gray.

"You're going to learn," he went on, "how he injected himself into Sandra Francis's life"—another rest—"pestered her"—rest—

"raped her when she wouldn't reciprocate"—rest—"killed her." Mark Lee paused longer at this point, putting a verbal period in his sentence instead of a comma. "Then told the Boston Police Department, when he was questioned, that he had no idea who she was." Pause. "All of which blew up in his face several months later when his DNA was found deposited on her body."

That was when Lee Perkins remembered having sex with her, when the cops told him they found his semen inside her. Still didn't prove anything, though. He stared at Mark Lee, watching him waving his arm around, watching the way his neck bulged over his collar, wondering if any of those people on the jury believed the words he was saying between those pauses.

SANDRA FRANCIS CLIMBED OFF THE BUS AT FOREST HILLS, HALF stumbling from the weight of the groceries in her arms and from the sting of the frigid January air. She was most of the way home. The Number 36 bus brought her from West Roxbury, the leafy, almost suburban neighborhood of Boston that backs up to Dedham and Brookline. At Forest Hills, a plaza of new bricks and cement where, under a clock tower built of thin metal poles, commuters traipsed on and off the final outbound stop of the Orange Line subway, she would switch to the Number 39 bus. The 39 replaced the trolley that used to run from Forest Hills north through Jamaica Plain, past the South Street projects and the bodegas on Centre Street, then forking left onto South Huntington Avenue before finally turning hard to the right onto Huntington Avenue. The trolley was always a smoother ride, especially since the buses had to bounce and tumble over the tracks left behind in the blacktop.

Sandra could catch a man's eye. She was nineteen years old with smooth, light brown skin and dark brown hair combed straight and parted in the middle, cut just above her shoulder. She had wide-set eyes and high-set cheekbones, and the corners of her mouth dipped down toward her chin. Lee Perkins, standing with a few of his friends on the plaza, watched her wrestling with her bags, her eyes squinting into the late afternoon sun. She looked almost waifish, a damsel who might want someone to ease her distress, or at least help with the bags. He gave her his best smile and asked if he could be of assistance, a touch of his native Alabama in his voice even though he'd left the Deep South more than twenty years earlier, when he was six.

Sandra blanched. She wasn't accustomed to talking to strangers waiting for the bus. But he seemed safe enough. He was with his friends, too, not a creepy loner lurking in the shadows of a bus terminal. And since he was riding the Number 39 anyway, and getting off at her stop, Brigham Circle . . . yeah, she could use the help.

They boarded the bus together and bumped along the pitted roads for almost two miles, making small talk. If she told Lee Perkins anything about herself, she probably would have started with Rakim, her son. She'd given birth in September 1989, at the beginning of her senior year at Boston Technical High School. She never married Rakim's father, but she wasn't going to let being a single mother steal her future. Rakim's future, really. So she finished high school and kept her grades up high enough to go on to the University of Massachusetts's Boston campus, where she was halfway through her freshman year. Eventually, she would study either psychology or sociology, but she wasn't positive which one yet.

Perhaps Sandra talked about her job at Au Bon Pain, a coffee-and-pastry shop where she often worked the evening shift. Or maybe she told him about her best friend, Emma Sampson. Emma was a year younger then Sandra, still a senior at Boston Tech. They'd met more than a year ago in a study group. Their friendship blossomed, though, in the spring, when they decided to play softball for the high school team. Emma pitched and Sandra played the infield, but their positions hardly mattered because they hardly got to play. Neither one was a particularly gifted athlete. But they could cheer on their teammates like nobody's business.

Emma was practically living with Sandra and Rakim, the three of them crammed into that shoebox studio on Huntington Avenue. There was only one room with a miniature kitchen along one wall and, next to that, a bathroom not much bigger than a closet. The view through the bars on the window was of the sidewalk and the clouds of diesel exhaust from the buses and trucks rumbling over the abandoned trolley tracks. But it was her own place, the first one she'd ever had.

Lee followed Sandra off the bus at Brigham Circle, lugging her grocery bags along the sidewalk and up six cement stairs to the front door of her building, then a few paces down the hallway to her apartment, which was on the left. Sandra opened the door. Lee leaned over and put the bags gently on the floor, said it had been nice meeting her, and left. Sandra thanked him and closed the door.

Emma glared at her. "Who was that?" she asked. After only one quick look, Emma knew she didn't like him. With his hood under his black coat and his dirty dungarees, he looked like a bum.

"Lee," Sandra said. "I met him on the bus."

Emma glared harder at her friend. "Sandra," she started, exasperated. "You don't do that. *Duh!* You don't just meet people on the bus and bring them over here."

Sandra dismissed her with roll of her eyes. "He was nice," she said. "He offered to help me with the groceries."

"But you don't do that," Emma said again.

Sandra ignored her, pulling groceries from the bags, trying to find someplace to put them all in her tiny kitchen.

THE NEXT TIME EMMA SAMPSON SAW LEE PERKINS WAS IN THE middle of February. She was at Sandra's apartment with her husband, Melvin, the two of them visiting with Sandra and keeping their voices low so they wouldn't wake up Rakim. It was late, almost eleven o'clock, when Lee knocked on the door.

Sandra pulled the door back only a few inches, not opening it wide enough to let anyone in. "What are you doing here?" she asked.

Emma couldn't hear the answer. Next, she heard Sandra say, "I have company."

Melvin got up from his seat and started toward the door. It took him only two strides to cross the small apartment. "Yo, man," he said, "she said she has company."

That seemed to work. Lee turned and left, and Sandra locked the door.

There were two more visits that Emma would remember. Lee invited himself into a shoebox apartment one night and sat at the kitchen table, lingering so long that Emma took to clearing her throat and scowling, trying to make him uncomfortable enough to leave. A few weeks after that, when Emma was already in bed at her own apartment, Sandra called her, frantic. Perkins had come over again, unannounced and uninvited, and he wouldn't leave. Emma, who was pregnant at the time, lumbered out of bed and across town to rescue her friend from being trapped alone with a bummy-looking stranger.

SANDRA FRANCIS DROPPED RAKIM AT HER MOTHER'S HOUSE shortly after 10:30 in the morning on Thursday, March 22, 1990. Sandra had a full day ahead of her—classes at UMass, then an evening shift at Au Bon Pain—so the plan was for Rakim to spend the night with his grandmother. Sandra would return for him on Friday morning.

She never showed up. Her mother waited. Hours passed, morning giving way to afternoon, then to dusk. Every time her mother dialed Sandra's phone number, the only answer was an endless series of rings.

Friday night, worried half sick, Sandra's mother called the police.

Saturday morning, a police officer knocked on Sandra's door. No one answered. The officer neatly printed a short note, asking Sandra to telephone either her mother or the police, let everyone know she was okay, and slipped it under her door.

Sunday morning, Sandra's mother went to 576 Huntington Avenue and convinced the building superintendent to open to the door to her daughter's apartment. Sandra was on the floor, her right arm bent at a ninety-degree angle up toward her head, which was lolling to the left. Her pants and underwear had been pulled down but not all the way off. In the center of her white top, surrounded by a sticky splotch of crimson, a steak knife stuck straight up, the blade anchored in the muscle of her heart. Fixing an exact time of death is a tricky business, but given the condition of her body and the fact that Sandra hadn't been heard from since Thursday, she most likely had been murdered before Friday's first light.

Thirty-seven other people had already been murdered in Boston in 1990. Another 115 would be shot, stabbed, or beaten to death before the year ended, the bloodiest twelve months in the city's history. In the decade beginning in 1985, the twenty-one detectives assigned to the homicide squad (assuming the unit was fully staffed) were investigating an average of ninety-nine murders every year. Yet the working theorem among homicide cops everywhere is the 48-Hour Rule—or, in some more optimistic jurisdictions, the 72-Hour Rule—which hold that if a case isn't solved within the first few days, it probably never will be.

It is a practical concept. In most cases, the only clues to a killing are spawned in one mean heartbeat, then deposited in the place and the instant of the crime: a weapon, perhaps, or maybe a fingerprint or some other miniscule trace of the killer. On a good day, a witness might emerge to recount some telltale details or supply a description or even the name of the killer. Those fragments of evidence, however, are generally collected in the first handful of hours. After that, cases begin to chill, eventually growing cold as the next inevitable corpse demands to be probed and prodded and, with luck, avenged. Cops don't give up so much as move on, swept along by a stream of blood and bodies. In a good year, the police only had enough time and enough clues to solve roughly six out of every ten murders.

The killing of Sandra Francis was one of the other four. The detectives had some evidence with which to work, including semen swabbed from Sandra's vagina. But they had no witnesses, no one who saw a particularly notable fiend prowling near her apartment. If there'd been a struggle—and, judging by the condition of her apartment, there had been—and screaming, no one noticed. Those sorts of sounds were a kind of white noise in 1990, a cacophony of sharp, shrill sounds that were numbing in their consistency. Emma was able to tell the police about a creepy guy named Lee, but she didn't know his last name. Even when the police were able to figure out they wanted Lee Perkins, they couldn't find him. And if they did, then what? They had no probable cause to ask him for a sample of his blood or sputum or semen to compare with the swabbings taken from Sandra's body.

Forty-eight hours came and went. Then seventy-two hours. A month. A year, another year. By 1996, Sandra Francis was buried in a filing cabinet, just one of thousands of yellowed and fading cases the police couldn't crack.

A LOT OF COPS DON'T LIKE CAPTAIN TIMOTHY J. MURRAY. IN fact, the Boston Police Department, as a matter of practice apparently rooted in spite, generally doesn't allow him to talk to the press, and hasn't for several years now. When he made captain shortly after his fortieth birthday—the same rank as the commanding officer in the homicide unit—they shipped him out. After a career working drug cases and murders, he was transferred to a decidedly unglamorous job inspecting the patrolmen, making sure everyone's uniform is up to snuff.

The reasons are partly personal. Murray's ego is arguably larger than his frame, which is big and beefy enough to have played safety on the football team at Stonehill College, where he majored in pre-med. He went on to graduate near the top of his criminal justice master's program at Northeastern University, and, after he followed his father onto the Boston force, rose rapidly through the ranks, eventually becoming the youngest lieutenant detective in the city. He's hyperkinetic and over-caffeinated, prone to speaking in rapid spasms, yet entranced by such time-consuming puzzles as correspondence chess. Combined with his still-dark hair and still-boyish face, those traits sometimes make him seem like an excitable, nerdy child. At the same time, though, he exudes a physical presence, a confidence so dense it can almost be felt when he enters a room, bouncing heavily on the balls of his feet, his barrel chest thrust out in front. Taken together, Murray appears to believe he is smarter than everyone else, which, truth be told, he usually is.

The other reason many police officers don't like Murray—or, at the very least, an aggravating factor—is that in the early nineties, when the supply of positive press rationed to the Boston Police was measured in thimbles, Murray and his partner, Lieutenant Detective Stephen A. Murphy, got nearly all of it. In 1991, not long after he was assigned to the homicide unit, Murray was told to organize the Cold Case Squad, to spend his shifts digging through musty cabinets and long forgotten killings. Murray's assignment likely had more to do with squirreling him away in a lonely office, isolated from any television cameras and newspaper reporters who might show up at a fresh and fantastic murder, than it did with actually solving anything. Plus, the chore might have pared his ego down, proving that he couldn't solve the cases other cops couldn't figure out, either.

Whatever the reasons, such squads were an emerging novelty among big-city departments, where commanders recognized that the advances in forensic science and computer technology opened new investigatory avenues. With even a rudimentary modem, for instance, a detective could pore over databases that, only five years earlier, would have required tens of thousands of man hours. Fingerprints lifted from a scene that didn't match an index card at the stationhouse used to be fruitless; by 1990, even partial prints could be matched against millions recorded on computers. In 1980, a killer whose blood type matched the smears found at a crime scene had a decent chance of beating the case, considering at least 2 percent of the population would have the same kind of platelets and cells running through their veins. Fast forward two decades, and DNA codes—drawn from a stray hair, a drop of spit—can incriminate or exonerate a suspect with unnerving certainty.

Murray and Murphy turned out to be quite good at using those new tools. Murphy joined the Cold Case Squad in 1993, marching into their shared office on the second floor of homicide headquarters carrying his Marine Corps flag, which he planted next to his desk. They couldn't have been more different, save for their Irish bloodlines and civil service rankings. Twenty years older than his partner, Murphy was the department's senior lieutenant detective and the prototypical gumshoe, albeit shorter and balder than the caricature. After slogging through more than a hundred murder investigations, his manner was deliberate and dispassionate, his eye trained to decipher crime scenes to figure out what happened and how and who likely did it. It's a grim task for which the standard set of tools is officially known at the police department as a Murphy Kit.

"This job is intellect and experience," Murphy used to say when he worked with Murray. "I've got the experience and he's got the intellect." They worked twenty-five cases at a time, a mix of unsolved killings and fugitives on the run for murder, debriefing fellow detectives and combing through old files looking for fresh clues that might have grown like mushrooms in a dark and misty place. They tunneled into their work from complementary angles, Murphy decoding the evidence and the crime scene photographs. "After Stevie tells me what time the crime went down," Murray explained once, when he was allowed to speak to reporters, "it's my job to get inside the killer's head."

He seemed to relish that particular aspect of the job. "To catch a killer," he used to say in his excitable way, "you have to think like a killer." So, over the years, he imagined himself committing all manner of depravity: executing an estranged wife, shotgunning a gambler over a two-dollar debt from a gas station craps game, clubbing a man with a two-pound ketchup bottle before slashing his throat with the shards. In the autumn of 1994, Murray drove the streets of West Roxbury after midnight, convincing himself he was drunk and horny and a sexual predator who, more than three years earlier, had raped and stabbed a single mother with multiple sclerosis after she let him into the house. That fit of mental gymnastics eventually led the two detectives to Gerald Craffey, who was later convicted of murdering Corinne Flynn in August 1991.

Craffey was only one of dozens. Five years after its formation, the Cold Case Squad had sent twenty-six killers to prison. Of the forty-two murder warrants that were outstanding in 1992, all but eighteen were disposed of—either by the suspect being captured or proven to have died—within four years.

IN THE EARLY WEEKS OF 1996, MURRAY AND MURPHY PULLED Sandra Francis's case from a filing cabinet. It was ripe with leads. For one thing, the pictures of Sandra's corpse and apartment were exceptionally vivid. "The best crime scene photos I've ever seen" Murphy says. "The classic rape-murder." From the corpse alone, Murphy could tell Sandra had been killed immediately after she had been raped. She was half-naked on the floor. "If there'd been time between the rape and murder," Murphy explains, "she would have tried to cover herself."

The case file also had a name of a potential suspect, Lee Perkins, who would be as good a starting point as anyone. The only problem was finding him, which the detectives six years earlier had been unable to do. Tracing felons, however, happened to be something Murray took an interest in because it gave him another chance to climb inside a bad guy's head, plumbing an imaginary psyche for some hint of an alias. He could sit for hours in front of his computer, the modem plugged into some database somewhere, typing variations on a theme until one of them bounced back through his monitor. Earl James Clark, for instance, shot a man over a pair of socks on February 22, 1969, then vanished, running away to a new name and a new life. Twenty-five years later, Murray renamed him more than a hundred times on his computer. James Clark. Clark Earl. James Earl. Nothing. Eventually, he got around to typing Stacey, which he had learned was Clark's boyhood nickname, and Griffin, which he knew was Clark's mother's maiden name. Fugitives always cling to some remnant of their past, which is how they get caught. Murray found a Stacey Griffin living a law abiding life in Dayton, Ohio. He was the right age, right physical description, and, in the end, the right man. Earl James Clark is now serving fifteen to twenty years in a Massachusetts prison after pleading guilty to manslaughter.

Finding Lee Perkins wasn't nearly so difficult. He was in the Massachusetts State Correctional Institution at Concord, where he'd been since April 4, 1996, after violating the terms of probation he was given in 1992 for an aggravated rape. There were still no eyewitnesses, though. There was still the DNA option, but, like the counterparts years earlier, Murray and Murphy didn't have enough probable cause to demand a sample of Perkins genetic code.

Homicide investigations, however, are often a matter of playing the odds. And the odds said Lee Perkins—a convicted rapist who wormed his way into the life of a woman who, shortly thereafter, was raped and murdered—was a prime suspect. "It's like what they tell pilots," Murphy explained once about another case. "You know what they tell pilots when they're first flying by the seat of their ass? *Believe your instruments."*

Their instruments said Lee Perkins was their guy. On the other hand, instruments are scary things. Murphy gave up flying after only fifteen hours of lessons.

ON MAY 31, 1996, LIEUTENANT DETECTIVES MURRAY AND MURphy drove north to the prison in Concord. Riding with them was Don Hayes, a criminologist who works in the Boston Police Department's crime lab and who is qualified to draw blood. A long shot, sure, but if Perkins agreed to give up an ounce or two of blood, it would be better to have Hayes waiting nearby with a needle.

Murray and Murphy also brought, as had become their standard by then, one pack of Newport cigarettes, a freshly scrubbed glass ashtray, a can of soda, and a tape recorder, the latter on the off chance that a suspect might agree to have his words imbedded on tape. At the prison, they were led through a series of thick doors and barred gates into a small interview room, only eight feet by ten feet, where the guards often eat their lunch. Murray wiped down the table and, in the middle, arranged the cigarettes and the soda. Then the two cops waited for Perkins.

They heard his voice outside the lunchroom, saying, Yes, when a guard asked if he wanted to talk to a couple of Boston cops. Then he came into the room. He wasn't wearing handcuffs or shackles. Murray and Murphy introduced themselves and shook Lee Perkins's hand.

"So what do you want?" Perkins finally asked.

"We want to talk to you about a friend," Murray told him. "But first I have to go over your Miranda rights."

Murray pulled a sheet of paper from his briefcase with the words, in large black type, "Boston Police Department Miranda Warning" and slid it across the table to Perkins. Murray kept a copy of the form in front of himself. After Perkins filled out the biographical information—name, age (thirty-three), and the like—Murray started reciting Perkins's rights, beginning with the one to remain silent. After he read each line, he asked if Perkins understood. He said yes every time, and Murray told him where to initial the form. When they'd gone through each line, Perkins studied the form, then signed his name at the bottom.

Now they were ready to talk.

"We want to talk about your friend Sandra," he said.

Perkins paused, but only for an instant. "Sandra who?"

"Sandra Francis."

"I don't know no Sandra and I don't know no Sandra Francis."

"Oh, I think you do," Murray said. "She had this really small apartment, remember? It was like that old joke: it was so small, if you put the key in the lock you'd break the window. Remember?"

"Nope."

Murray showed Perkins a picture of Sandra. Perkins studied it, then shook his head. "Nope, don't know her."

For two hours Murphy and Murray kept dropping hints, tossing out anything that might jiggle Perkins's memory or rattle his composure, asking if he'd ever dated a Sandra, slept with a Sandra. Nothing. When they told him Sandra's address on Huntington Avenue, all Perkins said was, "I don't know where that is. I lived in Brockton."

Eventually, Perkins asked if he could have a cigarette. "Yeah, sure," Murray said, gracious as he could be. Perkins took the pack, opened it, and pulled out a butt. They kept talking. Perkins, smoking his cigarette, kept insisting he didn't know Sandra Francis. He crushed out the butt in the ashtray. He drank a soda, smoked a second cigarette, then crushed that one out as well.

After ninety minutes, Murray and Murphy got around to telling Perkins the important thing, namely that Sandra Francis was murdered.

"Were my fingerprints there?" Perkins asked.

Murray told him the truth: "I don't know."

The next question was trickier. Would Perkins voluntarily surrender a sample of his blood? Murray pushed a consent form across the table, which Perkins actually read. He considered the idea, but only for moment before he declined. He also refused to speak into the tape recorder Murray and Murphy had lugged along. "I already told you everything I've got to say," he said. But he promised to ask his wife and his priest whether he should give up a vial of blood. He took the detectives' business cards and promised to call if he changed his mind.

Perkins stood to leave, hesitated, then turned back. "Can I have another smoke?" he asked. "Yeah, sure," Murray told him. "Take the whole pack." Neither Murray or Murphy smoke anyway.

The two cops lingered for almost twenty minutes, waiting to make sure Perkins wasn't having second thoughts about retrieving anything from the interview room. Then Don Hayes came out and, with the sterile precision of a practiced scientist, lifted the soda can into an evidence bag. Perkins's fingerprints were on the can. Next, Hayes carefully tipped the contents of the ashtray into a second bag. The ashtray contained two cigarette butts, a few dabs of Lee Perkins's saliva, and a sizeable number of his skin cells, sloughed off from his lips with each drag from the filter. It contained, in other words, the complete genetic profile of Lee Perkins.

DEOXYRIBONUCLEIC ACID, WHICH IS THE OFFICIAL AND CUMBERSOME way of saying DNA, is the blueprint of every human being, a combination of acids wrapped in a double helix, two microscopic strands twisted around each other in the nuclei of cells and connected by a distinct pattern of base chemicals. The sequence of combinations leave each person with his or her own unique double helix.

Though science identified DNA decades ago, distilling it into an effective investigatory tool wasn't possible until 1984, when a British geneticist named Alec Jeffereys figured out a way to isolate the underlying base pairs of acids that link a smear of genetic material to an actual human. The judicial system tends to be wary of complicated scientific evidence, fearing that jurors will put a layman's credulous faith into processes that they don't fully understand and that often allow for substantial margins of error. But DNA profiling—or DNA typing or fingerprinting, depending on what expert is testifying where—was embraced almost immediately as a sort of magic bullet for crime fighters. The United Kingdom allowed its use in court as early as 1985. By the late 1980s, DNA typing had crossed the Atlantic Ocean to the States.

There are a number of different techniques labs can use to coax a genetic profile from a smidgen of bodily tissue, each with its own strengths and weaknesses. Among the more reliable is Restriction Fragment Length Polymorphism, or R.F.L.P. for short, which involves applying enzymes to the DNA sample that home in on specific, letter-coded sequences in the double helix, then snip them apart into fragments. Those fragments are then immersed in a gel, to which a weak electrical current is applied, jiggling the snipped pieces around at different speeds depending on the size and heft of each one. After a few more steps—involving membranes and X-rays—the DNA profile is represented as a rough bar code, which can then be compared to whatever was retrieved from the crime scene. It's unnervingly accurate, but R.F.L.P. also requires a substantial amount of source material, often more than is available at a rape or murder. Plus, it takes weeks to complete.

So another method, P.C.R. or Polymerase Chain Reaction, was developed, allowing technicians to draw a DNA profile out of minute and aging samples of genetic material. The double helix is separated into single strands of DNA, which are then combined in a solution with primers, which are short strands of DNA that correspond to specific segments. Once combined in the lab, those markers can be multiplied, usually at least a million times, acting almost as a genetic photocopier and giving investigators enough material to make a comparison. An additional upside to P.C.R. testing is its speed; the process can typically be completed in a few days, sometimes in hours. The downside, however, is that it is less reliable, generally able to build the odds against a suspect into the hundreds of thousands or millions, compared to the one-in-several-billion sometimes achievable with R.F.L.P. What's more, because the initial samples tend to be smaller and older, there is a greater chance of contamination either in the stationhouse or the lab. That, in turn, gives savvy defense attorneys an avenue of attack, as in, for instance, the O.J. Simpson trial.

The Boston Police Department and Suffolk County District Attorney's Office have actually been a few steps ahead of most big cities in embracing new investigatory technology. As early as 1990, when DNA testing was available but both expensive—it still is: in fiscal year 1998, Massachusetts's eleven district attorneys paid half a million dollars to out-of-state labs— and so backlogged it was impractical, homicide detectives used a process called electrophoresis to build a case against a wolf pack of eight men and boys who tortured a prostitute to death on Halloween night. "The worst homicide I've ever seen," said Captain Detective Edward J. McNelley, who then commanded the squad. Kimberly Rae Harbour had been gang raped, then cut with a knife, smashed in the face with a forty-ounce beer bottle, clubbed with a tree limb, and repeatedly stabbed before one of her killers thrust his hands high above his head, leapt in the air and landed a two-footed stomp on her back. She had enough breath left to scream, but she was dead by the time police found her. "Bled out," McNelley said. "One hundred and thirty-two stab wounds and, you know, not one of them was fatal. She bled to death." With so many suspects, electrophoresis—which isolates proteins in bodily fluids, a process not as precise as DNA profiling but close enough—allowed detectives to sort out which suspect was responsible for which felony.

What's more, the Boston Police spent seventy thousand dollars in federal grant money to build a state-of-the-art DNA lab that will use, among other techniques, a relatively new process call Short Tandem Repeats, which has the advantages of P.C.R. yet produces almost twice as many genetic markers. And Boston was the first city to wire into the Federal Bureau of Investigation's national ballistics database, which allows different crimes to be linked by the guns used in them.

The FBI also linked together a series of DNA databases in 1997, giving law enforcement officers across the country instantaneous access to genetic profiles of felons in a dozen states. Massachusetts is expected to join the system shortly with its own collection of DNA fingerprints collected from some twelve thousand felons and from crime scenes dating back to 1986. Police have been building the database since January 1, 1998, when a state law allowed them to prick a drop of blood from people convicted of thirty-three felonies, including murder, rape, and armed robbery. Eleven hundred samples were collected in the first eight months, when a superior court judge ruled the law was an impermissible violation of the United States Constitution's Fourth Amendment against unreasonable searches, as well as the commonwealth's more stringent Constitutional protections. Eight months later, however, the Supreme Judicial Court overturned that ruling, and the collections began anew.

The advantage of such databases, obviously, is it allows investigators to almost instantly match a suspect on file with an unsolved crime. In Boston, for instance, police anticipate solving nearly one hundred dormant rape cases within days of logging into the system. In Virginia, forty-two old cases of have been disposed of since that state's bank of genetic code was computerized in 1996. Even so, the demand still far outstrips the supply of testing facilities. Virginia, which is one of the better-equipped states, has a backlog of almost a thousand cases that's growing by seventy-five a day. In Massachusetts, police expect some thirteen hundred rapes, beatings, stabbings, shootings, and killings will require DNA testing this year—and that's on top of a three-year log-jam of cases awaiting testing.

Yet while DNA has proven an invaluable aid to police and pros-ecutors, it can also be used to exclude people from a pool of suspects, or, more heroically, prove the innocence of a wrongly convicted—and sometimes condemned—prisoner. In the past eight years, according to the New York-based Innocence Project, seventy inmates have been released in the wake of DNA evidence that threw their convictions into question. Eight of those people were on Death Row.

LEE PERKINS NEVER TOOK HIS EYES OFF MARK LEE WHILE THE prosecutor argued to the jury, insisting the man in the gray sweater and sharp tie was a rapist and a killer. And his expression never changed, never lost that curious befuddlement, even when Lee brought up how Perkins's DNA was found on Sandra Francis.

His lawyer, a seasoned defense attorney named Larry Tipton who sat next to him scribbling notes on a yellow legal pad, would have his chance to tell the jury another version of the story soon enough. If his freedom rested on the strength of technical gibber-ish out of a laboratory, Perkins couldn't have drawn a better lawyer. Tipton, in yet another striking example of what a small big city Boston truly is, had been down this road before and only a year earlier, following the same sign posts, passing the same char-acters: Tim Murray, the cigarette ruse, specks of flesh tied to the most monstrous of crimes.

Tipton, who is a dead ringer for a brown-haired Martin Mull, was one of the attorneys who defended Jeffrey Bly in the assassi-nation of Assistant Attorney General Paul McLaughlin, a trial that didn't take place until May 1999. For more than a year, detectives had been badly divided into two camps, one convinced Bly was the killer, the other believing a gang-banger from Jamaica Plain had pulled the trigger. Murray was in the Bly faction. In June of 1996, he and Sergeant Detective William Mahoney visited Bly in prison, where he was only a few months into his ten-to-fifteen year sentence for carjacking Dana Alston. The conversation was different than the one with Perkins, of course, but the ruse and the pretense were precisely the same. While the detectives pestered him about a dead prosecutor, Bly smoked three cigarettes, all of which were extinguished in a spotlessly clean ashtray. Months later, the lab results came back: the skin cells retrieved from the cigarette butts provided enough genetic material to match another sample, a tiny piece of flesh taken from inside the ring finger of the left glove Bly had dropped along the railroad tracks.

The match wasn't perfect, however. The genetic profile fit Bly and one out of every 631,000 black people, give or take. Long odds—few people, and certainly not a half million people of one race, had a motive to kill McLaughlin—but the margin of error was enough for Tipton to work the jury. They deliberated for the three days, arguing and crying in frustration, passing around a gray hat to collect the votes for guilty or not, before finally convicting Bly on Saturday, May 29, 1999. The evidence, one juror told the *Boston Herald,* was "overwhelming," a parade of witnesses who either placed Bly at the scene or swore that he boasted about the murder in the hours and days afterward. But the verdict, to Tipton's credit, didn't hinge on DNA.

"Some of the people were uncomfortable with the results of the DNA, and a few of the people actually didn't factor it into their decision because they judged it to be potentially not credible," one juror told the tabloid. "I felt bad [for Tipton] because he did a good job. He served to confuse us."

Not surprisingly, Tipton has been among the members of the local defense bar who've complained about the techniques cops such as Murray use to gather evidence. So, too, has Stephen Hrones, Donnell Johnson's attorney. In 1994, he appealed a client's murder confession to the Supreme Judicial Court, insisting that Murray and another detective had illegally tricked Corey Selby into admitting he shot a man by suggesting police had found his handprint inside the house where the killing took place. Murray even used a prop: a photocopy of someone else's print that he took pains to make sure Selby saw. "Of course they don't use the rack and screw anymore," Hrones harrumphed to an appeals court judge. "The tactics are more subtle than in the old days." (The technique, while not embraced by the courts, was ruled to be permissible.) Likewise, defense attorneys maintain that swiping genetic material from cigarette butts—or empty soda cans or tossed-away tissues—amounts to an illegal search and seizure at worst, and sleazy trickery at best. Thus far, their protestations have not been successful. For one thing, cigarette butts and tissues are legally considered abandoned property, which means it's up for grabs. For two, police and prosecutors counter that their job does not include protecting suspects from their own careless ignorance.

But Tipton, defending Perkins for the second time, wasn't going to contest the scientific evidence, at least not the part that proved his client's semen was in a dead woman's vagina. Over the course of 1996, the police and district attorney's office had built a solid case that Perkins knew Francis. In November of that year, Emma Sampson had finally been able to give Murray a formal statement, and she was able to pick Perkins's mug shot out of a photo array, although she confessed his hair was styled differently than it was in 1990. So Tipton wasn't contesting the facts so much as the commonwealth's interpretation of them.

When Mark Lee finished his opening argument, Tipton rose from the oak table, took four strong paces toward the jury box, and began outlining his own theory of the crime. "The evidence will show, ladies and gentlemen," he said, holding his eyeglasses gently between the fingers of his right hand, "that, in fact, there was no forcible rape of Sandra Francis at some point leading up to March 25, 1990, but in fact, there was consensual sex."

Perkins propped his chin on his right fist, his elbow resting on the table. His face had shifted, but only subtly, drifting from confusion to a mild confidence. Sure, he'd had sex with her. There was no point denying that. After the initial DNA tests from his cigarette butt came back positive, a grand jury had subpoenaed a blood sample. They had him cold on the sex. "I did know Sandra at one time," he said during a break in the court proceedings. "And I had had a short term affair with her. But it was six years later"—his voice rose at this point, because he was clearly frustrated that the police would pester him about someone he'd slept with more than half a decade earlier—"and the pictures that they showed me I did not recognize as the person that I know." His voice softened for the second half of his sentence, as if he was finally recalling a long lost love.

"Do you remember every woman you ever had sex with?" Mark Lee was in his office late on Friday afternoon. He'd put his last witness on the stand a little while ago and, by now, most of Martin's staff was gone for the weekend, and a man with a large red machine was cleaning the pale carpeting in the hallway. Miller Thomas, one of the detectives who'd worked the Perkins case, had just walked in, and the question caught him off guard.

The detective smiled, then chuckled. "No comment," he said.

"I do!" Lee nearly shouted back. "I do. I do. I mean, I know every woman I've ever had sex with. How can you not remember?"

Lee was laughing, the glow of a good week in court bubbling out through his smile. He knew his opening argument had been strong and none of his witnesses had suffered any real damage. Tipton did a workmanlike job softening up Emma Sampson, harping on her recollection, almost nine years after the fact, of a fourth visit Perkins had made to Sandra Francis's apartment, which he used to build upon her admitted animosity toward the defendant.

"You testified yesterday," Tipton said when he cross-examined Sampson, "that the first time you saw Mr. Perkins you didn't like him."

"Um, I just didn't trust him."

"You stated yesterday that you felt he was a bum."

"I said he *looked* like a bum."

"He certainly didn't have any harsh words to say to you, did he?" Tipton persisted.

"No."

"And he didn't say, certainly, any alarming or harsh words to Miss Francis at that time, did he?"

"No."

"It's fair to say, Miss Sampson," Tipton continued, "that you never called the police regarding these visits Mr. Perkins had at Miss Francis's house."

"No," she said, "I did not."

"And it's fair to say that Miss Francis, to the best of your knowledge, never called the police. Is that correct?"

"Yes."

A glancing blow, nothing worse. If Sampson was to be portrayed as an embittered best friend, Lee already had his parry scripted. "I've thought long and hard about that," he told Sampson in a conference room after Tipton had finished with her. "And I think I've got a pretty good argument. Here's the difference: Emma Sampson forgot one of four events. She remembered three and the fourth came to her mind later on. It's an event. He [meaning Perkins], after two hours of questioning by the Boston Police Department, after having them do everything in the world to help him remember this person, he doesn't even remember the person. It's two different things. So don't worry about that."

Lee didn't have to worry about rehabilitating any other witnesses. Tim Murray, looking like an oversized Boy Scout as he swore to tell the truth, so help him God, had recounted how Perkins smoked his cigarettes in the prison conference room. Don Hayes had done a fine job explaining how semen would have leaked into Sandra Francis's panties if she'd moved around after having had consensual sex. Tipton's only counter was to ascertain that seminal fluid could remain inside her for twenty-four hours or so after having had sex.

Best of all, Lee had timed his case perfectly. Hayes, his last witness, closed out the testimony on Friday, January 14, the beginning of the three-day Martin Luther King Day weekend. "You do not want the defendant to get the last word," David Meier, the chief of homicide prosecutions and Lee's boss had told him after the first day of the trial. "You want the jury to sit for three days with your case. Particularly if Quill's at the end." Jack Quill, an FBI agent who specialized in genetic profiling, was Lee's key witness. "When does Quill come up?" Meier asked, the two prosecutors leaning against walls in the hallway outside Meier's office.

"Quill's my second to last...."

"Quill's not available, Judge, until Friday morning," Meier interrupted, outlining the excuse Lee would need. "He's an FBI agent, he flies all over the country...."

"Okay...."

"I'm sorry, Judge," Meier continued. "I made an effort to get him here Thursday, but rather than cut his testimony in half, bring him up late in the day Thursday, he's flying in first thing Friday morning, or flying in Thursday night, he'll be available nine o'clock Friday, whenever you get to him."

The next morning, which was Wednesday, Lee paced the red carpeted floor before the jury filed in, bantering with the court clerk. "So is your expert in?" she asked.

"Oh, no, no," Lee said. He feigned a slight edge of shame, or at least humility, raising his right hand to his mouth as if to acknowledge the awkwardness of the situation. "Here's the problem. In a pinch"—he spread his hands apart to emphasize the pinch part—"he can come tomorrow. But he's really wanting to come Friday."

"Well...."

"I know, I know," Lee interrupted, sounding like a schoolboy who'd forgotten his homework.

"...where will your case be? Over?"

"He would be the second-to-last witness," Lee offered quickly. "I mean, I'll show you. I'll go through the witness list...."

The clerk didn't seem to mind one way or the other. And when Quill took the stand, he was damning. Thin and gray-haired with a triangular face and a deep, mellifluous voice, he followed Lee's lead through the investigatory chain connecting Perkins and Sandra Francis.

"And what does that mean for us in this particular case?" Lee asked.

"We have a DNA match," Quill answered, "where I can't exclude Mr. Perkins as a contributor, and the chance that it would be an unrelated individual in the black population would be one in one-hundred-thousand."

FRIDAY WAS A BAD DAY FOR LEE PERKINS, EVEN BEFORE JACK Quill handicapped his odds of being a rapist. Actually, the nineties had been a bad decade, and the previous four days a disaster. Maybe the pressure finally got to him, which would explain the tantrum he threw in the courtroom that morning.

After Murray's testimony about the cigarette butts, an enterprising reporter at the *Boston Globe* named Sacha Pfeiffer started assembling a story about the debate over sneaky investigative techniques. As is their wont, her editors preferred to run the story with a photograph of the current smoking suspect, which would be Perkins. So, bright and early Friday morning, a *Globe* photographer was positioned in the front of the courtroom with a long lens on his camera pointed toward the defense table.

Perkins turned his back. In prison, cons don't have to admit what they did. Hell, most of them insist they're innocent anyway. If they can help it, no inmate will admit to being a rapist, which is only slightly less abhorrent, even to killers and thieves, than being a pedophile.

"My understanding was that PBS was gonna be here and that was it," Perkins told Tipton, who leaned over to hear him and kept glancing back over his shoulder toward the judge and the photographer. "I didn't hear anything about any camera, no one comin' in here takin' my picture." (PBS, by way of explanation, is not a big draw in the prison TV lounge.)

The court officers began to move closer, one of them putting his hand on Perkins's shoulder, leaning in close. He still refused to turn around. Finally, Judge Robert A. Barton stood up behind the bench. "Mr. Tipton, you listen to me," he said in his best, booming judicial tenor. "And you listen to me, Mr. Perkins. I'm not going to force you to sit in this courtroom. And if you want to absent yourself from the courtroom, the trial will continue in your absence, until you indicate that you would like to return." Barton turned to the clerk. "Line up the jurors please."

Tipton bent close to Perkins's ear. He knew, even if Perkins didn't, that his life was on the line. "C'mon Lee, keep your eye on the ball, man. Keep your eye on the ball."

"I'm gonna walk out the room...."

"Lee, don't do it...."

"I'm gonna walk out the room...."

"*Lee....*"

"Y'all better take me out then, 'cause I'm gonna walk out the room...."

Tipton turned back to the bench and asked Barton to reconsider. Which he did. He called a recess and summoned the *Globe* cameraman into his chambers.

"Okay," Tipton told Perkins. "He left."

"If this guy takes my picture," Perkins said, sounding like a man with nothing to lose, "all hell's gonna break loose in here."

It didn't happen. Barton dismissed the photographer, explaining he didn't want a verdict overturned because the defendant turned his back on the judge or, worse, fled the courtroom. Realistically, having his picture in the paper truly was the worst of Perkins's worries. The day's testimony—Quill, then Hayes—would only make spending the rest of his life in prison more probable. Better to go back and boast of being a killer than suffering being a rapist.

His defense would begin the following week, after the jury had digested the DNA evidence for three days. The only serious question was one of strategy, that being whether Perkins would take the stand. Tipton had managed to talk him into staying in the courtroom; now he had to talk him off the stand.

It began badly. "Now, are you gonna testify or not," Tipton whispered to Perkins on Tuesday morning. "I just explained all this to you in detail. Nothing's changed."

"Uh-huh," Perkins muttered. He pondered his options for a few moments, the fingers of his right hand resting against his mustache. "Okay," he said. "I'll take the stand."

Tipton stood up, turning away. "Oh-kay," he said. His tone belied his feelings.

Then Judge Barton interrupted. "I've been around for a few years," he said, "and I would like to think in my mind I know what you're talking about. If it relates to the issue of whether he is going to testify or not going to testify, you might want as much time as you think is necessary to discuss that issue with your client. We can adjourn for lunch if you would prefer that."

"I would appreciate that," Tipton said. Relief rolled from his shoulders. "Thank you."

Everyone stood as first the jurors, then Barton filed out. Court officers led Perkins away to a small holding cell where he could sit at a counter and, through a mesh screen, confer with his lawyer.

"The decision you have to make right now is whether you testify or not," Tipton told him. "You know how I feel about it. I don't have to go into it, right?"

"Uh-huh."

"And it's fair to say you didn't follow my advice at the first trial, correct?"

"Yes," Perkins answered, the first trace of a laugh slipping out.

"You went ahead and testified...."

"I went ahead and testified, Larry, because I am innocent of this crime and I want to get up there and let the people know that I'm innocent." He paused, considering a way out. "Um, on the other hand, I do have this stuttering problem that I've, that I've had all my life."

They talked for a little while longer, weighing the pros (none) and the cons (many) of Perkins walking up to the witness stand. In the end, he agreed to sit silently at the defense table, let Tipton try to argue his way out of a life sentence.

Which was fine with Tipton. "I'm happy he didn't testify," he told a colleague later that day. "He was going to be slaughtered."

On Tuesday afternoon Lee wore the look of a strained man as he sat behind his courtroom table, listening to Tipton pontificate to the jury. His hand kept creeping up to his head, massaging his temple and cheek, pushing every phrase and legal point deeper into his skull, where some synapse might ignite with an appropriate retort.

Tipton was right: Perkins would have been slaughtered on the stand. Swaying a dozen strangers to your side is best left to a professional. And Tipton, given the enormity of his task, did a masterful job.

"What I suggest to you," Tipton began, "what the evidence suggests, is that it is both illogical and unreasonable to continue to believe that there was a sexual assault of Miss Francis." He took a breath, gathering steam for his lungs. "Miss Sampson told you from the first second she laid eyes on Mr. Perkins she did not like him. She described him as a bum and dirty. Would Sandra Francis volunteer to Emma Sampson that she had spent some time with Mr. Perkins when she knows how Emma Sampson felt about Mr. Perkins when he carried her groceries home? Would she invite an argument with her best friend? Or would she simply say, as an independent young woman, I can see who I want to see and I'm not going to have another argument with my friend because she doesn't like this man.

"The death of Sandra Francis is a tragedy," Tipton went on. His voice was softer now, lower, both sympathetic and pleading. "But there is in fact, ladies and gentlemen, a tragedy of equal proportions looming. And that, I suggest to you, is to convict an innocent man based on bad science, on a bad investigation, and a bad assumption made on March 25, 1990. Thank you."

Mark Lee sat at the prosecution table for a few moments, gathering his thoughts. He'd already worked out most of his closing argument, recited it in his head a hundred times. He needed only a minute or so to massage Tipton's arguments into his own legal reasoning. By the time he stood up and took his first step toward the jury box, his body was tense with indignation.

"Mr. Tipton stood here and argued to you folks that there was no sexual assault in this case," he said. The pauses were back in his cadence, drawing out the dramatic points. No. Sexual. Assault. "I ask you, when you go back to deliberate on this case, the first thing you do is pick up this picture"—he whipped an eight-by-ten glossy crime scene photo from his hip to his chest, holding it up for the jury to see—"and ask your fellow jurors, if she wasn't raped, how did she get this way?" Another rest, two paces, pivot. "If she wasn't raped, how did she get this way. On the floor. Legs spread. Clothing around her knees. Dead."

Lee drew a breath, took a few more paces, then continued. Every picture, he told the jury, tells a story. And the story the picture of Sandra Francis's corpse told was of a fast and violent death. If she hadn't died immediately after the rape, the police would have found sperm in her panties. "Unless," Lee started again, just about to burst into a theatrical rage, "someone else came in after the rape and killed her before she had a chance to pull up her panties. Well, that sounds like what the defense is saying. Right after this either consensual sex, if you want to take it the way the defense has put it, or rape, right before Miss Francis could pull up her panties, the true killer came in—must have passed the defendant in the hallway—and for some unapparent reason killed Miss Francis right in her apartment."

Lee was throwing his entire body into his closer, squatting to imitate a woman pulling up her panties at the appropriate moment, slashing his left arm toward Perkins and Tipton to make a point, then halting for effect.

"That's ludicrous," he said next. "That doesn't make any bit of sense." He was soft-spoken now, deliberate in his cadence and pacing. "What is the more likely explanation for why there was no sperm in her panties?" he said. "Because she couldn't get them up." Pause. "Because she was dead."

Lee sat down. Judge Barton excused the jury. For the first time, Lee Perkins's brow quivered. Maybe it was fear.

MARK LEE SPENT THE NEXT DAY AND A HALF PACING THE COURT-house hallways. Deliberations are always the worst part for him. What if they acquit the bastard? Does that mean they didn't like Lee, that a dozen strangers thought he was an inarticulate putz? So he paced, working off nervous energy.

Perkins spent that time reading the Bible. God, or some convenient version of Him, seems to lurk in every prison cell. Somehow, He steered Perkins to the passages about the world forsaking him and evil men setting snares for him and the Lord being his only refuge. Quentin Tarantino couldn't write such hackneyed scenes.

The jury came back Thursday afternoon, after only a day and a half of deliberations. Guilty, the foreman said, of murder in the first degree. Guilty, he added, of rape. Then all twelve filed out of the courtroom. Tim Murray sat in the gallery next to Emma Sampson, nodding his head at each juror, solemn but glowing, mouthing the same words again and again: Thank you.

Lee was compassionate when he recommended a sentence for Perkins. Not that the law gave him much room—first degree murder carries a mandatory life sentence with no hope of parole. But he didn't ask for anything more than that on the rape conviction. Lee isn't one to get carried away with demanding harder time than is necessary. "If you can't respect and fear the power you wield, you're bound to abuse it," he likes to say.

Judge Barton, on the other hand, is not so lenient. Before he sentenced Perkins, he rattled off part of his criminal record. Assault and battery with a dangerous weapon in 1981, 1982, and 1995. Intimidation. Aggravated rape. "There is no question in my mind that this man is a danger to women and should not walk the streets," the judge said. Then he pronounced sentence. Life without parole for murdering Sandra Francis, plus another thirty to forty years for raping her.

CHAPTER 12

David Cherry

ASSISTANT DISTRICT ATTORNEY LEORA JOSEPH, WHO WORKS IN the Child Abuse Unit, shuddered in the courthouse hallway, pulling her bright blue sweater so closely to her body that her shoulders disappeared for an instant under her ebony hair. "This is so unbelievable," she muttered, shaking her hair off her shoulders. "I never thought he'd do this. It's obscene." She looked down the corridor, then turned back to Jack Zanini, the chief legal counsel for Ralph Martin's office. "He doesn't like the statute, that's what this is."

The shadow of a smile creased Zanini's face. "You think it's a conspiracy?"

"It's just, you know . . . ." Leora shuffled the phrases through her mind, finding the right one to put into words. "If this guy doesn't qualify," she finally said, "we're never going to get anywhere with this."

The guy who didn't qualify would be David Cherry, a hulking man of thirty-seven with a bald head who shambled across the marble courthouse floors in a set of prison blues that would have fit more loosely if he hadn't been so huge. Court officers flanked him on either side, and handcuffs kept his arms close around his waist. Leg irons clamped around his ankles just above his white, high-top sneakers. Cherry had spent the past fifteen years in prison after he pleaded guilty of raping one of his prepubescent cousins, a long decade-and-a-half that would have been an eternity if he'd also been convicted of raping his two other underage cousins, which he was accused of doing.

But David Cherry did his time, every hour of it, all 5,478 days, lingering in prison through the last minutes of the high end of a twelve-to-fifteen year sentence. After all that time, he was supposed to walk out a completely free man: no parole officer, no one with whom he'd have to check in every few days, no one to hover behind him, watching where he went, monitoring who David Cherry associated with. As long as he kept out of trouble, his days of being supervised by the factotums of the criminal justice system were supposed to be over.

Which was the part that Leora Joseph believed to be obscene. A few moments earlier, she'd stood up in front of Judge John C. Cratsley, her hands resting on the oak table in front of her, Cherry sitting at the table to her left, his mustache and goatee outlining the scowl contorted onto his face. On September 10, 1999, three weeks before he wrapped up his prison time, a new law took effect in the Commonwealth of Massachusetts that allowed prosecutors to file civil actions against people such as Cherry, convicted rapists and child molesters who might reasonably be considered a serious threat to continue raping and molesting. The legal term (a rare fit of legalese approximating English) is "sexually dangerous person."

Yet the legal concept behind that phrase—namely, that such people should be kept locked up until the state decides they are no longer dangerous—has been controversial for decades, a complicated and often unconstitutional attempt to balance public safety against due process. In Massachusetts, the new law already had gotten mixed reviews from judges in other counties, with at least one ruling that the statute violated the commonwealth's constitution by meting out retroactive punishment. David Cherry, as fate would have it, would be the inaugural case in Suffolk County. A week earlier, Zanini had marched into her office with a stack of papers stuffed into folders. "This guy's getting out in a week," he told her. "Do something about it."

So she stood in court, trying to do something. "Your Honor, if I could just address the court briefly," Joseph began. Her voice is high and vaguely raspy, which, considering she is also petite and only in her early thirties, makes her seem almost girlish in the courtroom. "The commonwealth's position on this case is that this defendant poses an immediate danger to the community at large," she said. "And as a result, we'd like the opportunity to present evidence to this court which would enable our having this defendant evaluated at the treatment center for what we consider him to be—an incredibly dangerous individual—before this court is prepared to release him to the community." She didn't break stride before outlining her second-best scenario, barely pausing for a breath. "Should the court be determined to release him notwithstanding that, the commonwealth is requesting the defendant be ordered to have no contact with any child under sixteen, the defendant be ordered to have no contact with any of the named witnesses in the case for which he did his fifteen year sentence, namely the victims that he anally, orally, and vaginally raped."

She stopped speaking, but only long enough for the last five words to echo in the courtroom.

"The commonwealth," she began again, "is also requesting that he not be allowed within two hundred yards of any day care facility, elementary school, junior school, and high school."

Judge Cratsley didn't waste any words shooting her down. "The burden of proof to commit Mr. Cherry"—Mr. Cherry, as opposed to "the defendant," a bad sign—"for these evaluation procedures remains on the Commonwealth of Massachusetts to give a sufficient showing to detain. And I am now of the opinion that he need not be detained. The commonwealth has not met its burden for temporary detention."

David Cherry wasn't quite free yet, but he was only hours away. He shambled back out of the courtroom, still cuffed and shackled, still flanked by court officers. Joseph and Zanini lingered in the hallway, talking about how obscene it all was.

"There are people with far worse records," Zanini offered.

"Yeah, you're right, there are worse," Joseph answered, which she knew too well after more than two years working child abuse. "But these are little girls, seven, eight, nine, whatever it is, and, like, all kinds of rapes. I mean, really disturbing."

"But because it's incest, it's not sexually dangerous," Zanini said. His tone was mildly sarcastic. "That doesn't make sense."

"Let me tell you something else," Joseph said. "That guy is big. How big is he? What is he, like, six-four? And he's, like, eight hundred pounds maybe."

She giggled at that. But she still thought it was obscene that big David Cherry would be walking free.

"BYYYYE...."

John Swomley's voice was high and singsong, teasing, almost mocking, as he drove away from the chain-link fence and razor wire surrounding Bridgewater State Hospital, which isn't so much a medical facility as it is a prison with doctors. The night was pale orange, the glow from the sodium lights along the prison perimeter reflecting off the clouds and the blacktop and the windshield of the lawyer's truck.

"Yes indeed," David Cherry said from the back seat. He was chuckling heavily, almost laughing. "See ya later." He chuckled again. "Hopefully I'm never coming back, either."

It was a clear and cool night in early November 1999, the first night of David Cherry's life as an ex-con and a free man. God, it felt good to be out. Beautiful, really. He did his time, tried to be as much of a model citizen as any man can be locked in a cage. Now his family was waiting for him to come home for good.

"David, are you hungry?" Swomley said.

"Yes." Every syllable came out in a heavy, happy sigh.

"Would you like a McDonald's hamburger?" Swomley said

"McDonald's" as if it were *haute cuisine,* which, compared to prison food, it is.

"Yes." Another happy sigh.

"If the answer's no, we can search around a little, but that's the closest thing.

"Listen here, listen here," Cherry said. "I heard McDonald's just don't sell hamburgers anymore," Cherry said. A man can miss a lot in fifteen years. "I just want a shake."

Then he leaned back in his seat, tilted his head, and turned his eyes toward the roof, or, more importantly, to the heavens beyond. "Oh, man. Oh, thank you, God," he said. He lowered his gaze to mortal level again. "Do you know what it's like to be in jail longer than some murderers? Longer than some people...." He didn't name another felony such as, say, rape, because that's what he did. But surely some people did worse things than David Cherry. "Oh, it's just unbelievable to me," he said.

Swomley pulled into a McDonald's drive-through. He ordered a large vanilla shake for his client, the ex-con in the back seat.

"Anything else?" the kid working the window asked over the tinny speaker.

"Yes!" Swomley said. Now he was starting to beam. "David, what else do you want?"

Cherry's appetite had returned. He ordered a Filet o' Fish and french fries. When the food was passed back to him, he marveled at the size of the shake, holding it in front of him like a lab experiment, as if a decade and a half had mutated fast food into giant replicas. "This is *big,*" he said. "They never made 'em this big, for real."

Not twenty years ago, when David Cherry was having sex with his seven-year-old cousin. And not thirty-seven years ago, when David Cherry was born to a girl who was only fourteen years old and who had been impregnated by an uncle. David didn't know that for years, though. Until he was almost a man, he never knew his father at all. Then, when he found out his father was his great uncle, there wasn't much point in knowing him too well.

When he became a man, he behaved the way he had been taught. As a child, when his mother would go to work and ask some of the neighborhood girls to look after him, those girls would take him up to their apartment and pull his pants down and fondle him and fellate him, all when he was barely seven years old. "He experienced what was essentially a pattern of predatory sexual activity, which, in his own mind, was not abnormal," Swomley says. "It's how he grew up, what he saw, what he was exposed to. So I don't think he had the same value structure that you or I might have had growing up."

Obviously. David Cherry was twenty-one years old when he was accused of raping his cousins, something he'd done for nearly five years, according to prosecutors. His crimes involved not only incestuous violence, but also pedophilia, considering how young the girls were when the abuse began. Pedophiles, moreover, are notorious serial offenders, molesting dozens, if not hundreds of children before they get caught, if they ever do. All of which made David Cherry a textbook case to test the limits of the state's attempts to civilly commit sexually dangerous persons.

"Mr. Cherry on paper looks like someone that they would think would be sexually dangerous," Swomley said on the ride out to retrieve his client on his first day of freedom. "And I think that they didn't give it much thought after that. They have compiled a list of every single person who's been convicted of a sex crime in the state of Massachusetts and they then will pick and choose from among that list whom they think warrants civil commitment. They had not seen his institutional record, had no idea whether or not he'd done anything wrong of a sexual nature during his fifteen years of commitment—in fact, they had no information at all over the last five years—but they went for it anyway just because they thought that his crime was disgusting enough that they wanted to have him civilly committed."

That's the part that, to David Cherry, in his first blessed moments on the other side of the fence, seemed so brutally and cruelly unfair. "I don't know," he said from the backseat. Another sigh, but not a happy one. "How in the world can they lay down a law three weeks before I wrap up, that I fit the criteria for? Subsequently, the people that got out the month before that law got put in, what are they gonna do?" he asked. By "they" he meant the prosecutors, the same ones or their interchangeable counterparts, who were coming after him. "They gonna go get them now?"

"No," Swomley answered from behind the wheel. "They're not."

"I know they're not," Cherry said. "I know they're not." Then he laughed again, but it was more sardonic than happy.

THE CHILD ABUSE UNIT OF THE SUFFOLK COUNTY DISTRICT AT-torney's Office is *sui generis* in that it is as much an investigatory agency as it is a prosecutorial one. In one respect, then, assistant district attorneys such as Leora Joseph wander acres of gray space, feeling their way, along with police officers and investigators from the Department of Social Services, through often cloudy claims of child sexual abuse. Indeed, only about 15 percent of the cases sent to the office for review end up being prosecuted.

In another respect, however, Joseph often is able to see the world in stark black and white, the gradations of gray blotted away into brief, solid lines of good and evil. "These are bad people doing things to innocent people," she says. "It's very clear to see who the bad guys are."

Prosecuting them, on the other hand, is not always easy—hence the 15 percent figure. Prosecutors in the office might, for instance, spend hours watching a fourteen-year-old girl on the far side of a plate of one-way glass, sobbing and rocking and choking out a terrible tale to a forensic psychologist. The child will sit in one plain armchair at a circular table with a box of tissues in the middle, the interviewer in another, both surrounded by walls painted a muted shade of beige with a touch of soothing pink.

The stories often begin with a variation on a chilling theme. "The first time I saw him," a fourteen-year-old named Denise[3]

---

3   The names of alleged child sexual abuse victims and their family members have been changed.

began one winter morning, "I thought he was a nice person." Nice enough to go to his apartment and watch a video in this instance, nice enough to join his Boy Scout troop in another, nice enough to perform altar service at Sunday Mass in another.

Then the narrative switches to the sickening. "He started touching me," Denise said.

"Where did he touch you?" the interviewer would ask, being careful to avoid any questions that could be considered leading, letting Denise unravel the tale in her own words, at her own pace.

"On the chest."

"What does that mean?"

"Um, my breast." That is an important distinction under Massachusetts law, and a compelling detail should Denise ever tell the same story in front of a judge and jury.

"Then he started getting on top of me," Denise went on. "By that time, he already had his penis inside my vagina." Her cadence was halting and distant, almost robotic, her lips barely moving and her eyes frozen to a patch of carpet in front of her feet. "He got off, and he was like, 'You see, that didn't hurt.' And I took my stuff and I went into the bathroom."

On the other side of the glass, the assistant district attorney and victim-witness advocate might want to know something specific like, for instance, how she felt. The question can then be relayed to the interviewer through a microphone in the booth and a small receiver in the interviewer's ear.

"How did you feel?" Denise is asked.

"He hurt me physically and he hurt me spiritually," she answers, "because I was still a virgin and after he did what he did, I wasn't a virgin." She reaches for a tissue. "I felt like I'm a whore, I'm a slut, I'm a bitch." Then she starts to sob.

Denise tells the story well, recounting details that are still fresh in her young mind. But to bring a case into court—where a traumatized child will have to retell the same story—requires physical evidence, smears of semen or drops of blood, something to connect Denise's older rapist to the younger victim. And the forensics people and the doctors can't always find that evidence. In Denise's case, they did not. The prosecutors believed her story, but they knew they couldn't prove it beyond a reasonable doubt. Denise became one of the 85 percent of alleged victims who never see their assailants stand trial.

All of the stories are wrenching, but sometimes the details, the small and otherwise innocuous afterthoughts, will tweak the horror. Like the young victim who happens to be wearing the exact same sweatshirt from the Gap in which Joseph had dressed her own toddler daughter that morning. Or the girl, all of ten years old, who spoke in calm and measured phrases about the relative who raped her and, when he finished, told her not to tell and gave her a cookie as a reward. "But I didn't want it," said the little girl on the other side of the glass. "So I threw it on the floor."

A scrap of dignity from a baby. Leora Joseph, watching from a darkened room illuminated only by the flickering monitor of a television screen recording the interview, wiped tears from her cheek.

MORE HAUNTING THAN EACH INDIVIDUAL STORY, HOWEVER, ARE the statistical and pathological models of sex offenders. In short, a staggering number of juveniles who commit sex crimes—a group that includes Cherry, considering his crimes began when he was sixteen years old—learned their behavior at the hands of another abuser. If not sexual assault, then physical or emotional trauma. And nearly all of the young offenders have at least witnessed serious assaults.

"The kids who are victimizers have a world view that victimization is the norm, that big people get to pick on little people," says Craig Latham, a Massachusetts psychologist who specializes in troubled kids. "They've been humiliated, they've been abused, they've probably been beaten, and they've seen this type of behavior in their home. And when they reach a certain age, they say, 'If I can be on the receiving end or the giving end of this behavior, the choice is clear.'" It is no coincidence, then, that many sex offenders choose victims who were roughly the same age as they were when they were abused. "In a sense," Latham says, "it's an attempt to go back and make it come out right this time."

Moreover, crimes of sexual abuse, whether physically violent or only emotional manipulative, tend to be addictive, reinforcing both a demented psychological sense of power and control and a normal biological urge of sexual release. "Sex offenses are the only crime, except for substance abuse, where there is a greater likelihood of the offense re-occurring over time," Latham says. "You get the sexual rush as well as the power rush."

The problem, then, is how to balance the needs of former victims, yet protect future victims from them. In the early nineties, a number of states began directing their efforts toward younger and younger offenders, trying to dismantle warped and predatory instincts before they could wreak immeasurable havoc. "The fact is," Ralph Martin said way back in 1994, when he was still an interim district attorney, "there is a young male population growing up with a very twisted view of what an appropriate relationship with someone of the opposite sex should be. We're turning out more sex offenders and more misogynists." The previous year, fifty-two juveniles had been committed to the Department of Youth Services for sex crimes, an increase of 57 percent from the year before that and more than double the number in 1983. What's more, 139 other children were on probation for sex offenses. And those were merely the ones who had been caught, tried, and convicted.

In the same decade that those numbers exploded, however, so did the treatment programs designed to deal with those kids. In 1984, there were a mere twenty programs for sexually abusive adolescents nationwide, and none for prepubescent youths. Ten years later, there were more than eight hundred for teenagers and an additional two hundred for younger children. At the time, Gail Ryan, who was an expert in the prevention of childhood sexual abuse who worked at the University of Colorado's Kempe Center, explained the vigorous attention as a matter of common sense. "What we know about this behavior is it doesn't just suddenly appear in a twenty-five-year-old father molesting his child," she said. "It's a behavior that develops over time."

Yet if perpetrating sexual abuse can be seen as a sort of behavioral disease or defect, there is not necessarily a correlative "cure." In fact, most experts in the field concur that rapists and pedophiles are never so much stripped of their underlying pathologies but instead are taught to control those impulses, to recognize the psychological cycles that lead to an assault, to understand the situations and emotions that trigger the commission of a heinous crime. Even accomplishing that much, however, is a long and expensive process. "If we want to stop this crazy cycle, it makes sense to put the resources into kids," said Carlos Morrissey, who used to be the director of clinical services for the Department of Youth Services. "But how much are we willing to invest in kids like this? There is no quick fix. But we do know what happens if we don't treat them—we start building more prisons."

THE COMMONWEALTH OF MASSACHUSETTS NEVER WANTED TO send David Cherry back to prison. Prisons are reserved for people who have been convicted of criminal offenses. David Cherry, by contrast, was being sued in the civil courts, where business disputes and slip-and-fall cases are heard. The state wanted to commit him, not convict him.

But those are all disingenuous semantics. What Ralph Martin's office wanted was for David Cherry to be locked up so he couldn't rape any more children, relatives or otherwise. He would have been committed to Bridgewater State Hospital, the same prison facility from which he'd just been released, and enrolled in a treatment program, some point after which a psychologist or psychiatrist might declare that he was no longer a threat to anyone outside of prison.

Libertarians and legitimate conservatives (as opposed to the dominant wing of the Republican party) immediately see beyond the practical veneer of societal protection to the frightening specter of crime and punishment run amok, of a judicial system teetering at the top of an extremely steep and greasy slope, determining which citizens should be allowed to walk the streets and which should be locked away. If the sexually dangerous can be shuttered and shackled today, are the car thieves and burglars—notorious recidivists themselves, not to mention far more numerous than sex offenders—the next to be targeted? Extrapolated to a theoretical extreme, the implications are Stalinesque.

The overwhelming majority of Americans, most of whom fall solidly in the middle of the political spectrum, however, see laws to deal with sex offenders as a salvation. Most popular, in no small part because they have the names of martyred children attached to them, are so-called community notification statutes, the most famous of which is Megan's Law, which is actually a package of nine separate codes. It was named for Megan Kanka, who was seven years old when she was raped and murdered on July 29, 1994 by a pedophilic ex-con who lived across the street from her. Three months later, Governor Christie Todd Whitman signed Megan's Law, requiring sex offenders to register with their local police department and update them on their whereabouts every ninety days. Those who don't can be sent to jail for seven months and fined seventy-five hundred dollars. The police, in turn, can then notify the rest of the populace that a sexual predator is in their midst.

Indiana has Zachary's Law, which requires a sex offender registry to be distributed to all schools and to agencies that license people to work with children. And on May 17, 1996, President Bill Clinton signed a federal version of Megan's Law, tying federal anticrime money to each state's willingness to release publicly information about convicted sex offenders.

In practice, however, those laws have been little more than media distractions, except, of course, for the flashers and rapists and molesters who have to keep checking in with the police. Left unanswered, for instance, is what the average resident is supposed to do when he discovers the nice young man across the street is a pedophile. Teach his children to be more careful around strangers? Organize a lynch mob? Stoning? The purpose of the information is so vague—and the thought of knowing it so disconcerting and confusing—that even Leora Joseph, a woman who wades through the worst tales of abuse every day and who has two young children, has never asked police in her hometown for the list of sex offenders living nearby.

A more dramatic, though not necessarily more effective, manner in which to neutralize sex offenders is castration, either chemically with drugs that dilute the hormones, or surgically. In California, for instance, pedophiles convicted of second sex crime against a child under thirteen years of age are required to take a drug called Depo-Provera. And Texas in 1997 gave recidivist child molesters the option of being surgically castrated.

Leading the call for that option was, curiously, a chronic pedophile from San Antonio named Larry Don McQuay. Actually, McQuay preferred to be called a "child-molesting demon," which, if he kept an accurate tally of the children he fondled, is true. Though he was sent to prison for assaulting only one child, McQuay, who used to drive a school bus, claimed to have molested 240 before he was caught. The only way to squelch his pedophilic impulses, he insisted to Texas prison officials, victims-rights groups, and newspaper editors, was to have his testicles cut off. "I will be walking the streets of your city, your community, your neighborhoods. And without a doubt, there will be children around," he wrote to the *Dallas Morning News* in March 1988. "You tell me what is likely to happen if I am not castrated before I am released." In another forum, he answered his own rhetorical question: "I am doomed to eventually rape and then murder my poor little victims to keep them from telling on me."

Whether castration is particularly useful, however, remains an open question. Though the procedure certainly lowers the levels of male hormones—and, thus, the sex drive—it does not address any underlying psychological issues. In other words, if rape is a crime more of power and control than sex, removing the gonads seems beside the point.

Civil commitment statutes, on the other hand, promise to attack the root of the problem: taking rapists and molesters out of circulation. "I think citizens have a right to be protected from child molesters," Leora Joseph says. "And I don't think that's a crazy, right-wing, Orwellian idea. The basic premise is that children need this protection."

CIVIL COMMITMENT STATUTES AREN'T NEW. IN FACT, LEGISLA-tures began tinkering with ways to eliminate sexual psychopaths as long ago as the 1930s, and by the beginning of the sixties more than half of the states had enacted one version or another of a sexual predator law. Over the next two decades or so, nagging concerns about the civil rights of offenders and the growing realization that the treatment centers they were confined to were largely failures led most of those states to scrap their statutes.

Massachusetts, in fact, repealed its civil commitment law in 1990 for precisely those reasons. Worse, some defense attorneys and other critics argued, such laws do more harm than good, dissuading convicted molesters from enrolling in treatment programs while they serve their prison time, since notes from those counseling sessions could be used against them by prosecutors later seeking a civil commitment. In the late nineties, following a series of particularly heinous sex crimes, including the rape and murder of a ten-year-old boy by two men in his neighborhood, the law was dusted off, updated, and reinstated.

By the time Suffolk County prosecutors got around to David Cherry, the statute had already opened to mixed reviews in other counties. Two judges ordered two ex-convicts, who they decided might pose a threat, to go through a civil commitment hearing. Another judge in another county, however, declared the law unconstitutional. "Finality in criminal punishments and pre-established punishment limits are part of our constitutional tradition. Newly enacted imprisonment measures for past offenses are not," Plymouth Superior Court Judge Charles Hely wrote in releasing Lawrence A. Bruno, who served eighteen years for raping an elderly woman.

Leora Joseph and Jack Zanini knew they had to clear a number of legal hurdles. One afternoon in the middle of November, they picked through Cherry's prison records and their strategic options. While Joseph dug through a small mountain of papers piled on a desk, Zanini bantered with Carol Feldman, a forensic psychologist who specializes in pedophiles.

"Let me ask this," Zanini said. "Do you think that this guy would be subject to a commitment, an emergency commitment, under section 12 right now?"

"No," Feldman told him.

"He's not mentally ill?"

"No," Feldman said again. "He has an antisocial personality, which is a personality disorder, so he's not psychotic . . . ."

"But he's got a personality disorder?" Zanini interrupted.

"But he's got a personality disorder," Feldman agreed, "which would be axis II. Axis I is psychosis, axis II is personality disorder."

Zanini pondered that for only an instant, then followed the line of legal logic. "Is it fair to say," he asked, "that a personality disorder could manifest itself by the sexual abuse of children?"

"Could be a part of it," Feldman said.

"So the personality disorder he has could result in a lack of power to control his sexual impulses?"

"It could."

"It could," Zanini repeated. "And, in fact, a more thorough examination at the treatment center by two qualified examiners for a period of sixty days would give us more information about whether his personality disorder is likely to result in a lack of power to control his sexual impulses."

Leora Joseph broke into the conversation, reading from a sheet of paper she'd found in Cherry's file. "'In my opinion, Mr. Cherry is not a sexually dangerous person'—signed from Dr. Moore, the guy that just died and we were going to hire," she said. She looked at Zanini, raised both eyebrows, then turned back to the page in her hand. "'And I do not recommend his commitment to the Massachusetts Treatment Center for a period of observation. I base this opinion on the fact that he has been convicted only of incest type offenses, and in our experiences such offenders do not, as a rule, constitute a danger to the community at large."

She drew the last three words out with disgust and flopped the letter down on the desk. Silence lingered in the office for a moment until Feldman broke it by stating the obvious. "Anybody who, as we would say, *shtups* somebody who's that little is a pedophile. And a pedophile is a pedophile is a pedophile."

"Yeah," Zanini said. "I agree."

Miles away, in an apartment in a yellow house with a mansard roof a block from the beach, where David Cherry was staying with his brother, he knew the prosecutors were trying to figure out a way to keep him locked up. And he knew they were calling him a pedophile, which seemed to wound him more than having his freedom taken away.

"The prosecutors' job is simple," he said, launching a short dissertation on the adversarial system of justice. "It's just, their whole reason for being in existence is to lock people up. They're not into fixing things that are broken in a person, they're not even into how that person thinks. They don't care about that. That's not their job." He was animated, waving his hands as he spoke. But he didn't sound angry. "I understand the public outcry," he went on. "Now, if I was a man that they let out of prison and I kept doing things, that would be different. But that's not the case with me. I don't chase day-care kids. I don't. That's not what I did, that's not what I do, and that's not who I am. So I don't give a damn if there's a day care right downstairs. It doesn't affect me. Understand what I'm saying? I'm not sexually dangerous, that's number one. Children don't turn me on, which is number two. And number three is, I'm going on with my life."

Or trying to, anyway. He still had one more day in court.

LEORA JOSEPH LOOKED LIKE SHE COULD TELL WHAT WAS COMING. She was dressed in a tailored red suit over a white blouse, good, professional courtroom fashion, but she sat slumped behind the prosecution's table, fiddling with her hair and frowning. As soon as

Judge Cratsley said he wanted to hear arguments on the "legal questions" raised by the civil commitment proceedings, she could sense which way His Honor was bending. John Swomley had filed a motion to dismiss the commonwealth's attempt to lock up Cherry, and the judge wanted to hear his reasons.

Swomley stood. He is a plain-faced man with short cropped brown hair, neither particularly stylish nor striking. But when he began to speak, he nearly shook with conviction, starting off low and calm, then rising to an indignation barely contained beneath his dark blue suit.

"Proceeding with my motion to dismiss," he began, "the commonwealth has introduced or alleged no facts from which a reasonable person could conclude that Mr. Cherry presently suffered from a mental abnormality or personality disorder. Furthermore, the finding in 1986 that Mr. Cherry was not a sexually dangerous person, I would suggest, is binding on the commonwealth as a matter of law. To the extent that he was found"—this is when the indignation could be heard—"to be *not* sexually dangerous by the commonwealth's own expert, they should not be able to come in here some thirteen years later, ten years later, and say he is."

It was succinct and passionate, logically sound. Zanini had to counter, which he did calmly, almost dispassionately, letting the graphic adjectives carry their own unbearable weight.

"I think that allegations, which if proved, that a person engaged in multiple acts of anal, oral, and vaginal intercourse with minor female children, a reasonable person . . . would be led to conclude that there was a personality disorder or a mental abnormality there," he told the judge.

But that—arguing that pedophiles are weird—was the easy part. Now Zanini had to contort his tongue through the legal gymnastics necessary to put David Cherry back behind bars after he'd done all of his time. "I would suggest," Zanini said, "that if you have a particular condition in the present day, and if the statute is changed or amended or altered in some way so that your condition today subjects you to commitment, no vested right has been taken from you. The notion of a vested right simply is misplaced as applied to someone in the mental health, mental commitment field. None of us sort of have that vested right."

He had led with his legal chin. In plain English, he had argued that anyone could be locked up if the state decided he or she was bonkers. Swomley had a clean counterpunch, a right cross a blind man could see coming a mile away.

"I would suggest," Swomley said, though he suggested things more vigorously and loudly than Zanini, "that everyone has a vested right not to be civilly committed. And I would suggest that the notion that everyone here doesn't have a presumption to be walking the streets, as Mr. Cherry had a presumption to be walking the streets, is wrong. Wrong. Bad law, poorly constructed." He nearly shouted the final syllables.

"I think I'll ask you to conclude if you could," the judge told him.

"Basically," Swomley said, his voice back to a conversational level, "I'm concluded."

Judge Cratsley announced he would take the matter under advisement, which is how judges say they will think about something. Leora Joseph fiddled with her hair some more. Everyone knew what the judge was thinking.

AS EXPECTED, DAVID CHERRY'S MOTION TO DISMISS WAS AL-lowed. No one was surprised, least of all Leora Joseph. "It's very over," she said a few hours after the decision was released. "The judge, as we predicted, joined many other judges across the state in finding the statute unconstitutional. But that happens." She dropped heavily into her chair, propped her elbows on her desk, clasped her hands in front of her. She pulled the corners of her mouth back into a dimpled grimace. "I don't like wasting my time," she said. "Something's going to happen to David Cherry, though. I would be shocked if he never got arrested again. I think the statistics are so powerful, I can't imagine that he won't."

David Cherry can imagine as much. He had spent the previous weeks trying to catch up on fifteen years he'd whittled away in prison, looking at old photo albums, piecing together the lives of his family and friends. Taunting him, haunting him, was the chance, no matter how slim, that he might have to go back to prison, and not even know for how long. So maybe he was surprised by the decision. Or, perhaps, he was so relieved he was afraid to believe it was over.

He was at his girlfriend's house, a fortyish blonde, laying in bed when the phone rang on Friday morning. It was David's brother, who was supposed to have called the day before with the news. When he explained it, David didn't believe him at first. Finally, he hung up the phone, looked at his girlfriend and said, "It's over. I don't have to go back."

CHAPTER 13
The Downey Brothers

IN A CITY DEFINED BY ITS NEIGHBORHOODS, AND THEN USUALLY
in broad brush strokes that change texture and shade from one
block to the next, South Boston is an anomaly, an isthmus that, to
cheapen a well-worn snippet of literature, embodies both the best
of Boston and the worst of Boston, depending on the perspective
from which it is viewed.

In the early morning, when the sun begins to climb above the
gray horizon where Boston Harbor meets the sky and the first
soft light of day tickles the sand of Carson Beach, it is possible to
see a virtuous enclave. The shore, or at least the road closest to
it, is lined with grand Victorians and colonials and, farther
south, the low-rising bricks of the Mary Ellen McCormack projects, the first public housing development in the country. The
streets fall back from there in a grid, lettered ones running one
way, crossed by numbered blocks the other, all anchored by the
wide spine of Broadway. The side streets are narrow and lined
with three-story homes joined side-to-side, save for the odd
driveway carved through the curb, where families have lived for
generations, apartments and townhouses passed on from father
to son to grandson.

Southie is an island, not physically but psychically, bordered on two sides by the harbor and cut adrift from the mainland of downtown by a shipping channel spanned by only two bridges. In the softer light, it is a place of loyalty, a place where someone's always watching your back in the name of Southie Pride. It is also a decidedly Irish enclave, despite an influx of black and Latino tenants into the D Street and Old Colony and McCormack projects during the past decade. Southie knows all the words to "Danny Boy" and the best lines from *The Quiet Man,* and enough Gaelic to write "Welcome to South Boston" in both English and the nearly forgotten mother tongue on a mural at the foot of the Broadway Bridge.

As the sun rises higher in the sky and the light becomes brighter, the shadows deeper, Southie appears less an island than simply isolated, insulated, shut off from the wider world around it. Farther east, the larger homes and brick rowhouses are rapidly gentrifying, bought up by younger and richer infiltrators. The projects are deteriorating, scarred by barren patches of dirt that used to be lawns. Loyalty becomes fear, or, lacking that, a foolish concept of acquiescence that leaves no room for rats and snitches. The Irish heritage becomes an Irish caricature, and a mean one at that: Southie has always been a die-hard supporter of the Irish Republican Army, a pack of murderous thugs whom most Irish citizens wish would stop shooting people and bombing pubs. Indeed, when entrepreneurs from the Ould Sod began migrating to South Boston and buying new businesses, carried ashore by an economy so robust it is called the Celtic Tiger, the locals dubbed them the FBI, which stood for Foreign Born Irish, as opposed to, apparently, the legitimate Irish born in South Boston. The former editor of *Boston* magazine, a transplant from New York City, always believed the kind Gaelic words on the mural were a secret code directed toward him and his kind that read, "Jews Keep Out."

For nearly thirty years, the neighborhood has seen itself as under siege, which was often not untrue. In the seventies, court-ordered desegregation tore native children from their local schools and replaced them with black children from Roxbury, who were promptly stoned when they rolled up in yellow buses. In the nineties, the venerated St. Patrick's Day parade was so deeply threatened by gay men and lesbians who wanted to march that the local burghers fought the issue all the way to the Supreme Court. (It was lost on the Bostonians that gay groups were happily welcomed in the parades in Cork and Dublin and Galway.)

More subtly, yet far more insidious and poisonous, were the small demons from within and the swirling mistrals from without, forces micro and macro that ate away at the neighborhood like acid. Internally, James J. "Whitey" Bulger, the older brother of the erudite former president of the state senate, William Bulger, enveloped himself in a Robin Hood mythology. He was the gentleman who passed out turkeys to widows come Thanksgiving, the paternal tough guy who could straighten out a wife-battering husband, the menacing protector who kept drugs out of Southie. But a 1986 presidential commission on organized crime called Whitey, quite accurately, a reputed bank robber, drug dealer, and murderer although, after his stint in Alcatraz, the bank robbery part was more than simply reputed. And he certainly didn't prevent heroin and cocaine and angel dust from coursing through the neighborhood. Whether he sold any dope is unclear. Yet he clearly either collected tribute from dealers (the government's version) or ripped them off (his lieutenant's version).

In any case, Southie's young men and women are a chemical stew, jacked up either on cheap beer and liquor or, in more recent years, strung out on heroin. Meanwhile, the rest of urban America's woes descended heavily upon the neighborhood. As blue collar jobs declined and substance abuse increased, marriages fell apart and poverty deepened. By the middle of the nineties, according to statistics compiled by *U.S. News & World Report,* almost three quarters of the families on the southern tip of Southie were headed by single white females, marking it the most desperate white ghetto in America. At the close of the millennium, suicide was becoming a teenage epidemic.

Jimmy Murphy grew up in South Boston, the fourth child
and first son born to James Murphy and Marianne LeClair. In
1972, the brood moved into an apartment at 319 East 8th Street,
which was in the Old Colony projects, a drab collection of pale
brown buildings. Marianne loved it. She'd spent a few years in
Southie as a child, but then moved to Roxbury (which was still
predominantly white then). She welcomed the return to the isthmus. Her daughters had a tougher time making the adjustment, at
least early on. As the new kids in the project, they were taunted
mercilessly by the other children, then roughed up in courtyard
fistfights that would send them scurrying home in tears. Their
mother finally told them to toughen up. "If you come in here crying one more time," Marianne LeClair said, "*I'm* kicking your ass."

The marriage didn't last long. Jimmy's father was a Southie
stereotype, a seventh-grade dropout who found good work cutting meat and found a good time in a bottle. He would stay sober
for a while, three, maybe four months, and then go out to the
store for a pack of cigarettes or something and be gone, lost in an
alcoholic haze for the next six weeks. In 1989, on his forty-second
birthday, Jimmy's father died, drank himself into such a stupor he
either fell down and froze to death or got whacked on the head
and froze to death.

Marianne remarried, this time to a borderline sociopath named
Francis McGuirk. "Bad to the bone," Marianne says, though not
without his reasons. Frankie's mother died when he was seven years
old, leaving his alcoholic father to raise him and his five sisters. He
didn't do a very good job. Some mornings, he would whip Francis
with the cord from an iron, and force the boy to stand under a cold
shower to wash the blood away before he got dressed for school. He
grew up to be as mean as his old man, and also a drinker with a
taste for bad drugs. Francis would come home some nights cranked
up on angel dust and start screaming at his wife, "I'm going to kill
ya, you bitch!" He came close, pushing her against a wall and
squeezing her throat so tightly Marianne would black out. Still, she
bore him a son, Frankie Jr., her eighth and final child. He was still

a toddler when his father died, fresh out of rehab and out buying a pack of Marlboros. Somehow, he got tangled up in a fight—either rescuing a woman from a beating or arguing over drugs, depending on which story is true—that ended with Francis taking a knife in the back. His last words, which he spoke in the fading light of a spring night in 1979, were, "God, I don't want to die."

His namesake, ten years younger than his half brother Jimmy Murphy, probably doesn't want to die either, though it's not from lack of trying. He was always the bad seed of the family, the kid never afraid to throw a sucker punch or a stiff uppercut to the face of anyone who pissed him off. Plus, he was a thief. "My Frankie, he'd go out and steal a bike, go out with his friends and grab a bike and screw—he's been arrested for that, too," his mother says, the instructive word being "too" because Frankie's been arrested a lot. Then he got himself hooked on the heroin Whitey Bulger was sup-posed to be keeping out of South Boston, which meant he stole more, even from his mother. "Come into my house and steal from me?" she says. "That's a different story." Frankie Jr. tried to kick the dope a couple of times, laying on his mother's couch, weeping and wailing, gobbling Clonapins Marianne would feed him to try and calm his nerves. But he never stayed clean for very long.

Jimmy, by contrast, was the more gentle soul. He was the worker in the family, the eleven-year-old boy who'd take his shoeshine box to the bars on Broadway and come back with a hundred dol-lars in his pocket, which he dutifully turned over to his mother. He was a funny kid, too, always trying to be the class clown. His teach-ers would call Marianne down to the school, even though Jimmy could never understand why. "Honest, Ma," he'd tell her, "I didn't do nothin'." A few hours later, Marianne would be sitting across from a teacher, saying, "Oh, I'm so sorry." When he was older, he would flex his biceps in a muscle beach pose, half mocking himself because his arms were never as thick as he wished they were.

He was never tough, though, not like Frankie. "His sisters fought his battles for him," Marianne says. "Sure, many times Jimmy would get into arguments out there, get into fights. But mostly

Jimmy got beat up." And he did manage to get himself into some trouble, but nothing ever too serious. When he was seventeen years old, he was pinched for the first time selling a small bit of weed in the courtyard outside the apartment. Later, he was arrested for drunken driving, which seemed to put a scare into him, seeing as how he quit drinking for four years, not one drop. "He was no prize package, don't get me wrong," his mother says. "There was no halo over him. He'd been through his things. But he never hurt anybody but himself."

JIMMY WAS DRINKING AGAIN BY THE SPRING OF 1997. ST. Patrick's Day is a high holy holiday in South Boston, a raucous celebration of the patron saint of Ireland, to whom homage is paid with a long, squawking parade of bagpipers and drummers and through the consumption of frothy fermented beverages. Indeed, it is such an important day, and politicians from South Boston have long held such enormous power, that a state holiday was declared to coincide with it. Technically, state workers celebrate Evacuation Day, marking the occasion 225-odd years ago when the hated British fled Boston; realistically, a great number of people, South Bostonians and otherwise, swill copious amounts of beer wearing green plastic hats.

Boston Beer Garden is a relatively upscale pub on Broadway along the parade route that is inevitably lined a dozen deep with spectators, children perched on the curb, toddlers clinging to their fathers' shoulders. After the last floats and marching bands pass by, the families retreat somewhere safer and saner. Everyone else stays to drink. Jimmy Murphy ended up inside the Beer Garden.

Inside the bar and well into a drunken haze, he ran into a young man named Joe Downey, another South Boston native with roots stretching back three generations. They got into an argument over a girl—these things always begin over girls—which led to the bouncer barking at them, "Take it outside." So they staggered out to the sidewalk, argued some more, and then started punching. It's unclear who swung first. But for perhaps the only time in his life, Jimmy Murphy didn't get his ass kicked. Joe Downey went down hard before someone broke up the melee.

A beer-sotted brawl on St. Patrick's Day is nothing to be ashamed of, at least not in some quarters of South Boston. Nor, really, is losing, what with all the alcohol throwing off your balance and your timing. No shame in that. But another Southie trait, one born through generations of isolation and frustrated faux pride, is enmity. Irish Alzheimer's, the old joke goes: forget everything but the grudge.

Joe Downey suffered that particular disease. So did his brother, Danny. Family loyalty and all. One week later, on March 24, 1997, it was still fresh in their minds.

Jimmy was out drinking again that night, shooting pool at a bar called Sully's with his best friend Lance Smith, another young man with a taste for alcohol and a variety of drugs. Somehow, word got back to his family that Jimmy was driving around in his sparkling Grand Marquis with a few beers under his belt. Considering he had to drive south to Quincy, where he was living with one of his sisters, his brother and his mother tried to head him off.

"Ma," Frankie said when he called her that night, "Jimmy's out drinkin' and he's drivin'."

"Go find him," Marianne said. "Take his keys."

"Ma, I'm not gonna take his keys. I don't want to fight with Jimmy."

"Just take his keys," she said. "If you have to fight him, fight him."

Marianne hung up and called the desk sergeant at the South Boston precinct. She told him her boy was out driving when he shouldn't be, and maybe the cops could go track him down. They couldn't do that, the cop told her, but they'd keep a close eye out for a weaving Marquis.

Jimmy's sister was chasing after him, too. Shortly after 1:30 in the morning, she dialed his pager and punched in her telephone number. By that time, Jimmy and Lance were pulling into the parking lot outside Kelly's Cork 'N Bull, a notorious bucket of blood a few blocks from the Old Colony projects. In the old days, a man could die inside only to be dumped out the back door. No-body ever saw anything, and if they did it was only the dead guy trying to stick up the joint. In the present day, it's still a punch palace but, more importantly, open the latest in Southie, so it's a fine place to head for one last call.

Kelly's is a long, wedge-shaped barroom, wider at the front door, then narrowing as the bar on the right and the booths on the left converged toward the back, where the toilets and a payphone were tucked into a small anteroom. At the end of the bar, a doorway opens into a dining room, but at that hour of the night the door was locked. Jimmy Murphy walked down the center of the room toward the back, past the Downey brothers sitting in the last booth. Who knows if he saw them. Then Jimmy continued toward the payphone. Joe and Danny Downey followed.

Martin Kelly, the grandson of the original owner was working behind the bar that night. He heard the sounds of a scuffle rapidly escalating into a fight. At Kelly's, a man learns to discern an argument from a brawl. He came around the bar in time to see Danny Downey holding onto the door jamb, his torso swaying, taut and rhythmic, as if he was kicking something on the floor. Then the Downey brothers screwed. Jimmy Murphy hauled himself to his feet and stumbled back toward the front door, his hands clutching the crimson smears spreading across his shirt. He had been stabbed twice, once so hard the blade cut into his liver, the other so deep it sliced a five-inch wound through his heart. Jimmy Murphy, thirty years old, collapsed by the front door.

Somehow, Frankie heard about that, too. He called Marianne again. "Ma," he said, "I heard Jimmy got stabbed."

She took it in stride. Stabbed was better than shot and much better than dead. "Okay," she told Frankie, "you call one hospital and I'll call City Hospital."

Marianne hung up and dialed the number for Boston City Hospi-tal. She got a nurse on the line and asked if Jimmy Murphy was there.

"Are you his mother?" the nurse asked.

"Yes."

"I'm sorry," the nurse told her. "He expired."

Marianne dropped the phone and screamed, a deep primal wail. "Hang that fucking phone up," she shrieked at one of her daughters. "Hang the fucking phone up!" She gulped a breath of air, refueling her lungs. "He's dead," she cried. "He's dead, my Jimmy's dead."

She cried through the night. Kelly's Cork 'N Bull opened for business at eight o'clock the next morning.

JOE AND DANNY DOWNEY STOOD TRIAL FOR MURDER IN NOVEMber 1999. Building a case against them strong enough to get an indictment had been easy enough. Witnesses were hauled in and, in proceedings kept secret from the public, outlined enough of a motive—the St. Patrick's Day fight—and enough of a narrative—the Downey brothers following Murphy toward the phone—to have them charged with murder. It took almost exactly a year until both brothers surrendered, though, at which point they were ordered held on $1 million cash bail, the realistic equivalent of no bail at all.

Assistant District Attorney Dennis Collins, a slim and boyish man with a button nose, had a straightforward theory of how the killing went down. After cornering Murphy in a tight hallway, Danny Downey grabbed him in a bear hug from behind. Joe then stabbed him twice. Convincing a jury of that, however, would be no easy feat. The first hallowed commandment of South Boston— Thou Shalt Not Rat—was wreaking havoc with his case.

The first obstacle Collins had to overcome was putting Jimmy Murphy and the Downey brothers in the hallway by the phone. He used Martin Kelly for that.

"Did you hear or see anything unusual?" Collins asked him.

"I heard a commotion going on," Kelly told him.

"And by commotion, can you describe the noise you heard?"

"Just thuds, like a thudding and banging," Kelly said. "It sounded like there was an altercation going on. I know because from being there so long and at night, there's just a certain sound when a fight starts."

"Have you been in Kelly's before when fights have started?"

"Yes, many times."

Collins asked Kelly to explain exactly what he saw next. "I could see Danny Downey motioning like he was kicking something on the ground," Kelly said.

"What movement could you see?" Collins asked.

"Just the motion of a body." Kelly got up from his seat and moved to his right, holding on to the half-wall that surrounds the witness box. "He was holding on doing this," Kelly said, pumping his right leg up and down, bending at the knee, "holding onto the side of the door."

Point for the prosecution. But Roger Witkin, a balding man with an intimidating gray mustache who was defending Danny Downey, had his counterattack well planned. Witkin asked Kelly if he'd told the first officer on the scene the night Murphy was killed about seeing Danny in the doorway.

"No," Kelly said. "I did not tell him."

"You didn't tell him," Witkin repeated. "Then another officer by the name of Michael Griffin, you didn't recount to him about Daniel Downey being at the door, did you?"

"No, I never mentioned it."

"You're telling us," Witkin said next, "that like fine wine your memory has improved over the almost three years since this incident?"

"No," Kelly answered. "I'm telling you I didn't want to be this involved in it."

Jack Cuhna, who represented Joe Downey, had his crack at Kelly next. And he had more ammunition.

"There was a warrant out for your arrest, correct?" he began, not so much asking a question as reporting a fact.

"That's correct."

"And that case charged you with possession of cocaine, did it not?"

"Correct."

"And on the night of March 23 through March 24, there was a warrant out for your arrest, correct?"

"That's correct."

"Were you arrested?" Cuhna asked.

"Nope."

"Okay, you spoke to the police two days later, correct?"

"Correct."

"Were you arrested then?" Cuhna inflected the question with just a hint of incredulity.

"No."

"And you're still on default in that case, aren't you?"

"No," Kelly said.

Cuhna's eyes opened wider. An unexpected answer, but it could play to his favor. "When did you clear it up?" he asked.

"This morning."

"Okay," Cuhna said, his tone suggesting a convenient coincidence. "And when you went up to the Boston Municipal Court this morning, what was your expectation?"

"I actually thought I was going to spend the day in jail," Kelly said. It didn't sound sincere. Men scheduled to testify in murder trials don't typically get sent to jail a few hours before.

"Oh, you did?" Cuhna said. He didn't think Kelly was sincere either. "Well, did you bring a lawyer with you?"

"No."

THE DEFENSE STRATEGY INVOLVED A HODGEPODGE OF CONFUSION and miscreants and drunkards, starting with the bartender with the coke charge who doesn't want to talk to police but, miraculously, is never arrested and never sent to jail. And Kelly would be the most difficult witness to rough up. The others looked like a cakewalk.

Tommy Shields, for instance. He was in Kelly's that night drinking with Lance Smith, facing the room where the killing took place. Roger Witkin corralled him in the hallway before his testimony and gave him a basic primer in courtroom etiquette. "Be calm, because they're going to put you on the stand, babe," he told him. "You know what you're going to be asked, the same shit. Don't get angry. It's all right out here, but not in there. Just answer what you're asked.

'What's your name?' 'Thomas Shields.' 'Are you the same Thomas Shields who this, that, and the other thing?' Yes or no. Whatever the answer is, 'yes sir,' 'no sir.' Just be calm. Do your best."

Shields didn't need too much prepping. He slouched in the witness box, his broad shoulders rolling forward, his eyes blank and heavy under his buzz cut. And he didn't remember anything.

"Do recall ever seeing Joseph or Daniel Downey in the bar?" Dennis Collins asked.

"No," he answered.

"Can you say whether or not your memory of those events was affected in any way by your drinking alcohol?"

"Yes."

"How so?"

"I was drinking all day that day," Shields said.

"And what effect, if any, did that have on your memory?"

"Usually when I drank, I usually blacked out, you know," Shields said. "So I really don't recall anything, you know."

So began a parade of drinkers, witnesses so intoxicated they couldn't remember seeing a man knifed to death in a small bar.

"Do you remember how much you had to drink?" Collins asked one woman who'd been in Kelly's.

"Well, no," she said.

"Could you approximate?"

She laughed. "I started about four."

Even better was the next guy on the stand, doing his best to sound erudite. "I do remember a little bit but not too much," he said. "I was very intoxicated on alcohol and drugs."

Collins was getting frustrated. The witnesses knew more than they were saying, drunk or not. But if they weren't telling the jury, it didn't do him any good. His best chance of redeeming it fell to Lance Smith, Jimmy Murphy's drinking buddy and purportedly best friend. "Mr. Smith," Collins sighed as he gathered his papers for the day, "makes or breaks the case."

Smith took the stand in a blue jailhouse jumpsuit, which he had to wear because he'd spent the past few months locked up on drug charges. He was surly, looking like Matt Dillon in *The Outsiders,* only with hollower cheeks and with a faltering memory.

"What did you see when you got into Kelly's?" Collins asked him.

"Nutin'," Smith nearly sneered. He even sounded like Matt Dillon.

"Did you see what Mr. Murphy did after you went in?"

"He went to use the phone."

"And where's the phone located?"

"Back of the bar."

Do you remember whether or not you saw him go back there?"

"He was back there." Smith was insolent, like a snotty teenager.

"What did you do?" Collins asked.

"I sat down and talked to my friend Tom," Smith said, meaning the blacked-out Shields.

"Where was he sitting down?"

"One of the booths."

"And what happened after you sat down? What did you see or hear?"

"Little fight goin' on, back in the phone area."

"What did you do?" It was like pulling teeth.

"I went back there."

"What did you see?"

"Fight." An impacted wisdom tooth, fused to the jawbone.

"Who was fighting?"

"Jimmy and . . . ." Smith's voice hitched. "And the Downey brothers."

Finally. "Do you recall what you did after you saw that?" Collins asked.

"I grabbed Danny."

"Do you remember if he reacted in any way when you grabbed him?

"Yeah, he pushed me away."

Jack Cuhna was ready for Lance Smith. The witness was a fish, the courtroom a very small barrel, and Cuhna was loaded with a sniper's rifle. He stood up with a sheaf of papers in his hand, a transcript of Smith's grand jury testimony, which he summarized. He

asked Smith if he remembered the first story he told, the one where
he had his back to the phone area and, next thing he knew, Jimmy
Murphy was stumbling toward him, then tumbling to the floor.

"Yes," Smith said.

"And you were under oath at that time, were you not, sir?"

"Yes."

"And that was true, wasn't it?"

"Yes."

"And when you were brought in here today, when you first testified, when Mr. Collins asked you the questions, you just tried to
say what you thought he wanted to hear, isn't that correct?"

"Yes."

"I have no further questions," Cuhna said.

Collins had a chance to rehabilitate Smith. He cut straight to the
heart of South Boston. "Have you ever heard the word rat used in
reference to something besides an animal?" he asked.

"Yes."

"What's it mean when you're not referring to an animal?"

"A snitch," he said. "Someone who tells on someone."

"Has anyone called you a rat or a snitch before you came in to
testify today?"

"Couple of arguments with a few people," Smith said.

"And what did they call you?"

"A rat."

"Did that happen once or more than once?"

"A couple of times," Jimmy Murphy's best friend said. "Twice."

"You've been in jail now for several months, is that correct Mr.
Smith?"

"Yes."

"In the more recent past," Collins continued, still yanking at
teeth, "leading up to your testimony today, have any friends
started to treat you differently?"

"Yes."

"How so?"

"Just don't associate with me like they used to."

"Have any of the events, including being called a rat, a snitch, and losing friends, affected your testimony today?"

"No," Smith said.

Later, after the trial and after he was out of jail, Lance Smith would try to make amends with Marianne LeClair, his best friend's mother. He got down on his knees and kissed her hand. "I'm sorry," he said. Marianne LeClair answered, "Get the fuck away from me."

THERE WAS STILL FRANKIE MCGUIRK. HE WAS THERE AT THE Beer Garden on St. Patrick's Day. He could recount the fight Jimmy had, which would give the jury some sense of motive, of why the Downeys would want more trouble with Murphy. "The crutch," as Roger Witkin put it, "from which you can get from point A to point B."

But that was only if he would testify. His mother begged him to, pleading with him over the phone when Frankie called from jail, where he was locked up for heroin. "Ma, it's not easy bein' a snitch when you're locked up," he would tell her.

"Frankie, just tell the truth," she would counter. "It's your brother."

"Ma," he insisted again, "you just don't give your friends' names. I'm locked up in here. It's not easy."

Collins feared Frankie would lie on the stand, just clam up about everything. But he could use the same trick Cuhna had used on Smith, dredging up his past testimony from the grand jury to rehabilitate him on the stand. That way, Collins could stick in the jurors' mind two important images: the Beer Garden fight for the motive and the near-universal fear of testifying. If the dead guy's own brother was spooked, then surely Shields and Smith and all the others would be as well. In order to do that with his own witness, however, Collins first had to put Frankie through a hearing without the jury. If the judge decided Frankie would say enough to allow the defense to cross-examine him, Frankie would be allowed to testify. If, on the other hand, he insisted he didn't remember anything—which would neuter any attempts to trip him up on cross—he would be kept off the stand.

Frankie started badly. Collins asked him if he remembered testifying before the grand jury about being at the Beer Garden. No, Frankie mumbled, he didn't. His eyes were sunken under his brow, a dark slash across his face, contrasting with the white T-shirt that hung too loosely over his junkie frame. Collins gave him his testimony to read. Did that refresh his memory? No.

"Do you remember testifying in April of 1997?" Collins asked.

"Yeah, I guess so," Frankie said. "Since I read that."

"Okay," Collins said. It was a start. "Do you remember whether you told the truth when you testified?"

"I don't know. I was messed up on drugs back then, you know?"

"Well, why don't you explain what you mean by that."

"Mean, uh, strung out on heroin."

"Well," Collins started again, "can you explain to the court what that means in terms of your ability to answer questions?"

"Means, uh, say what you want to hear so I can just get out of there."

"Were you telling the truth?" Collins asked. The money question.

"Prob'ly not," Frankie said. He snickered. "No."

All the lawyers went to the bench for a sidebar conference, then broke for a short recess. Collins would get one more chance to ask Frankie McGuirk if he knew the truth. So he asked the same questions. Do you remember testifying? Were you telling the truth?

He got two different answers. "Yes" and "Yeah, most likely yeah. Yes."

In the back of the courtroom, Marianne LeClair nodded. She was relieved. Frankie would tell the truth. But then Judge Daniel A. Ford jumped in. "Why did you tell me earlier you just were saying what you thought people wanted to hear and it probably wasn't true?"

"I don't know," Frankie said. "I was confused."

"What were you confused about?"

"About what's going on."

"You didn't know what's going on?" the judge said. "What did you think's going on here?"

"Well, I know what's going on."

"So why did you tell me an hour ago..."

"Well it's hard to tell you something," Frankie interrupted, "when I don't remember it, you know?"

He was led away in handcuffs, past the Downey brothers. They looked relieved. Their lawyers were smiling. Out in the hallway, Marianne LeClair was somewhere between rage and misery, hoping her last living son would be prosecuted for perjury. "If they don't, I'll be very upset," she said. "Give him five years. Let him know what it's really like, not to be in the kiddie camp. Put him in a good one. No more canteen money. No more visits. See, he doesn't realize, we're all he's got." And soon he would not even have that. His mother would tell him later, "It should've been you, Frankie, not Jimmy." And she meant it.

DENNIS COLLINS WAS SCRAMBLING TO SALVAGE HIS CASE. FRANKIE wouldn't be allowed to testify, which meant Collins didn't have a motive to present to the jury. Getting a conviction was looking like a long-shot gamble.

He sat down on a hard hallway bench and pulled out his cell phone. It was Friday, November 12, the last day of testimony. Monday morning he would give his closing argument, then leave the Downeys' fate to the jury. Unless he cut a deal.

David Meier answered the phone in his office. "Got a minute?" Collins asked him. "The defense was interested in an offer, so I've extended manslaughter offers conditional on your approval." Collins would offer Danny Downey seven-to-ten years and, for his older brother Joe, who wielded the knife, eighteen-to-twenty years. The condition, though, was that both of them had to agree. If Joe wouldn't go down for eighteen years, Danny couldn't take the seven.

Cuhna tried to lower the numbers for Joe. "Would you give him twelve?" he asked in a hallway conference.

Collins shook his head. "If it was one wound, you'd have a twelve-to-fifteen. But not two," he said. "You know, there's no conceivable way this was a mistake. Whoever put that knife in him meant to kill him."

Witkin went to Danny Downey, leaned in close to him at the defense table, and whispered the hard truth. "The offer made to you is absolutely reasonable, it really is," Witkin told him. "You can't turn it down in good conscience, not facing what you face. The problem is him."

Witkin tipped his head over his left shoulder, toward Joe Downey. Cuhna was whispering too in his ear. "It's a serious offer," he said, "in that he's essentially offering you the rest of your life. And I don't know what to tell you in terms of how you want to play that gamble."

And it was a huge gamble. A murder conviction means life, and with no hope of parole if the jury votes for first degree. Joe wanted time to think about it, to talk with his family. At the very least, Collins assumed the defense would make a counteroffer. He waited by his phone past five o'clock that Friday night. No call. No counteroffer.

By eight o'clock Monday morning, the Downeys had decided to gamble. "Today's our big day," Joe said before he changed out of his orange jailhouse jumpsuit into a clean white shirt and black sweater vest. "Going to the jury. Scary."

"We'll see what happens," Danny said. He looked terrified.

Both men dressed and filed into court, taking their seats next to their attorneys. Just before the judge entered, Joe Downey leaned over and whispered to Cuhna. The lawyer looked mildly startled, a faint smile on his face. "You want me to ask?" he said to Joe, already rising to his feet. Joe nodded.

Cuhna met Collins between the two tables. "Would you go lower on Joe?" he asked the prosecutor.

Collins had the same startled look Cuhna had flashed. "Can't do it now," he said. Then he laughed, a nervous, disbelieving chortle. He'd spent the weekend preparing his closing argument, working up the best speech he could cobble together from a collection of drunkards and felons who'd been his witnesses. He couldn't break his train of thought now. Plus, if the morning session was delayed, he knew the jury would take it out on him. Jurors always blame the prosecutors when they are left waiting on some hard chair, bored. "Judge wants to start at 9:30, I can't do it," Collins said. "If you wanted to make a counteroffer the time to do it was Friday. That's why I thought I'd hear from you Friday."

"Court, all rise," the court officer barked.

"I just got the word now," Cuhna said, turning back to his seat. "And I did make a counteroffer Friday. You said you couldn't do it."

Collins looked confused. That's right: the defense wanted twelve-to-fifteen for Joe, too low for two wounds. He looked at Cuhna. "Yeah."

So they gave their closing arguments. Witkin attacked the evidence and the witnesses, hardly any of whom were credible or, at the time of the crime, sober. Cuhna did the same, starting with Martin Kelly, a man "trying to please the police."

As for Collins, he went with the best thing he had: a corpse. "Mr. Murphy's body says, 'I was murdered,'" he said. "He's stabbed twice in the chest and never gets his hands up to defend himself. How could that happen? Two people. Someone grabs him from behind, another person stabs him in the front. Two people acting together. Two people who have to be near where the victim is going to be when he goes back to that phone. Which other two people know each other well enough to act quickly together, who are near enough to get Mr. Murphy when he finally gets alone?" Collins took two dramatic steps toward the center of the courtroom and spread his arms, his left one sweeping toward the Downey brothers. "They're sitting right here," he said.

The jury deliberated for a long six hours. Marianne LeClair was sure they would be acquitted, what with the way her own son had behaved. "I know they're going to walk," she said. "I hope they walk into the ocean, but that's beside the point." At least she'd kept her sense of humor.

THE JURY RETURNED ON TUESDAY MORNING. BOTH MEN, THEY decided, were guilty of murder in the second degree. The judge has no discretion in sentencing, so he ordered the clerk to read the words. Danny swallowed hard at the phrase "the term of your natural life." Joe didn't even blink. As the court officers pulled his arms behind his back and snapped on the handcuffs, he looked straight at the judge. "Thank you, you honor," he said.

He'd gambled and lost. But he was still a gracious loser.

CHAPTER 14

Justice Delayed

THREE DAYS BEFORE THANKSGIVING 1999, STEPHEN HRONES smiled from behind a heavy wooden table in a courtroom on the fifth floor of the new building, still glittering with marble and polished oak, that houses the juvenile division of the Suffolk County courts. Donnell Johnson, his client for five years, shambled from the front of the room, out of the prisoners' dock, a blue T-shirt hanging from shoulders that had filled out from those of a scrawny teen to those of a prison-conditioned young man. His hair was braided in tight rows, and he wore a pair of scholarly gold-rimmed glasses. He managed a wan wave to his mother, sitting in the first row of the gallery, before settling into the chair next to his lawyer.

Hrones leaned in close, whispering into Donnell's right ear. "What's the first thing you want when you get out, I mean that you couldn't get in prison," Hrones asked. "I mean, in terms of food, for instance."

Donnell's face erupted in an awkward smile. "I don't know," he answered, nearly laughing with relief and awe.

"What about a turkey, Thursday, a nice turkey dinner? That'd be nice wouldn't it? Not that crap in the cafeteria." Hrones was grinning madly. The Mad Czech looked giddily insane.

The past few months had been agonizing for Hrones and Johnson, weeks spent on the edge of jubilation, yet mired in frustration. Nearly five years after Manny Goffigan died—years in which the case had faded from the collective memory, receding deep enough that there was no real gain in dredging it back up—Martin's office started to suspect that Donnell might be innocent. In August, Elizabeth Keeley and David Meier had suggested as much to Hrones. The investigation had been reopened, they told him, but they needed more time to develop the evidence against a new suspect. Hrones gave them three weeks. Twenty-two days later, Hrones went public, demanding that Johnson be released. It didn't happen, couldn't happen, at least not right away. So for weeks, tensions between Hrones and Martin's office repeatedly flared, the former accusing the D.A. of stalling, the latter countering that Hrones was jeopardizing the very investigation that could set Johnson free.

But all that was in the past. Today Johnson was going home.

"Court, all rise," an officer in a crisp white uniform barked. Hrones stopped asking about turkey dinners and stood up, Johnson at his side, the smile replaced by weary stoicism.

THE REASON DONNELL JOHNSON HAD ALWAYS BEEN A REASONable suspect in the killing of Manny Goffigan had everything to do with his stunning ability to be in the wrong place at the wrong time. Like when he was in that rented limo in April of 1994 when Brandon Bass popped through the sunroof and started shooting .357 slugs at Kareem Tyler. Mostly, the wrong place Donnell Johnson was usually at was the Bromley Heath projects, and the wrong time was ... well, anytime for as long as anyone can remember.

Bromley Heath has always been a schizophrenic place, fifteen hundred apartments stacked into short red brick towers and filled with poor Bostonians, most of them black, a handful Hispanic. A generation ago, it was an open, festering wound, a place of misery and violence and neglect, which made it exactly the same as every other project where the poor had been warehoused. The cops weren't afraid to cross Heath Street and wander into the interior of the project—they were armed, after all—but they were exceptionally cautious. Ambulance drivers, who do not carry firearms, were sometimes more hesitant, waiting for a police escort to cart away the dead and dying in the early seventies.

About that same time, the project began to change, to rejuvenate from within, slowly at first, then at the rapid pace that draws the attention of the media and the accolades of liberals. "Tenant management" was the fashionable word, an experiment in giving control of housing developments to the people who lived in them, rather than leave tenants to the whims of bureaucrats with suburban homes and government jobs. From the bowels of Bromley Heath emerged, like a modern-day Moses, a savior, a stout, feisty and forty-ish black woman named Mildred Hailey. She would lead her people, who also happened to be her neighbors, to a metaphysical promised land where they would control their own homesteads.

In 1974, the Tenant Management Corporation was formed, officially transferring control of the development from the Boston Housing Authority to the people who lived there. Led by Hailey and governed by a board of directors, the T.M.C. transformed the project. Broken windows—harking back to the theory of shattered glass leading first to the fear of crime, then actual crime—were repaired. The T.M.C. hired its own police force, over which it would have authority. Drug-treatment centers were established. The health care center was state of the art, which, cruelly, is a novelty for the urban poor. Hailey, who exuded a sort of grandmotherly kindness (most everyone called her Nana, anyway) gathered the formerly dispossessed residents of Bromley Heath under a slogan that was both hopeful and subtly defiant: We Are Family.

By the middle of the eighties, Bromley Heath was being heralded across the nation as an icon of what the urban poor could do for themselves. If it is true—and it is—that the poor are fundamentally no different than the wealthy, Bromley Heath was the proof that impoverished people could take as much pride in the environs as the middle-class homeowners of Brookline and even tonier Wellesley. After all, a housing project is not so radically dif-

ferent than a gated community for the rich: each is segregated by
class, and outsiders are kept at bay, either by decorative iron or an
invisible fence of fear and loathing.

As for Hailey, she became a celebrity. She was flown all over the
country, and even across the Atlantic Ocean, to extol the virtues of
returning power to the people. The press adored her, a gray-haired
grandmother so tiny she sometimes had to climb on a table to be
heard as loudly as she wanted to be at a noisy conference, a charming savior from the depths of the ghetto who just might have
found the solution to the sprawling acres of litter and terror that
define many of the nation's tracts of public housing. Indeed, she
had been anointed, and by more than one fawning scribe or politician, as "the Mother Theresa of public housing."

Yet Hailey also proved that the poor are no different from the
rich in a less noble way, as well. Power and fame, especially when
they accrue to one person or a concentrated handful of persons,
can be eerily corrupting forces, corrosive elements that slowly eat
away at their own source, cannibalizing the meat of good intentions into the hard bones of self-perpetuation. Bromley Heath's de-
liverance came from We Are Family; its downfall came from We
Are Clans, and not all clans are considered equal.

That, in turn, exposed the other side of Bromley Heath's split
personality: the pack of thugs who sold crack and shot at the boys
across Columbus Avenue in the Academy Homes project. On the
wall outside of Mildred Hailey's apartment, scribbled in big black
letters, was the word "Chill" and the initials "H.S.P." The latter
stood for Heath Street Posse, which was interchangeable with the
Heath Street Boys, depending on which hoodlum was proclaiming
fealty to the gang. The former, Chill, was the name Eugene
Damian Martin used on the street, seeing as how it is more intimidating than either Eugene or Damian. Chill was a bona fide thug,
a backstreet business man who helped operate a relatively large-
scale cocaine operation that was not only illegal but dishonest;
Chill was notorious for putting his thumb on the scale when he
was packing his drugs. As with most such entrepreneurs, he used

violence as a business tactic, allegedly ambushing customers who were bitter after being shortchanged, even killing one of them, police and other sources suspect. He has never been accused of any violent crime, however, save for an accusation in 1993, when he was eighteen years old, that he stabbed one of his H.S.P. boys in the head during an argument. That case was later dismissed.

The other thing Chill was notorious for was his lineage. Mildred Hailey is his grandmother. In Bromley Heath, where Hailey was the queen presiding over the Tenant Management Corporation, that endowed Chill with an enormous amount of clout, especially among the police officers who were employed by the T.M.C. Mildred Hailey tried to keep him in line, tried to push him into the military and college. But Chill stayed in the projects, making bootleg money and strutting about the courtyards as if he were invincible, taunting Bromley Heath officers who would try to, and sometimes actually would, arrest him. "Do you know who I am?" he told one officer, who recounted the episode to the *Boston Globe*. "You better dress warm. You're gonna be working in Alaska."

Chill wasn't the only one of Hailey's clan to run on the wrong side of the law, either. Another grandson, Eugene "Gino" Martin, was in the drug business, as was a nephew, Samuel Girard. And her son, Stephen Hailey, was arrested on July 17, 1999, by officers from the Youth Violence Strike Force, who found him inside Nana Hailey's apartment after they surrounded it with their guns unholstered. The charge: beating a man to death a month earlier in an apartment in Brockton, a deteriorating city twenty miles south of Boston.

Those were the people with whom, and that was the place where, Donnell Johnson chose to spend much of his free time. That he could shoot a child to death was not inconceivable to the police, to prosecutors, to a judge, and, finally, to a jury.

AT ABOUT THE SAME TIME DONNELL WAS BEING SENT TO PRISON for eighteen years, the Boston Police Department and the Suffolk County District Attorney's Office were getting weary of making routine arrests in Bromley Heath, dragging out the occasional gang-banger and crack dealer and shuffling him through the state court system, knowing he would either return to the streets in short order or, lacking that, that some other aspiring hoodlum would quickly step into the vacuum left behind.

So they upped the ante. After decades of open hostility between local authorities and their federal counterparts, Commissioner Paul Evans—who already had a proper working relationship with Ralph Martin—began mending fences with the local bosses of the federal agencies charged with enforcing various laws. George Festa of the Drug Enforcement Agency was both a friend and a pragmatic cop. The city also learned to work and play well (albeit with the occasional ruffling of individual feathers) with the Bureau of Alcohol, Tobacco, and Firearms, the Federal Bureau of Investigation, United States Attorney Donald K. Stern, and the Massachusetts State Police, the Massachusetts Bay Transportation Authority Police, and the Boston Housing Authority Police. Rather than battling over turf, competing for busts and statistics, the city of Boston became, in effect, a multi-jurisdictional precinct, with each agency bringing in a certain expertise, be it intelligence or, in the case of the federal agencies, criminal statutes that bordered on draconian.

During the past two decades, Congress has ratcheted up the sanctions for a myriad of crimes, imposing mandatory sentences that are measured in decades for everything from cocaine trafficking to being a felon in possession of some contraband or another. Systematically, those laws have largely been an utter failure, crowding prisons with low level drug pushers and handcuffing judges who in theory should mete out punishment with vast discretion, depending on the mitigating and aggravating circumstances of each person convicted. Taken together, the ever-more-severe rules are a de facto attempt to eliminate crime by building more prisons.

Used surgically, however, federal punishment can be enormously effective, neutralizing the baddest of the bad for extended periods of time and sending a sharp shock wave through the streets. Consider, for example, the plight of Freddie Cardoza, who in the summer of 1995 was considered a leading menace in an ongoing shooting war between the Humboldt Raiders and another local gang. He'd shuffled through the district court system a few times, picked up on a variety of charges, but never going away for a terribly long time. The last time he was arrested was on July 15, 1995, when a carful of Boston police officers saw him walking along the street late at night with a sixteen-year-old apostle. The police patted down the kid, who had a nine millimeter pistol stuck in his waistband. Cardoza, on the other hand, had only a single bullet, which he toyed with while the police chatted with him, rolling it between his thumb and forefinger. "You're not gonna bust me for one bullet are you?" he asked the cops.

No, they weren't. Under state law, possession of a bullet, even for a convicted felon like Cardoza, is a misdemeanor. At worst, Cardoza would spend the night in jail, perhaps spend a few months in the county jail, then return to the streets with his reputation freshly glossed. The feds, on the other hand, could arrest him as a felon in possession of ammunition, which is precisely what they did. A few months later, a federal judge sentenced Cardoza to spend nineteen years and seven months in prison. And federal time is real time: no early parole, no time off for good behavior. A hard sentence, to be sure, but Cardoza was a hard man. And probation officers in Dorchester District Court wasted no time printing up flyers announcing the arrest, conviction, and sentencing, which they distributed to every now-spooked miscreant they could find.

When Evans and Martin turned their attention to Bromley Heath, they called in both state troopers and DEA agents to help. Beginning in the autumn of 1996, the joint task force spent two years mining the seedier veins of Bromley Heath. The thrust of the operation was to ferret out a crack cocaine ring that the police suspected was making some three thousand dollars a day. For Martin's office and Evans, however, there was a secondary mission: even with Donnell Johnson in prison, there were two accomplices—another shooter and the getaway driver—who'd never been called to account. Perhaps one investigation would help crack the other.

On October 30, 1998, almost four years to the day after Manny
Goffigan was shot dead while counting his Halloween booty, U.S.
Attorney Stern and Ralph Martin's office unsealed indictments
against thirty-eight people allegedly involved in cocaine trafficking
in Bromley Heath. Eleven of the suspects would be prosecuted by
Martin's office for distributing crack cocaine. Twenty-seven others
would be handled by federal prosecutors. Among that group, in addition to Mildred Hailey's grandsons, were two interesting charac-
ters. One was Kamiya Santos, who'd been shotgunned four years
earlier, which police had always surmised was the reason for the
counterattack at Academy Homes. The other was Algernon Wilson,
who Donnell had named as one of the alleged shooters on Halloween night 1994, right after he named Neico Santos as the other.

Wilson knew that federal time was hard time. And hard time
can make even the hardest men turn soft.

THERE ARE TWO DIFFERENT VERSIONS OF WHAT TRANSPIRED ON
August 31, 1999, though both begin with the same basic fact. On
that afternoon, David Meier, the chief of homicide prosecutions,
and Elizabeth Keeley, the number two person in Martin's office,
called Stephen Hrones and said they wanted to meet with him.
They met at Hrones's office on the second floor of an old granite
wharf that was renovated into expensive waterfront offices with
ceilings held up by heavy wooden timber two centuries old. At
that meeting, Meier and Keeley either said they now believed Donnell Johnson was innocent (Hrones's version) or that they had reopened the case and might have new information but needed time
to develop it (the other version). In any case, Hrones gave the two
prosecutors three weeks to get his client out of prison.

Hrones was firm about the deadline. On Tuesday, September 21,
he summoned reporters to his office, seated the print and radio reporters at a long table, and lined the television cameras in a semi-
circle near the back of a small conference room. Then he squeezed
into the room and took a seat at the head of the table, a bank of

microphones in front of him. He smoothed his tie while one reporter positioned a tape recorder in front of him.

"Ladies and gentlemen," he began, "I've called you here today
to announce that I'm filing this afternoon a petition with the state
supreme court, the single justice session, demanding the immediate release of Donnell Johnson, my client, who was convicted of
the killing of the youngest victim in Boston history."

He explained a few pertinent details, such as the sympathetic
victim and the weakness of the case against Johnson. Then he cut
to the point. "The assistant to Ralph Martin, Miss Keeley, and the
head of homicide"—he pronounces the word *home*-i-side, an odd
tic for a man who's defended so many accused killers—"called me
up on August 31 and said, 'Can we come to your office?' And they
came here and sat down with me and basically told me that they
believe now that Johnson was not involved. And they asked me for
time for more investigation in order to build a case against the real
culprits. I agreed and I've given them some three weeks. But nothing seems to be happening."

The assembled reporters had already pestered Martin for a re-
buttal. "Ralph Martin," a television reporter told Hrones, "denies
that anyone in his office represented to you that your client was
innocent."

Hrones was annoyed. "Well, his chief of *home*-i-side did, and his
chief assistant. I mean, why would they come to my office?"

"What, precisely, did they say?" another reporter asked.

"Meier did the talking," Hrones answered. "He basically said, 'If
you give us a little time, we'll go to a judge and work this out.' So
they were well along the way to basically saying we need time only
to get the other culprits, we believe your man is innocent. And,
fortunately, we got the lucky break we needed in terms of the federal prosecution of the Bromley Heath drug dealers. Several of
those defendants are cooperating witnesses and have given information indicating Johnson was not involved. The feds called up
and said, 'Look, we have evidence that Johnson didn't do it.'"

It was at once a subtle backtrack—conceding Meier was only "well along the way" to calling Johnson a wrongly convicted man—and an obvious swipe at Martin's office—"the federal prosecution."

Then Hrones switched gears, faintly praising the district attorney to the point of damning him. "What they have done, they pulled all the original police officers off the case," he said. "There's a whole new squad of Boston police reinvestigating the case." Which was true, if somewhat miscast. New detectives in homicide had taken the case, but only because the squad had had so many fresh faces move in since 1994, and the original cops were working more recent killings.

Finally, Hrones got to the indisputable point. "He"—meaning Martin's office—"is the one that has all the information, and I think we have a right to know it. We've been patient long enough, and I think we've got enough that it's time to move. If you were in prison for five years, you'd always claimed you're innocent, there was no evidence except eyewitness testimony, no corroboration, you'd want to get out, and get out soon."

HRONES HAD PLAYED HIS CARDS WELL. HE FILED HIS MOTION LATE on that day, shortly after his press conference, knowing Wednesday was when only one justice from the Supreme Judicial Court would be there to entertain arguments. His brief was mostly a history of Johnson's travels through the court system and a summation of the sins Hrones maintains police and prosecutors committed. He also invoked the name of Marlon Passley, who was as jarring a precedent as he could find.

Passley had been convicted by one of Martin's prosecutors on October 16, 1994, for a brutal shooting on a Dorchester street corner that left one man paralyzed, another injured, and a third, Tennyson Drakes, dead. Passley had an alibi—he claimed, and seven witnesses agreed, that he'd been in Wellesley, more than fifteen miles away, when the shots were fired at ten o'clock on the night of August 15, 1995. But the prosecutor countered sharply. "He may have been out there at eight o'clock, at nine o'clock, at eleven o'clock," she argued to the jury. "At ten o'clock, he was the cold-blooded killer who took a young life on Nelson Street."

The jury had agreed. Passley was sentenced to life in prison and, as a matter of routine, started working the appeals courts. On February 9, 1999, the Supreme Judicial Court proclaimed his trial had been fair, that there was no legal reason to grant him a new one. Yet three months later, David Meier, flanked by the original prosecutor, homicide detectives, and other police officials stood up at a press conference and said, in essence, we goofed. "New and sufficient information" had bubbled up from the streets, he said, compelling enough to set Passley free. Meier did not elaborate on that information. In his brief, however, Hrones credited the feds with digging it up. And if Passley could be sprung without the real shooter being arrested, Hrones argued in his petition, then so could Donnell Johnson.

Moreover, Hrones had timed his filing with the precision of a Navy SEAL team. Martin's office scrambled to counter. Late in the afternoon, Meier and Keeley and Jim Borghesani, Martin's press liaison, sat down to strategize.

"When I talked to him, he was apologetic," Meier said, meaning Hrones.

"You talked to him?" Keeley asked. She was agitated, flapping a sheaf of papers in her lap.

"Yeah, I called him this afternoon."

"After this?"

"Yeah," Meier said. He was nonchalant, infused with the same subdued style as his boss, leafing through the papers Hrones had filed. "Ralph called me and said, 'Is there anything going on with this case, I've just gotten besieged with reporters.' I said, 'Yeah, I was supposed to sit down with Hrones.'"

"So what did he say?"

"He goes, he said, 'David, I'm sure you know I'm holding a press conference.' I said, 'No, I don't know.'"

Keeley flapped her sheaf again. "I can't believe it."

"I said, 'Steve, you know, it's only gonna hurt your client.'"

"Yeah, his innocent youngster."

"You know, not for nothing," Meier went on, "but he's also laid out Passley. I mean, no one knows that . . . . It says in Passley a federal drug investigation also resulted in new evidence that revealed the defendant's innocence . . . ."

"How does he know that?" Keeley interrupted.

"That was reported," Borghesani interjected. "Not officially, but it was in the paper. I'll bet he just saw that in the *Globe*."

Meier continued rifling through the Hrones filing, which included his five-page letter to Martin and Keeley's response. "Did he turn this letter over to the press?" he asked.

"Not that I'm aware of, no," Borghesani said. "In fact, I don't think any of that is ever going to be reported in the press."

"This is going to be filed with the S.J.C," Meier said.

"And the problem," Keeley said, picking up the theme, "is what he files is public information, and there's some really sensitive information in those letters. We need to get somebody up there first thing in the morning to impound it."

The reasoning, she explained later, was simple enough. "There are a finite number of people who know what really happened and a finite number of people who know who was involved," she said. "And those people, with the exception of one possible suspect, are all on the street. And they also can narrow down the possible suspects who are talking." She dropped into role playing, animated. "Okay, we're on the street. I'm not talking, you're not talking. Who's not on the street? Oh, it's our friends X, Y, and Z who are locked up in a federal pen. And who has a greater motive to help themselves out than someone locked up facing a federal sentence?" Keeley sighed, somewhere between disgust and agitation. "Not that these individuals are necessarily the brightest bulbs," she went on, "but it doesn't take much to figure out and narrow down who they're going to come looking for and who's doing the talking."

David Meier repeated that same line of reasoning in a courtroom a few days later. He had convinced the single justice to impound Hrones's filing, keeping secret the names of various hoodlums and potential suspects the lawyer had typed into his five-page letter to Martin. Instead, the justice bounced the petition down to Boston Juvenile Court, where it was heard by Judge Paul H. Lewis.

"On behalf of the juvenile," Meier began in arguing against releasing Johnson on bail, "if Mr. Hrones takes it upon himself, or anyone else takes it upon himself to attempt by speculation, most respectfully, to attach names to any of those individuals made reference to in the commonwealth's notice of discovery, I suggest, most respectfully, that that could very well lead to physical harm, at a minimum, to any individuals who might be forthcoming with information."

Hrones started to speak. Meier increased his volume, drowning out his words. "Which most respectfully, Judge," he said, "would only undermine anyone's attempts to get to the truth of this matter."

It was a compelling argument, which Lewis accepted. Johnson would remain in jail while the investigation continued. Yet if a dead nine-year-old is news, so, too, is a wrongly convicted sixteen-year-old. The inertia of an old conviction was overcome by a thrust of fevered media. The reporters and cameramen were waiting in the hallway outside the courtroom, first for Johnson's relatives, who expressed a routine outrage, and then for Meier. He was surrounded by press people, leaning in close with their notepads and tape recorders and microphones, his face awash in the bright white lights of the cameras.

"Do you feel any public pressure?" a television reporter asked Meier.

"None whatsoever," the prosecutor replied. His words were clipped, the reply more reflexive than contemplative. It was only a matter of time.

JUDGE LEWIS CLIMBED BEHIND THE BENCH A MONTH LATER, three days before Thanksgiving. Hrones and Donnell Johnson stood behind one table on the right side of the courtroom from Lewis's bench. Meier rose behind the table on the left side.

A perpetually rumpled man with a mop of brown hair that seems stripped from a rag doll, Meier cleared his throat and shuffled some papers on the table in front of him. "Judge, if it please the court, in the name of the commonwealth and on behalf of the Suffolk County district attorney's office, I file a motion to stay execution of sentence and admit the juvenile to bail."

Twenty-two years old and the system still called Donnell Johnson "the juvenile." Meier went on to recite five years of history, each time referring to the juvenile who was identified by three witnesses, the juvenile who was convicted of first degree murder, the juvenile who was sent away to prison for eighteen-to-twenty years. The juvenile who was now a full-grown man blinked his eyes hard and slow as he listened to Meier.

"The Boston Police, the Suffolk County District Attorney's Office, and various other law enforcement agencies have been actively investigating"—he paused, cleared his throat again, as if he were afraid the words would get stuck in his windpipe—"the identity of each and every individual who was responsible for the shooting death of Jermaine Goffigan. That ongoing investigation led to the discovery of certain new information, alleged exculpatory information. The commonwealth convened a special grand jury and, as Your Honor knows, over the last several months that grand jury has been hearing evidence. It suggests ultimately, Your Honor, that there may be other individuals, not including the juvenile, who may in fact have been responsible for the shooting death of Jermaine Goffigan. The nature of the evidence is such that there is a very real possibility that the juvenile Donnell Johnson did not commit the crimes for which he was convicted. And, in fact, the grand jury investigation, the police investigation, suggest and has identified individuals who may well have taken a role in the shooting death of Jermaine Goffigan. For those reasons, your honor, I ask the court respectfully to allow the commonwealth's motion to admit Donnell Johnson to bail."

The judge thanked Meier, then turned to Hrones, who stood up.

"Thank you, Your Honor. Donnell has always professed his innocence," Hrones began, his words halting, long pauses where the periods fell in the sentences. Hrones had waited years to speak these lines, practiced them in his head so many times that now, his lips forming the syllables, they seemed almost surreal. "Juries do make mistakes. And in this case, they convicted an innocent man. But in this case, the system has worked. So we certainly have no objection, Your Honor."

Judge Lewis took only a moment to allow Meier's motion to release Donnell on bail. "Mr. Johnson," Lewis went on, looking directly into Donnell's brown eyes, "I consider what I have done today to be a crowning jewel in the system. At this juncture, the court is going to release the defendant on personal recognizance." The lowest level of supervision, the best Donnell could have hoped for. His family and pastor let out a small rumble of joy, then quickly quieted themselves, as if afraid to offend the judge and see Donnell whisked back to jail. "The advice I have for you, sir, is don't look back to the despair of the past. You must look forward to the hope of the future."

Donnell nodded. "I will, your honor," he said, his voice barely above a whisper. "Thank you."

Epilogue

THE POLITICAL PROBLEM WITH A CRIME RATE THAT DROPS steadily and steeply is that it will eventually bottom out and, in all likelihood, sharply spike upward from time to time. Most noteworthy crimes—that is, the ones that capture the attention of reporters and, thus, the public—are at some primal level uncontrollable. Murder and assaults, for instance, are most often emotional outbursts, flashes of anger or rage or fermented machismo that explode in a bloody instant. (Exhibit One: *Commonwealth versus the Downey Brothers,* which followed the *Downey Brothers versus Jimmy Murphy.*) So long as angry people populate the planet, a few fellow citizens are going to die violent deaths. Cain slew Abel and it's been downhill ever since.

Any increase is quite naturally seen as a worsening of social woes, of a return to lawless times, no matter how dwarfish the benchmark against which the spike is measured. The same press and populace who celebrate a decline in crime are eager to assign blame for a later rise. So it was in Boston in the summer of 2000 when children again began to die on the city's streets. Two killings, one by gun and one by knife, both became major news stories.

Chris Resende made the front page of the *Boston Herald* on July 31. Barely twenty-four hours earlier, in the first dark minutes of July 30, Resende left a Sweet Sixteen party on the third floor of an apartment building on Magnolia Street to smoke a cigarette in the vestibule. He was a sixteen-year-old of Cape Verdean descent and, by all accounts, a good kid: polite, well mannered, and employed as a cashier and stock boy at a local grocery store. He also happened to be standing in a terribly wrong place when a white Dodge Neon drove by, gunfire blazing from the window. A bullet hit Resende in the stomach, killing him. "Birthday party ends in teen's murder," the *Herald* announced in its headline. "Sweet 16 gathering turns deadly in Dorchester."

The same week, Cedric Ennis was stabbed to death in Jamaica Plain. "A fifteen-year-old Roxbury youth, described by his neighbors as 'everybody's little brother,' was fatally stabbed early yesterday," the *Globe* began its report, "becoming Boston's second juvenile murder victim in a week, fueling fears that youth violence is on the rise."

By the time these killings ocurred, Ralph Martin's grace period, that lag time between the black token being appointed and the veteran D.A. getting poked, had expired. Privately a good number of the local press corps were suggesting that Martin's handling of Donnell Johnson was evidence of colossal incompetence. Moreover, there was increasing grumbling about morale slipping inside the office. Now these killings, while not reflectling directly upon Martin, hinted at and reinforced a broader sense that the city's gains against crime were faltering. If Martin, Evans, and Menino can be considered generals in a successful war on crime, they also can be tainted as failures if that war appears to be reversing.

But two murders, though tragic, don't annul the progress that Ralph Martin and his colleagues have made in eight years. If police and prosecutors are essentially powerless to prevent sporadic murders, they—along with youth workers, counselors, ministers, and a host of other people—can control the fallout, isolate the damage, and stem the cycle of bleeding. Recent history, in fact, provides the instructive lessons. For years, gang killings tended to be retaliatory, a fatal and near fatal tit-for-tat. Jermaine Goffigan, the most shameful killing in the city's history, was a direct result of such demented logic. Even the street where Resende died once suffered an ongoing cycle of back-and-forth violence. In the spring of 1995, Rasheed Fountain, who ran with a crew called the Magnolia Street Steelers, got into a petty squabble in a school hallway with rivals from the Fayston Street Boys, who chased him all the way home that day. From those humble beginnings sprang a shooting war that, by July, had left Fountain dead and eight other people shot. In one horrific three-day stretch, police chased after three separate shootings between the two gangs.

By 1995, with both Ralph Martin and Paul Evans running their respective outfits, the city already was tacking toward finding a way to short circuit the gunplay. "The gang problem never stopped being a problem, but it flared up again," Evans said at the time, a concession that alone put him light-years ahead of the brass circa 1988. "Part of our dealing with the gang problem is getting a handle on what's going on from the intelligence angle so we can prevent the violence.... We're working on a daily basis to monitor the problem and prevent the violence, not react to it."

Over eight years, the manner in which Boston is policed, the manner in which criminals are prosecuted, has evolved in such a way that the city's occasional spasms can now be calmed, that the swirls of mayhem can be amputated before they stretch into a spiral of violent revenge. The justice system—the entire organic structure, from the streets to the courts—has earned a curious credibility. When a district attorney will admit he did the wrong thing by imprisoning a boy for five years, it is easy to believe that same D.A. wants to do the right thing. When detectives will hunt a killer six years after the fact, it is easy to believe they really do want to catch the bad guys. The effect multiplies. When Superintendent Joyce says he is concerned about a dead child, it is impossible not to believe him, not to believe that the justice system, so often an oxymoron, will truly attempt to dispense justice.

And when people believe in the justice system, they are less likely to establish their own vigilante system. To date, nearly one month after Chris Resende was killed for standing in the wrong place, no one has exacted revenge on his behalf.